Julia Kusznir, Heiko Pleines (eds.)

Trade Unions from Post-Socialist Member States in EU Governance

CHANGING EUROPE

Edited by Dr. Sabine Fischer, Dr. Heiko Pleines and
Prof. Dr. Hans-Henning Schröder

ISSN 1863-8716

1   *Sabine Fischer, Heiko Pleines, Hans-Henning Schröder (Eds.)*
    Movements, Migrants, Marginalisation
    Challenges of societal and political participation in Eastern Europe and the
    enlarged EU
    ISBN 978-3-89821-733-0

2   *David Lane, György Lengyel, Jochen Tholen (Eds.)*
    Restructuring of the Economic Elites after State Socialism
    Recruitment, Institutions and Attitudes
    ISBN 978-3-89821-754-5

3   *Daniela Obradovic, Heiko Pleines (Eds.)*
    The Capacity of Central and East European Interest Groups to
    Participate in EU Governance
    ISBN 978-3-89821-750-7

4   *Sabine Fischer, Heiko Pleines (Eds.)*
    Crises and Conflicts in Post-Socialist Societies
    The Role of Ethnic, Political and Social Identities
    ISBN 978-3-89821-855-9

5   *Julia Kusznir, Heiko Pleines (Eds.)*
    Trade Unions from Post-Socialist Member States in EU Governance
    ISBN 978-3-89821-857-3

Julia Kusznir, Heiko Pleines (eds.)

Trade Unions from Post-Socialist Member States in EU Governance

ibidem-Verlag
Stuttgart

Bibliografische Information der Deutschen Nationalbibliothek
Die Deutsche Nationalbibliothek verzeichnet diese Publikation in der
Deutschen Nationalbibliografie; detaillierte bibliografische Daten sind im
Internet über http://dnb.d-nb.de abrufbar.

Bibliographic information published by the Deutsche Nationalbibliothek
Die Deutsche Nationalbibliothek lists this publication in the Deutsche Nationalbibliografie;
detailed bibliographic data are available in the Internet at http://dnb.d-nb.de.

This book presents the results of the research project 'Already arrived in Brussels? Interest
representation of trade unions from the new EU member states at the EU level'. The project
has been carried out by the Research Centre for East European Studies at the University of
Bremen in collaboration with the Sociological Institute of the Czech Academy of Sciences,
the Sociological Institute of the Slovak Academy of Sciences and the Koszalin Institute of
Comparative European Studies. Brigitte Krech was responsible for the conduct of interviews
in Brussels. The project has received financial support from the Otto Brenner Foundation
(Frankfurt/M.).

Language editing: Hilary Abuhove

Style editing: Judith Janiszewski

Technical editing: Matthias Neumann

∞

Gedruckt auf alterungsbeständigem, säurefreien Papier
Printed on acid-free paper

ISSN: 1863-8716

ISBN-10: 3-89821-857-0
ISBN-13: 978-3-89821-857-3

© *ibidem*-Verlag
Stuttgart 2008

Printed in Germany

Contents

List of Tables

List of Abbreviations of Relevant Organizations

A

ASO	Association of Independent Trade Unions (Asociace samostatných odborů), Czech Republic
ASZSZ	National Federation of Autonomous Trade Unions (Autonóm Szakszervezetek Szövetsége), Hungary
ATTAC	Association for the Taxation of Financial Transactions for the Aid of Citizens
AWS	Solidarność Electoral Alliance (Akcja Wyborcza Solidarność), Poland

B

BCC	Business Centre Club, Poland

C

CEEP	European Centre of Enterprises with Public Participation and of Enterprises of General Economic Interest
CESI	Confédération Européenne des Syndicats Indépendants (English version: European Confederation of Independent Trade Unions)
ČMKOS	Czech-Moravian Confederation of Trade Unions (Českomoravská komora odborových svazů), Czech Republic
COPA	Committee of Professional Agricultural Organisations
CoR	Committee of the Regions, European Union

D

DGB	German Confederation of Trade Unions (Deutscher Gewerkschaftsbund)

E

EAKL	Confederation of Estonian Trade Unions (Eesti Ametiühingute Keskliit)
ECF-IUF	European Committee of Food, Catering and Allied Workers' Unions within the International Union of Food, Agricultural, Hotel, Restaurant, Catering Tobacco and Allied Workers' Associations
ECOSOC	United Nations Economic and Social Council
EESC	European Economic and Social Committee

EFBWW	European Federation of Building and Woodworkers
EFFAT	European Federation of Trade Unions in Food, Agriculture and Tourism Sectors
EMCEF	European Mine, Chemical and Energy Workers' Federation
EMF	European Metalworkers' Federation
EP	European Parliament
EPSU	European Federation of Public Service Unions
ERDF	European Regional Development Fund
ESF	European Social Fund
ÉSZT	Confederation of Unions of Professionals (Értelmiségi Szakszervezeti Tömörülés), Hungary
ETF	European Transport Workers' Federation
ETMAKL	Estonian Confederation of Food Producers and Rural Workers (Eesti Toiduainete ja Maatöötajate Ametiühingute Keskliit)
ETUC	European Trade Union Confederation
ETUI-REHS	European Trade Union Institute for Research, Education and Health and Safety
ETUF-TCL	European Trade Union Federation – Textiles, Clothing and Leather
EU	European Union
EUROCADRES	Council of European Professional and Managerial Staff
EUROFOUND	European Foundation for the Improvement of Living and Working Conditions

F

FERPA	European Federation of Retired and Older People
FZZ	Trade Unions Forum (Forum Związków Zawodowych), Poland

I

ICEM	International Federation of Chemical, Energy, Mine and General Workers' Unions

K

KNSS Neodvisnost	Confederation of New Trade Unions of Slovenia Neodvisnost (Konfederacija Novih Sindikatov Slovenije Neodvisnost)
KOK	Christian Labour Confederation / Christian Trade Union Coalition (Křesťanská odborová koalice), Czech Republic
KOZ SR	Confederation of Trade Unions of the Slovak Republic (Konfederácia odborových zväzov Slovenskej republiky)

KPP	Confederation of Polish Employers (Konfederacja Pracodawców Polskich)
KUK	Confederation of Arts and Culture (Konfederace umění a kultury), Czech Republic
KZPS	Confederation of Employers' and Entrepreneurs' Associations (Konfederace zaměstnavatelských a podnikatelských svazů), Czech Republic

L

LBAS	Free Trade Union Confederation of Latvia (Latvijas Brīvo Arodbiedrību savienība)
LDF	Lithuanian Labour Federation (Lietuvos darbo federacija)
LIGA	Democratic League of Independent Trade Unions (Független Szakszervezetek Demokratikus Ligája FSzDL), Hungary
LPSK	Lithuanian Trade Unions Confederation (Lietuvos Profesinių Sajungų Konfederacija)

M

MEP	Member of the European Parliament
Metalowcy	Federation of Metalworkers' Trade Unions (Federacja Związków Zawodowych 'Metalowcy'), Poland
MGYOSZ	Confederation of Hungarian Employers and Industrialists (Munkaadók és Gyáriparosok Országos Szövetsége)
MOSZ	National Federation of Workers' Councils (Munkástanácsok Országos Szövetsége), Hungary
MSZOSZ	National Association of Hungarian Trade Unions (Magyar Szakszervezetek Országos Szövetsége)

N

NGOs	Non-governmental organizations
NSZZ Solidarność	Independent and Self-Governing Trade Union Solidarność (Niezależny Samorządowy Związek Zawodowy Solidarność), Poland

O

OPZZ	All-Poland Alliance of Trade Unions (Ogólnopolskie Porozumienie Związków Zawodowych)
OS ČMS	Trade Union Association of Bohemia, Moravia and Silesia (Odborové sdružení Čech, Moravy a Slezska), Czech Republic

OS KOVO	Czech Metalworkers' Federation KOVO (Odborový svaz KOVO)
OS PHGN	Union of Workers in Mines, Geology and Oil Industry (Odborový svaz pracovníků hornictví, geologie a naftového průmyslu), Czech Republic
OZ KOVO	Slovak Metalworkers' Federation KOVO (Odborový zväz KOVO)
OZ PBGN	Union of Workers in Mines, Geology and Oil Industry (Odborový zväz pracovníkov baní, geológie a naftového priemyslu), Slovakia

P

PERGAM	Confederation of Trade Unions of Slovenia Pergam (Konfederacija sindikatov Slovenije Pergam)
PKPP Lewiatan	Polish Confederation of Private Employers Lewiatan (Polska Konfederacja Pracodawców Lewiatan)

R

RHSD	Council of Economic and Social Agreement (Rada hospodárskej a sociálnej dohody), Slovakia
ROH	Revolutionary Trade Union Movement (Revoluční odborové hnutí), Czech Republic
RUZ	National Union of Employers (Republiková únia zamestnávateľov), Slovakia

S

SLD	Democratic Left Alliance (Sojusz Lewicy Demokratycznej) [Polish political party]
SP ČR	Confederation of Industry and Transport of the Czech Republic (Svaz průmyslu a dopravy ČR)
SZEF	Forum for the Co-operation of Trade Unions (Szakszervezetek Együttműködési Fóruma), Hungary

T

TALO	Estonian Employees' Unions' Confederation (Eesti Teenistujate Ametiliitude Keskorganisatsioon)
TUTB	Trade Union Technical Bureau [now **ETUI-REHS**, q.v.]

U

UNICE	Union of Industrial and Employers' Confederations of Europe

W

WFTU	World Federation of Trade Unions

Z

ZPS	Entrepreneurs Association of Slovakia (Združenie podnikateľov Slovenska)
ZRP	Polish Craft Association (Związek Rzemiosła Polskiego)
ZSSS	Association of Free Trade Unions of Slovenia (Zveza Svobodnih Sindikatov Slovenije)
ZZG	Trade Union of Miners in Poland (Związek Zawodowy Górników w Polsce)

Part I. Introduction

Heiko Pleines

1. Trade Unions from Post-Socialist Member States in EU Governance. An Analytical Framework

1.1. Introduction

The central question the contributions in this book try to answer is whether trade unions from the post-socialist member states are capable of adequate interest representation on the EU level. At issue is not only their purely formal integration into umbrella organizations and EU bodies; of much greater concern is their actual participation in political decision-making processes.

To this end, the authors of this book focus on the following guiding questions:

- To what extent and in which form are trade unions from the new member states integrated into political decision-making processes on the EU level?
- How do the participatory levels of trade unions from the new member states compare to those of trade unions from the old member states or other interest groups (in particular employers' associations) from the new member states?
- How does the trade unions' engagement on the EU level influence the national (and sub-national) level?

Three of the larger new member states, Poland, the Czech Republic and Slovakia, were chosen for the empirical analysis. The major trade unions from these three countries are among the strongest in the post-socialist EU member states. Accordingly, the analysis presents a best-case-scenario for the potential influence of trade unions from the post-socialist member states in EU governance. The trade union studies were thus consciously selected as cases of maximum influence potential rather than as representative of the new member states. This is due to the prevailing assumption of weak representation of trade unions from the new member states on the EU level. If even the strongest trade unions fail to gain traction on the EU level, then the assumption will have been validated. At the same time an analysis of the strongest trade unions offers the best possibilities for an analysis of the effects of integration and Europeanization.

1.2. The Competences of the EU

The competences of the EU in labour market regulation and social policy are limited in scope and largely focus on establishing health and safety regulations in the workplace, regulating labour migration within the EU and equalizing the status of female labourers. Collective bargaining, one of the major tasks of trade unions, is still done exclusively below the EU level.

Nevertheless, the competences of the EU in the field of social policy have been systematically expanded since the beginning of the 1990s. And by means of the Open Method of Coordination (OMC), a more sweeping EU-wide harmonization of social integration, pension funds and health care has been pursued since 2000. Moreover, the EU competences in the economic sphere also possess implications for labour market regulation, as e.g. the EU Service Directive has shown.[1]

1.3. Trade Unions in EU Multilevel Governance

Economic concerns have traditionally shaped interest representation on the EU level, numerically as well as politically. To some extent, this phenomenon has arisen from the EU's history as an economic community. The Commission's dialogue with employers' and employees' representatives organized at the EU level (the Social Dialogue) is based on legal foundations. The Social Dialogue is rooted in Articles 138 and 139 of the Treaty establishing the European Community; these endow the social partners with legislative and executive competences. The European Trade Union Confederation (ETUC), the European Centre of Enterprises with Public Participation and of Enterprises of General Economic Interest (CEEP) and the Union of Industrial and Employers' Confederations of Europe (UNICE) are recognized as social partners by the European Commission and are involved in the Social Dialogue.

The current regulation of decision-making in the area of social policy on the EU level grants the social partners the right to initiate regulations within nine months if they express interest. If the social partners can reach a consensus within this period, they can request that it be incorporated into the Council of Ministers' decision via the Commission. Formally speaking, the EU institutions cannot take any actions in this policy field without consulting the social partners. It is only in the case that the social partners decline to negotiate that responsibility reverts back to the EU institutions.

However, labour relations continue to be strongly organized along national lines. Due to the different national concerns, consensus between the social partners is diffi-

---

1   A concise analysis of the expansion of EU social policy initiatives furnishes Falkner, Gerda: Forms of Governance in European Union Social Policy. Continuity and / or Change?, in: International Social Security Review, 2006 (Vol. 59), No. 2, pp. 77–103. Overviews of the policy field are provided by Edquist, Kristin: EU Social-Policy Governance. Advocating Activism or Servicing States?, in: Journal of European Public Policy, 2006 (Vol. 13), No. 4, pp. 500–518; Falkner, Gerda: The EU's Social Dimension, in: Cini, Michelle (ed.): European Union Politics, 2nd edn, Oxford: Oxford University Press, 2007, pp. 271–285 and Stuchlík, Andrej: Sozialpolitik in der erweiterten Europäischen Union, in: Bos, Ellen / Dieringer, Jürgen (eds): Die Genese einer Union der 27. Die Europäische Union nach der Osterweiterung, Wiesbaden: Verlag für Sozialwissenschaften, 2008, pp. 213–225.

cult to reach. In addition, national interest groups are often reluctant in their support for European umbrella organizations.[2]

Another institutionalized possibility for trade union participation in the EU decision-making process is via the European Economic and Social Committee (EESC). Since its inception in the 1957 Treaty of Rome, the EESC's position has been steadily gathering strength. It unites representatives from employee associations, including those of civil servants (Group I), employees (Group II) and other sectors of organized civil society (Group III). The 317 members of the EESC are nominated by the national governments for a renewable four-year term of office.

In certain cases, the European Commission or the European Council is obliged to consult the EESC; in other instances, consultation is voluntary. In addition, the EESC can also issue opinions unilaterally. The Single European Act (1986) and the Maastricht Treaty (1992) broadened the scope of issues that require EESC consultation, above all those concerning regional and environmental policy. Furthermore, the Treaty of Amsterdam (1997) expanded the regulations for reporting to the EESC and also provides that the European Parliament can consult the EESC. However, the EESC is endowed solely with an advisory capacity.[3]

---

2   This assertion is corroborated in Falkner, Gerda: The Council or the Social Partners? EC Social Policy Between Diplomacy and Collective Bargaining, in: Journal of European Public Policy, 2000 (Vol. 7), No. 5, pp. 705–724; Grande, Edgar: How the Architecture of the EU Political System Influences Business Associations, in: Greenwood, J. (ed.): The Challenge of Change in EU Business Associations, Basingstoke: Palgrave, 2003, pp. 45–59; Greenwood, Justin: Interest Representation in the European Union, New York: Palgrave Macmillan, 2003; Hartenberger, Ute: Europäischer Sozialer Dialog nach Maastricht. EU-Sozialpartnerverhandlungen auf dem Prüfstand, Baden-Baden: Nomos, 2001; Hyman, R.: Trade Unions and the Politics of the European Social Model, in: Economic and Industrial Democracy, 2005 (Vol. 26), No. 1, pp. 9–40 and Rojot, Jacques: European Collective Bargaining. New Prospects or Much Ado About Little?, in: Neal, A. (ed.): The Changing Face of European Labour Law and Social Policy, The Hague: Kluwer, 2004, pp. 13–38. An analysis of the positions of national trade unions with respect to European economic and social policy provide Busemeyer, Marius R. / Kellermann, Christian / Petring, Alexander / Stuchlík, Andrej: Overstretching Solidarity? Trade Unions' National Perspectives on the European Economic and Social Model, Friedrich Ebert Stiftung, Berlin, 2007.

3   An overview on the inclusion of the EESC in the decision-making process on the EU level provide Obradovic, Daniela / Vizcaino, Jose M. Alonso: Good Governance Requirements for the Participation of Interest Groups in EU Consultations, in: Working Papers of the Research Centre for East European Studies, 2006, No. 76, pp. 19–44. The Social Dialogue and trade union engagement on the EU level has already been thoroughly researched for the EU 15. Greenwood, Justin: Interest Representation in the European Union, New York: Palgrave Macmillan, 2003, pp. 149–174; Leiber, Simone / Falkner, Gerda: Sozialer Dialog der EU und nationale Sozialpartnerschaft. Chronik einer paradoxen Beziehung, in: Karlhofer, Ferdinand / Tálos, Emmerich (eds): Sozialpartnerschaft. Österreichische und europäische Perspektiven, Wien: Lit, 2005, pp. 159–183 and Eising, Rainer: Interessenvermittlung in der Europäischen Union, in: Reutter, Werner / Rütters, Peter (eds): Verbände und Verbandssysteme in Westeuropa, Opladen: Leske+Budrich, 2001, pp. 453–476. All provide a concise overview. Other important recent studies include Compston, H. / Greenwood, J. (eds): Social Partnership in the European Union, Basingstoke: Palgrave Macmillan, 2001; Edquist, Kristin: EU Social-Policy Governance. Advocating Activism or Servicing States?, in: Journal of European Public Policy, 2006 (Vol. 13), No. 4, pp. 500–518; Erne, Roland: European Trade-Union

1.4. Trade Unions in the Post-Socialist Member States

With the Eastern enlargement of the European Union, eight post-socialist countries were incorporated in 2004,[4] and two more joined in 2007.[5] Due to their Socialist legacy, many trade unions in the new, post-socialist EU member states indeed boast large numbers of members, but are organizationally limited in their ability to represent trade union interests in the political arena. The trade unions are only associated in comparatively loose umbrella associations. Trade union representatives often shy away from political responsibility and have barely any experience in working with supranational committees.

The weakness of the post-socialist trade unions is also manifest insofar as none of the national-level tri-partite committees has led to successful trade union participation in political decision-making processes in the new EU member states.[6] The trade unions' influence on national politics is generally perceived as minimal.[7] On the basis

Strategies. Between Technocratic Efficiency and Democratic Legitimacy, in: Smismans, Stijn (ed.): Civil Society and Legitimate European Governance, Cheltenham: Edward Elgar, 2006, pp. 219–240; Hartenberger, Ute: Europäischer Sozialer Dialog nach Maastricht. EU-Sozialpartnerverhandlungen auf dem Prüfstand, Baden-Baden: Nomos, 2001; Martin, A. / Ross, G.: Trade Union Organizing at the European Level, in: Imig, D. / Tarrow, S. (eds): Contentious Europeans. Protest and Politics in an Integrating Europe, Lanham: Rowman & Littlefield, 2001, pp. 53–76 and Neal, A. (ed.): The Changing Face of European Labour Law and Social Policy, The Hague: Kluwer, 2004. The impact of EU-level social policy initiatives on the member states has been less intensively researched, however. First analyses on this topic provide Falkner, Gerda / Hartlapp, Miriam / Leiber, Simone / Treib, Oliver: Die Kooperation der Sozialpartner im Arbeitsrecht. Ein europäischer Weg?, in: Eising, Rainer / Kohler-Koch, Beate (eds): Interessenpolitik in Europa, Baden-Baden: Nomos, 2005, pp. 341–362, Leiber, Simone / Falkner, Gerda: Sozialer Dialog der EU und nationale Sozialpartnerschaft. Chronik einer paradoxen Beziehung, in: Karlhofer, Ferdinand / Tálos, Emmerich (ed.): Sozialpartnerschaft. Österreichische und europäische Perspektiven, Wien: Lit, 2005, pp 159–183 and Lopez-Santana, Mariely: The Domestic Implications of European Soft Law. Framing and Transmitting Change in Employment Policy, in: Journal of European Public Policy, 2006 (Vol. 13), No. 4, pp. 481–499.

4   Estonia, Latvia, Lithuania, Poland, Slovakia, Slovenia, the Czech Republic and Hungary.
5   Bulgaria and Romania.
6   See Casale, Giuseppe: Experiences of Tripartite Relations in Central and Eastern European Countries, in: International Journal of Comparative Labour Law and Industrial Relations, 2000 (Vol. 16), No. 2, pp. 129–142; Kurtan, Sandor: Gewerkschaften und Tripartismus im ostmitteleuropäischen Systemwechsel, in: Merkel, Wolfgang / Sandschneider, Eberhard (eds): Systemwechsel 4. Die Rolle von Verbänden in Transformationsprozessen, Opladen: Leske+Budrich, pp. 115–135; Mailand, Mikkel / Due, Jesper: Social Dialogue in Central and Eastern Europe. Present State and Future Development, in: European Journal of Industrial Relations, 2004 (Vol. 10), No. 2, pp. 179–197; Reutter, Werner: Tripartism without Corporatism. Trade Unions in Eastern and Central Europe, in: Agh, Attila / Ilonszki, Gabriella (eds): Parliaments and Organized Interests. The Second Steps, Hungarian Centre of Democracy Studies, Budapest, 1996, pp. 59–78.
7   See the overviews by Ost, David: After Postcommunism. Legacies and the Future of Unions in Eastern Europe, in: Phelan, Craig (ed.): The Future of Organised Labour. Global Perspectives, Oxford: Lang, 2006, pp. 305–331; Pleines, Heiko: Sozialpartner, Oligarchen und graue Eminenzen. Zur Rolle nicht-staatlicher Akteure in wirtschaftspolitischen Entscheidungsprozessen, in: Höhmann, Hans-Hermann / Pleines, Heiko (eds): Wirtschaftspolitik in Osteuropa zwischen ökonomischer

of a comprehensive study, Stephen Crowley concludes that labour relations in the new EU member states tend to resemble the American model, and therefore might not be compatible with the EU's system.[8]

Many analyses of trade unions and labour relations in the post-socialist EU member states have been conducted to date.[9]

Kultur, Institutionenbildung und Akteursverhalten. Russland, Polen und Tschechische Republik im Vergleich, Bremen: Edition Temmen, 2003, pp. 225–245 and Sil, Rudra / Candland, Christopher: Institutional Legacies and the Transformation of Labour. Late-Industrializing and Post-Socialist Economies in Comparative-Historical Perspective, in: Candland, Christopher / Sil, Rudra (eds): The Politics of Labor in a Global Age. Continuity and Change in Late-Industrializing and Post-Socialist Economies, Oxford: Oxford University Press, 2001, pp. 285–308. A more differentiated perspective, citing numerous successful examples of political influence by trade unions provide Avdagic, Sabina: State-Labour Relations in East Central Europe. Explaining Variations in Union Effectiveness, in: Socio-Economic Review, 2005 (Vol. 3), No. 1, pp. 25–53 and Matthes, Claudia-Yvette / Terletzki, Peggy: Tripartite Bargaining and its Impact on Stabilisation Policy in Central and Eastern Europe, in: International Journal of Comparative Labour Law and Industrial Relations, 2005 (Vol. 21), No. 3, pp. 369–403. However, they do not challenge the widely held view that trade union interest representation is extremely weak in comparison to Western Europe.

8   Crowley, Stephen: Explaining Labor Weakness in Post-Communist Europe, in: East European Politics and Society, 2004 (Vol. 18), No. 3, pp. 394–429. In a similar vein argues Vanhuysse, Pieter: Workers without Powers. Agency, Legacies and Labour Decline in East European Varieties of Capitalism, in: Czech Sociological Review, 2007 (Vol. 43), No. 3, pp. 459–522.

9   An overview of this topic present Kohl, Heribert / Platzer, Hans-Wolfgang: Arbeitsbeziehungen in Mittelosteuropa. Transformation und Integration. Die acht neuen EU-Mitgliedsländer im Vergleich, 2nd edn, Baden-Baden: Nomos, 2004. More important, however, are the numerous individual studies, which taken together provide a rather comprehensive body of knowledge. Examples pertaining to the countries covered in this publication (Poland, the Czech Republic and Slovakia) include Čambáliková, M.: Tripartismus in der Slowakei – Leere Struktur oder außerparlamentarische Form der Interessenvertretung?, in: Zeitschrift für Gemeinwirtschaft, 2001 (Vol. 38), No. 6, pp. 27–46; Cox, Terry M. / Mason, Robert: Interest Groups and the Development of Tripartism in East Central Europe, in: European Journal of Industrial Relations, 2000 (Vol. 6), No. 3, pp. 325–347; Deppe, Rainer / Tatur, Melanie: Rekonstitution und Marginalisierung. Transformationsprozesse und Gewerkschaften in Ungarn und Polen, Frankfurt/M.: Campus, 2002; Dvorakova, Z.: Trade Unions, Works Councils and Staff Involvement in the Modernising Czech Republic, in: International Journal of Public Sector Management, 2003 (Vol. 16), No. 6, pp. 424–433; Frege, Carola M.: The Illusion of Union-Management Cooperation in Postcommunist Central Eastern Europe, in: East European Politics and Societies, 2000 (Vol. 13), No. 3, pp. 636–660; Gąsior-Niemiec, Anna: Civil Society and New Modes of Governance in Poland, in: Polish Sociological Review, 2007, No. 157, pp. 65–85; Kubicek, Paul J.: Organized Labor in Postcommunist States. From Solidarity to Infirmity, Pittsburgh: University of Pittsburgh Press, 2004; Kroupa, Aleš / Mansfeldová, Zdenka: The Democratisation of Industrial Relations in the Czech Republic – Work Organisation and Employee Representation. Case Study from the Electronic Industry, in: Smith, S. (ed.): Local Communities and Post-communist Transformation. Czechoslovakia, the Czech Republic and Slovakia, London: Routledge, 2003, pp. 126–142; Mansfeldová, Zdenka: Social Partnership in the Czech Republic, in: Kirschbaum, S. J. (ed.): Historical Reflections on Central Europe, Basingstoke: Macmillan, 1999, pp. 207–218; Myant, Martin / Slocock, Brian / Smith, Simon: Tripartism in the Czech and Slovak Republics, in: Europe-Asia Studies, 2000 (Vol. 52), No. 4, pp. 723–739; Myant, Martin / Smith, Simon: Czech Trade Unions in Comparative Perspective, in: European Journal of Industrial Relations, 1999 (Vol. 5), No. 3, pp. 265–285; Ost, David: The Weakness of Symbolic Strength. Labor and Union Identity in Poland, in: Crowley, Stephen / Ost, David (eds): Workers

1.5. Trade Unions from the New Member States in EU Multilevel Governance

Interest representation on the EU level poses formidable challenges to the trade unions from the post-socialist countries. The quantitative representation of non-governmental organizations from the new member states is weak. While German, Belgian, French and Italian organizations are represented in 90% of the relevant umbrella organizations with respect to social policy, the new member states lie at the other end of the spectrum with only 40–50% representation, as an analysis by Wasner demonstrates.[10]

For trade unions from the new member states, the EESC constitutes a central channel of participation on the EU level. Organizations from the new member states received observer status in the EESC by the mid-1990s. Since the EU enlargement, Poland has had twenty-one members in the EESC, while the Czech Republic and Slovakia are represented by twelve and nine members, respectively. Several trade unions from the new member states were already involved in EU-wide umbrella organizations prior to the accession and were thus included in the Social Dialogue. A further aspect of international engagement is the participation in European Work Councils in multi-national firms.[11]

However, up to now, no serious empirical studies have been conducted about the integration of the post-socialist trade unions in EU decision-making processes. The few existing academic analyses have largely been limited to a description of the general conditions and related problems.[12] A systematic, empirically-based survey of the

after Workers' States, Lanham: Rowman & Littlefield, 2001, pp. 79–96; Ost, David: The Defeat of Solidarity. Anger and Politics in Postcommunist Europe, Ithaca: Cornell University Press, 2005; Pańków, Włodzimierz / Gąciarz, Barbara: Industrial Relations in Poland. From Social Partnership to Enlightened Paternalism?, in: Blazyca, George / Rapacki, Ryszard (ed.): Poland into the New Millenium, Cheltenham: Edward Elgar, 2001, pp. 72–90 and Pollert, Anna: Labor and Trade Unions in the Czech Republic, 1989–2000, in: Crowley, Stephen / Ost, David (eds): Workers after Workers' States. Labor and Politics in Postcommunist Eastern Europe, Lanham: Rowman & Littlefield, 2001, pp. 13–36.

10 Wasner, Barbara: Europäische Institutionenpolitik und die Vernetzung sozialpolitischer Verbände, in: Knodt, M. / Finke, B. (eds): Europäische Zivilgesellschaft. Konzepte, Akteure, Strategien, Wiesbaden: Verlag für Sozialwissenschaften, 2005, pp. 129–152.

11 A detailed study of their role in the countries under study here can be found by Tholen, Jochen: Labour Relations in Central Europe. The Impact of Multinationals' Money, Aldershot: Ashgate, 2007.

12 Borragán, Nieves Pérez-Solórzano: The Organisation of Business Interests in Central and East European Countries for EU Representation, in: Greenwood, J. (ed.): The Challenge of Change in EU Business Associations, Basingstoke: Palgrave, 2003, pp. 213–225; Mansfeldová, Zdenka: Czech Trade Unions and Employers' Associations in the European Social Dialogue, in: Obradovic, Daniela / Pleines, Heiko (eds): Civil Society Groups from the New Post-Socialist Member States in EU Governance, Stuttgart: Ibidem, 2007 and Einbock, Joanna: The Participation of Polish Trade Unions in EU Governance, in: Obradovic, Daniela / Pleines, Heiko (eds): Civil Society Groups from the New Post-Socialist Member States in EU Governance, Stuttgart: Ibidem, 2007, pp. 231–241.

experiences, modes of participation, successes and pitfalls of the new member state trade union representatives on the EU level is thus lacking.

1.6.   Integration and Europeanization

In this book the role of trade unions from post-socialist member states in EU governance will be investigated from two angles. On the one hand the actual (and not merely formal) inclusion of trade unions from the new member states in decision-making processes on the EU level is concerned. Here we will differentiate between the different methods of exerting influence and forums of decision-making. And the subjective self-evaluation of the trade union representatives with respect to their participation will be compared with the evaluation of other actors and objective criteria. On the other hand the Europeanization of trade unions, i.e. the influence of the EU on the relevant actors, will be examined.

Political engagement on the EU level requires three abilities from interest groups, including trade unions. The first is the general ability to engage in political decision-making processes. The second is the ability to actively participate on the EU level, and the third is the fulfilment of the EU criteria that regulate access to the various consultation processes on the EU level.

From a chronological perspective, most interest groups first develop the basic ability to engage in political decision-making processes. In most cases, they commence their work on the national or regional level and develop a position that they wish to communicate to political decision-makers. Therefore, they have to know who the relevant decision-makers are and seek the appropriate way to communicate, that is, they must develop a thorough understanding of political processes. Strategies for easier access to political decision-makers include the procurement of expert knowledge, public protests and media attention. All of these strategies require resources, which range from technical expertise to active members and from financial resources to savoir-faire in public relations.

Engagement on the EU level requires additional personnel as well as new skills. The latter include basic skills like English language ability and knowledge about the decision-making structures in the EU, but also other more specialized abilities like networking on the multinational level. The difficulties inherent to the multilevel system are evident in the inability of nearly all interest groups to orchestrate protest actions on the EU level (in contrast to the national level). This means that engagement at the EU level cannot simply be understood as the logical extension of national political activities. Engagement at the EU level requires new capacities.

At least on paper, the European Commission has erected an additional barrier by introducing minimum qualifications for interest groups wishing to participate in EU decision-making processes based on the principles of transparency, accountability and representativeness. Trade unions wishing to submit feedback to the Commission's draft regulations must therefore be prepared to furnish the Commission and the public at large with the necessary information.[13]

Based on the structure of trade union organizations, channels of influence and relevant institutions on the EU level, different categories can be established in order to evaluate how effectively trade unions from the post-socialist member states have been able to integrate themselves into decision-making processes at the EU level. In terms of organizational structures, Greenwood differentiates (1) national organizations that exert influence on the EU level via national cooperation with their governments, (2) national organizations that have direct contact with EU organs, (3) transnational organizations and (4) international trade union umbrella organizations represented in Brussels.[14] This differentiation is relatively general, and the division between (3) and (4) is not conclusive. It therefore makes more sense to categorize according to channels of influence or forums of decision-making.

In principle, there are six ways for trade unions to exert influence on political decision-making processes at the EU level: (1) direct consultations with the European Commission, (2) consultations with national representatives in the Council of Ministers, (3) direct consultations with the European Parliament, (4) participation in the Social Dialogue, (5) involvement in the EESC, (6) engagement in transnational umbrella organizations and networks. An office in Brussels is also frequently cited as a channel of influence. While an office does not automatically guarantee involvement in decision-making processes, it can facilitate the pursuit of all the avenues listed above.

According to the channels of influence, there are four relevant forums for political decision-making for trade unions: (1) the European Commission or the appropriate Directorate-General, (2) the Council of Ministers or the appropriate national representation at the Council of Ministers or the relevant working group, (3) the EU Parliament or the responsible parliamentary committee and (4) the Social Dialogue. The fifth and sixth channels listed in the previous paragraph represent organizations (EESC or European umbrella organizations) that offer an alternative form of access to the relevant four forums of decision-making.

In addition to addressing the trade unions' integration into decision-making processes, the book also examines their Europeanization. This concerns not only the extent to which the EU level is being integrated into trade union activity and what

---

13   For a conceptualisation of the required capacities, see Obradovic, Daniela / Pleines, Heiko: The Capacity of Civil Society Organisations to Participate in EU Multi-Level Governance. An Analytical Framework, in: Obradovic, Daniela / Pleines, Heiko (eds): The Capacity of Central and East European Interest Groups to Participate in EU Governance, Stuttgart: Ibidem, 2007, pp. 13–24.

14   Greenwood, Justin: Interest Representation in the European Union, New York: Palgrave Macmillan, 2003, pp. 160–161.

significance the trade unions accord to interest representation on the EU level: It must also be examined if ideas, concepts or values from the EU level are being transferred to the national and sub-national levels, i.e. if an exchange is taking place between Brussels and the new member states' trade unions.

Europeanization will be defined here according to Radaelli:

Europeanisation consists of processes of a) construction, b) diffusion and c) institutional-isation of formal and informal rules, procedures, policy paradigms, styles, 'ways of doing things', and shared beliefs and norms which are first defined and consolidated in the EU policy process and then incorporated in the logic of domestic (national and subnational) discourse, political structures and public policies.[15]

Such a Europeanization is only possible when there is cross-linking between the levels. With respect to the trade unions, the first condition for Europeanization is integration into the EU level in trade-union-related work and the perception of the EU as an important decision-making level.

If this condition is met, it can be investigated whether ideas, concepts or values from the EU level are indeed transferred to national (and subnational) levels, that is if a true exchange is occurring between Brussels and the new member states concerning the trade unions. This exchange should encompass the discussion of issues and behavioural and normative harmonization. This issue is not only important for an understanding of national trade union activity, but it is also relevant for the long-term capacity of trade unions to effectively integrate themselves into decision-making processes on the EU level.

In the empirical analysis, these two aspects, integration in decision-making and Europeanization, will largely focus on the actors, that is on the trade unions, and to a lesser degree on individual policy fields. The primary objective is to evaluate the overall situation of the trade unions. Our policy research will therefore be interaction-oriented rather than problem-oriented.[16] However, the focus on trade unions will automatically result in a concentration on the policy fields of labour market regulation and social policy.[17]

---

15   Radaelli, Claudio M.: Europeanisation. Solution or Problem?, in: European Integration Online Papers, 2004, No. 16, pp. 3–4. An overview of the current state of research is given by Quaglia, Lucia et al.: Europeanization, in: Cini, Michelle (ed.): European Union Politics, 2nd edn, Oxford: Oxford University Press, 2007, pp. 405–420; Axt, Hans-Jürgen / Milosoki, Antonio / Schwarz, Oliver: Europäisierung – ein weites Feld. Literaturbericht und Forschungsfragen, in: Politische Vierteljahresschrift, 2007 (Vol. 48), No. 1, pp. 136–149.

16   Scharpf, Fritz W.: Games Real Actors Play. Actor-Centered Institutionalism in Policy Research, Boulder/CO: Westview, 1997, pp. 10–12.

17   A research project initiated by the Friedrich Ebert Foundation provides an overview of the trade unions' positions with respect to economic and social policy. An overview of the results is provided by Busemeyer, Marius R. / Kellermann, Christian / Petring, Alexander / Stuchlík, Andrej: Overstretching Solidarity? Trade Unions' National Perspectives on the European Economic and Social Model, Friedrich Ebert Stiftung, Berlin, 2007, http://library.fes.de/pdf-files/id/04751.pdf

While our focus is on the trade unions, the analysis of their influence is also valuable for an analysis of the EU political system. An investigation of the experiences of trade union organizations from Central and East European member states offers a missing link between the research on post-socialist trade unions and EU governance.

First, the Eastern expansion presents the first big test of how accessible the post-Maastricht system is for newcomers. This concerns the openness of European umbrella organizations as well as the capacity of EU institutions to organize comprehensive consultations in light of the rapid increase in the number of interest groups.

Second, the investigation of the participation of the relatively weak trade unions from the new member states in decision-making processes will help to clarify the relationship between formal representation and actual participation on the EU level.

Third, the new post-socialist member states pose interesting cases for an analysis of the influence of EU multilevel governance on the political role of trade unions. Because the accession negotiations were protracted and formal, the European Commission initiated a series of programmes for interest groups from the candidate countries in order to prepare them for collaborative work in the EU. As a result, they were able to build new coalitions on different EU levels.

Fourth, the recent integration into EU governance offers a chance to have a new look at forms and causes of Europeanization.

1.7.   Structure of the Book

The contributions in this edited volume examine the integration of trade unions from the post-socialist member states, namely from Poland, the Czech Republic and Slovakia, in decision-making processes on the EU level and resulting Europeanization effects. The contributions are grouped into two parts.

The first part analyses the rules and actors. The chapter by Janna Wolff gives an overview of the involvement of trade unions in EU governance, focusing on the formal channels of influence. The following three chapters then examine the trade unions from the post-socialist member states as actors in EU governance. The contribution by Aleksandra Lis assesses the capacity of trade unions to engage in politics based on quantitative indicators. Brigitte Krech then goes on to describe the formal representation of Czech, Polish and Slovak trade unions on the EU level. Andrej Stuchlík, Christian Kellermann, Alexander Petring and Marius R. Busemeyer finally put the policy positions of trade unions from the new member states into a comparative perspective. The first part ends with a case study by Katarzyna Gajewska on the engagement of Polish trade unions on the EU level during the debate on the EU Service Directive.

The second part of the book then presents three country studies based on the results of an interview project conducted in summer 2007. The first chapter in this part by Heiko Pleines describes the research design of the project. The results of the country studies are summarized by Heiko Pleines in the conclusion. The interview results are documented in the appendix. The following three chapters provide country studies of Poland written by Joanna Einbock, of the Czech Republic by Zdenka Mansfeldová and of Slovakia by Monika Čambáliková. Each country study gives an overview of the relevant trade unions and their engagement in national politics before elaborating on the integration into EU-level decision-making processes and Europeanization effects based on the interview results.

Part II. Rules and Actors

Janna Wolff

2. Going a Long Way to Europe – Trade Unions in EU Governance

Indeed, to some unions, Europe risks being seen as the cutting edge of globalisation's worst effect [...] and there is a mood less willing to recognise that globalisation has benefits, as well as draw-backs
ETUC, 'Seville Manifesto 2007'[1]

2.1. Introduction

Trade unions across Europe have never constituted a homogenous group. They have developed against different socio-economic backgrounds and under varying political systems. As a result, considerable differences exist with respect to their history, their political and economic importance, the activities they carry out, as well as the interests they represent. Today, most unions have to interact with an increasing number of political actors at the national as well as at the European level.

Against this background it is quite difficult to draw up a consistent picture of 'Trade Unions in the European Union'. This task has become even trickier since the formerly communistic countries acceded to the European Union (EU) in 2004. Nevertheless, some general remarks on the development of European organized labour interests can be made.

After World War II, trade unions in Western Europe played an important role in promoting democratization and social rights. Regardless of their traditional allegiances to different political parties or religions, unions have generally been considered representatives of the working class. They were generally involved in tripartite negotiations between the national government, employers and workers. Given their growing number of members and their corresponding ability to mobilize electoral pressure, their national political influence increased continuously in most Western European countries until the 1970s.

However, the process of European economic integration as well as the increasing international interdependency of economies has substantially lowered the political and regulatory control of the nation state over its now transboundary economies. The first oil shock in 1973 made it clear that neither European nor global economic integration remained exclusively under national political control. Growing international interdependency and proceeding liberalization as realized through the Single

---

1   European Trade Union Confederation: The Seville Manifesto, 2007, p. 1, http://www.etuc.org/ IMG/pdf_CES-Depliant_Manifeste-EN.pdf

European Market (1987) intensified competition between European labour markets and led to a significant decline in the influence of nationally based labour movements. To compensate these losses, unions were compelled to develop strategies that reach far beyond domestic politics.

Today, unions have to face even more challenges. An increasing level of education and rising economic wealth for large parts of European societies have diversified and separated interests and lifestyles, which in turn has led to increasing individualisation and to a decrease in social cohesion.[2] In addition, the working population's interests have become more diverse, which complicates their representation by unions.[3] As a result, unionization has decreased throughout the last decades in most EU member states, especially in the new member states.[4]

Even though there currently is 'no uniform trend of union embeddedness in political systems across member states'[5], one potential instrument for coping with the described challenges is the improvement of unions' interest representation at the European level. How such structures have developed over the last decades and what the different channels of influence look like will be described in the following sections.

2.2. Getting started

European economic integration was set up in the early 1950s; according to some authors, European unions failed to create appropriate structures at this new level for quite some time.[6] Only two institutions were created in this decade: the European Regional Organisation of the International Confederation of Free Trade Unions (ERO-ICFTU), founded in 1950, and, in response to the creation of the European Coal and Steel Community (1951), the Trade Union Committee of Twenty-One, established in 1952. However, their influence and competencies remained very minor.

The pertinent reason identified for this lack of engagement is the way in which the unions of that time estimated the potential gains of creating international, i.e., European unions. Whilst unions that were weakly incorporated into domestic politics perceived the European level as a promising new channel of influence, strongly incorporated

---

2   Klammer, Ute / Hoffmann, Reiner: Unvermindert wichtig. Gewerkschaften vor alten und neuen Aufgaben, in: Aus Politik und Zeitgeschichte, 2003, B 47-48/2003, pp. 23–29, here p. 23.
3   ETUC: Strategy and Action Plan 2007 – 2011, Sevilla, 2007, p. 16, http://www.etuc.org/IMG/pdf_ Rapport_congress_EN-2.pdf
4   Visser, Jelle: Trends in Unionisation and Collective Bargaining, International Labour Office, September 2000, http://www.ilo.org/public/english/bureau/exrel/global/ilopub/tucb.pdf
5   Greenwood, Justin: Interest Representation in the European Union, New York: Palgrave Macmillan, 2007, p. 103.
6   Buschak, Willy: Der Europäische Gewerkschaftsbund und die Europäischen Gewerkschafts-verbände, FES library 2003, p. 1, http://library.fes.de/library/netzquelle/eugew/geschichte/pdf/ buschak.pdf

unions explicitly hesitated to shift competencies.[7] Moreover, national traditions and interests among member states' unions prevented effective cooperation and thus thwarted the formation of European unions.[8] Consequentially, unions have continually failed to cooperate effectively and set up common positions against a Europeanized economy. European unions are still grappling with this problem today.[9]

Nevertheless, the organization of European labour interests has advanced and improved continuously over the recent decades: One year after the signing of the Treaty establishing the European Economic Community (EEC) in 1957, the Trade Union Committee of Twenty-One was absorbed by the European Trade Union Secretary (ETUS), which was founded by ICFTU's European affiliates. In 1969, ETUS adopted a new name, the European Confederation of Free Trade Unions in the European Community (ECFTU). As it was composed only of EEC member states, however, the Trade Union Committee for the European Free Trade Area (EFTA-TUC) emerged the same year. To overcome this division, in 1973 ECFTU and EFTA-TUC merged into the European Trade Union Confederation (ETUC), which still exists today.

2.2.1.   European Trade Union Confederation

The European Trade Union Confederation (ETUC) is located in Brussels and has about sixty employees. Membership in ETUC has never been restricted to EU member states. It currently comprises eighty-two member organizations from a total of thirty-six European countries and twelve industry federations.[10] It claims to represent the interests of sixty million trade unionists.

The supreme authority of ETUC is its Congress, which meets once every four years and elects the members of the Executive Committee, which meets four times a year; it also elects the President and the General Secretary. The Congress and Executive Committee are composed of representatives from the affiliated organizations in proportion to their number of members.

---

7   Greenwood, Justin: Interest Representation in the European Union, New York: Palgrave Macmillan, 2007, p. 109.
8   See Streeck, Wolfgang: Gewerkschaften zwischen Nationalstaat und Europäischer Union, Max-Planck-Institut für Gesellschaftsforschung, Working Paper 96/1, 1996.
9   See Buschak, Willy: Der Europäische Gewerkschaftsbund und die Europäischen Gewerkschaftsverbände, FES library, 2003, http://library.fes.de/library/netzquelle/eugew/geschichte/pdf/buschak. pdf and Armingeon, Klaus: Die doppelte Herausforderung der europäischen Gewerkschaften, in: Gewerkschaftliche Monatshefte, 1991 (Vol. 42), No. 6, pp. 371–381.
10   Industry federations represent separate industrial sectors such as agriculture, food or the steel industry. Most of the twelve European federations that are members of ETUC today were founded around the millennium. For further information see: www.etuc.org/a/17 and Buschak, Willy: Der Europäische Gewerkschaftsbund und die Europäischen Gewerkschaftsverbände, FES library, 2003, http://library.fes.de/library/netzquelle/eugew/geschichte/pdf/buschak.pdf

Additionally, ETUC supports the European Trade Union Institute for Research, Education and Health and Safety (ETUI-REHS), whose three branches specialize in different areas and provide useful preparatory work for ETUC's political decisions. ETUC's prime objective is

> to promote the European Social Model and to work for the development of a united Europe of peace and stability where working people and their families can enjoy full human and civil rights and high living standards.[11]

Further, it

> aspires to represent all European working people and promotes the extension and consolidation of political liberties and democracy, respect for human and trade union rights and the elimination of all forms of discrimination.[12]

One of ETUC's important tasks is to build up public political pressure. Its primary means of doing so is to initiate large-scale public protests and demonstrations. Given the fact that cross-border protests require enormous logistical efforts, ETUC has been relatively successful. One of the most visible actions undertaken was a recent demonstration in Strasbourg attended by approximately 50,000 protesters, who expressed their resentment towards the European Service Directive in 2006.[13]

As indicated above, the main problem confronting ETUC is the different expectations of its affiliates. Some of them, mostly the stronger national unions, still prefer ETUC to hold a mere coordination function, reflected in its current confederal structure, whilst others support the idea of ETUC as a supranational organization, including a broader mandate from its members.[14] Reconciling these different views is still one of ETUC's major challenges. Furthermore, ETUC is only one of the many interest groups European decision-makers have to deal with. To be heard and to gain access to the responsible decision-makers under such circumstances requires an especially coherent structure as well as excellent expertise. Currently, ETUC is approaching these challenges with a vigorous change of strategy. Last year, at its eleventh Congress in Seville, it adopted a new Manifesto for action that is 'committed to going on the offensive on behalf of European workers'.[15] It identifies five main areas of action: (1) the European labour market; (2) the Social Dialogue, collective bargaining and worker participation; (3) better European economic, social and environmental governance; (4) a stronger European Union; (5) stronger trade unions and a stronger ETUC.

---

11   ETUC: Our Aims, http://www.etuc.org/r/2, accessed 1 February 2008.
12   International Institute of Social History: ETUC Archives. History, http://www.iisg.nl/archives/en/files/e/10748348.php, accessed 1 February 2008.
13   Greenwood, Justin: Interest Representation in the European Union, New York: Palgrave Macmillan, 2007, pp. 100–112.
14   Ibid., p. 109.
15   ETUC: Manifesto, http://www.etuc.org/r/1223, accessed 1 February 2008.

Corresponding to the Manifesto, a new 'Strategy and Action Plan'[16] has been published in which ETUC outlines in detail its foreseen strategies and goals for 2011. It includes a declaration that defines in round terms ETUC's future plans and present self-conception:

The ETUC will be taking the initiative with new strategies, new campaigns, and improved organisation going well beyond monitoring and reacting to initiatives of employers and European institutions [...]. We must move from a defensive strategy to an offensive one.[17]

2.3. Social Partners / Social Dialogue

It has been stated that organized European labour interests' long-standing weakness has led to a 'paradoxical strength of business' and thus to the conclusion that 'business did not need a highly developed employer organization'.[18] Nevertheless, at least two organizations have emerged, such as the Union of Industrial and Employers' Confederations of Europe (UNICE)[19], founded in 1958, and the European Centre of Enterprises with Public Participation and of Enterprises of General Economic Interest (CEEP), founded in 1961. Whilst it had been difficult for European unions to organize their interests at the European level, it was even harder for European business, given the wide range of existing products, markets, and its endemic fragmentation.[20]

The European Commission recognized ETUC, UNICE and CEEP as European social partners in 1965, but the European Social Dialogue remained a noncommittal discussion group until the 1980s.[21] This was fundamentally changed when Jacques Delors took office as president of the European Commission. Delors, a trade unionist and former socialist minister in the French government, initiated the 'Val Duchesse'[22] process in 1985. This process aimed at incorporating social aspects into the European single market structure. Delors encouraged social partners ETUC and UNICE to participate in

---

16   ETUC: Strategy and Action Plan 2007–2011, Sevilla, 2007, http://www.etuc.org/IMG/pdf_Rapport_ congress_EN-2.pdf
17   Ibid., p. 19.
18   Greenwood, Justin: Interest Representation in the European Union, New York: Palgrave Macmillan, 2007, p. 95.
19   UNICE changed its name into BUSINESSEUROPE, The Confederation of European Business, in 2007.
20   Greenwood, Justin: Interest Representation in the European Union, New York: Palgrave Macmillan, 2007, p. 105
21   Leiber, Simone / Falkner, Gerda: Sozialer Dialog der EU und nationale Sozialpartnerschaft. Chronik einer paradoxen Beziehung, in: Karlhofer, Ferdinand / Tàlos, Emmerich (eds): Sozialpartnerschaft, Österreichische und Europäische Perspektiven, Wien, Münster: LIT Verlag, 2005, pp. 159–183, here p. 160.
22   Named after the Chateau near Brussels where the first meeting was held.

a bipartite labour market dialogue.[23] The intention was to achieve agreements at the European level that would bypass the veto-dominated negotiations in the Council at that time. It was the first time that the national organizations were excluded; solely the European business and labour confederations were addressed. However, because employers refused to enter into binding agreements and therefore preferred a non-committal exchange, this ambitious project failed in a medium-range perspective.

However, when it became clear in the preliminaries to the Maastricht Treaty that qualified majority voting (QMV) in the Council would be extended to a broader range of political issues of social relevance, employers finally abandoned their strategy of the 'empty chair'[24]. As a result, an agreement between the three social partners (ETUC, UNICE and CEEP) could be achieved, in which reforms to the Treaty decision-making provisions in the social policy field were proposed. This 'Protocol on Social Politics' was added to the Maastricht Treaty as an appendix in 1992 and incorporated as Articles 138 and 139 of the Treaty Establishing the European Communities (TEC). Following from this legal basis, the social partners were promoted to co-legislators in European social politics.

The European Social Dialogue embodies two forms: the bipartite dialogue consists of formal consultations, exchanges of views and negotiations and refers to the dialogue between the European employers and trade union organizations. The tripartite dialogue involves interaction with public authorities.[25] For more than ten years the social partners have been meeting regularly with the EU troika[26] on the eve of European Council meetings. This seems to be an attractive channel for social partners' interests but 'rapid turnover of the office bearer, together with the contrasting variations in culture and agendas of each Presidency, mean that the possibilities introduced by these relationships fluctuate considerably.'[27]

During the Convention drafting the Treaty establishing a Constitution for Europe, which took place in 2003/2004, the social partners were allocated observer status and

---

23 For further information see: Leiber, Simone / Falkner, Gerda: Sozialer Dialog der EU und natio-nale Sozialpartnerschaft. Chronik einer paradoxen Beziehung, in: Karlhofer, Ferdinand / Tàlos, Emmerich (eds): Sozialpartnerschaft, Österreichische und Europäische Perspektiven, Wien, Münster: LIT Verlag, 2005, pp. 159–183, and Greenwood, Justin: Interest Representation in the European Union, New York: Palgrave Macmillan, 2007.

24 Streeck, Wolfgang: Politikverflechtung und Entscheidungslücke. Zum Verhältnis von zwischen-staatlichen Beziehungen und sozialen Interessen im europäischen Binnenmarkt, in: Bentele, K. / Reissert, B. / Schettkat, R. (eds): Die Reformfähigkeit von Industriegesellschaften, Frankfurt, New York: Campus, pp. 101–130.

25 European Commission: European Social Dialogue, http://ec.europa.eu/employment_social/ social_dialogue/index_en.htm, accessed 1 February 2008.

26 That is the present and future Presidency of the Council and the European Commission.

27 Greenwood, Justin: Interest Representation in the European Union, New York: Palgrave Macmillan, 2007, p. 28.

they succeeded in drafting a Treaty clause aimed at protecting the status of the Social Dialogue.

Because the Constitutional Treaty failed to be adopted in 2005, the text was transformed last year into the so-called Reform Treaty (also known as the Lisbon Treaty). In general, ETUC appreciates the new Treaty and recognizes

> that there are important improvements in the text [...] when compared to the Nice Treaty like the introduction of full employment as a goal and the concept of social market economy.[28]

At the same time, ETUC fears that 'there could be a lower profile recognition of the role of social partners than was the case in the former EU constitutional treaty'[29] because of potential changes in terms of the legal value of the Social Dialogue / partners section.[30]

In summary it can be said that European social partners 'are the civil society players which have achieved most access to intergovernmental EU decision-making.'[31] Over the last decade, some of the successful negotiations between social partners and the European political actors have been implemented by directives. Respective negotiations have had a substantial influence on the directives concerning part-time work (1997), fixed-term work (1999), the adoption of the telework agreement (2002) and the adoption of the agreement on work-related stress (2004).

2.4. Formal channels of influence / institutions

For ETUC as well as for national unions there are various channels of influence in the European Union. Given that policy making in the EU is a 'complex interplay between the national and the European level'[32], the 'national route' and the 'European route' will be distinguished in the following. The former refers to traditional governmental channels and the latter to approaches through European institutions.

2.4.1. National route

Traditionally, trade unions in the European Union have preferred the 'national route' over the 'European route' to influence European politics, which is to convince national

---

28 ETUC: Statement, http://www.etuc.org/a/4176?var_recherche=%20reform%20treaty, accessed 1 February 2008.
29 Ibid.
30 To compare these texts: The Lisbon Treaty and the European Constitution. A side-by-side Comparison, Openeurope, 2008, http://www.openeurope.org.uk/research/comparative.pdf
31 Greenwood, Justin: Interest Representation in the European Union, New York: Palgrave Macmillan, 2007, p. 27.
32 Streeck, Wolfgang / Hassel, Anke: Trade Unions as Political Actors, in: Addison, John T. / Schnabel, Claus (eds): International Handbook of Trade Unions, Cheltenham, Northampton: Edward Elgar, 2003, pp. 335–365, here p. 361.

governments to adopt the unions' interests as their own in European interstate negotiations. Typical measures are individual consultations and negotiations with national
ministers and heads of governments. Since the Comité des représentants permanents
(COREPER) gained significance in the preliminary stage of Council decision-making,
the national diplomats in Brussels have also become important connecting factors.

These national channels have proven attractive for 'strong unions' having solid
relationships with political parties. But, although traditional union-party connections
have remained relatively stable over time,[33] the 'national route' has been challenged
by multiple factors: First, governments and parties change and unions thus have to
make continuous efforts to ensure adequate party support. Second, intergovernmental negotiations rely upon consensus and governments are therefore regularly forced
to sacrifice some issues. Finally, even where member state governments are willing to
defend unions' interests, the fact that more and more decisions are taken by quality
majority voting (QMV) raises the risk that specific interests will be overruled.

Unions that are rather weakly incorporated into domestic politics have generally
perceived the 'European route' as an auspicious opportunity to transport their interests more effectively.[34]

2.4.2.   European route

The 'European route' encompasses several options. The institutions available differ
regarding the degree of involvement in the European decision-making process.

2.4.2.1.   European Commission

The European Commission is divided into forty Directorates-General (DGs) that are
arranged around the present twenty-seven Commissioners, one of which is responsible for 'Employment, Social Affairs and Equal Opportunities'. Given its power to initiate and draft legislation, it has always been a relevant target for interest representation in the European Union. However, for a long time, interactions between the
Commission and civil actors were unstructured and informal. As a result, unions had
difficulties approaching the Commission, which led to some criticism concerning the
issues of transparency and legitimacy. To overcome these shortfalls, the Commission
recognized in its 'White Paper on Governance' (2001) the need to open up for a closer
dialogue with non-governmental actors, particularly with trade unions.[35]

---

33   Ibid.
34   Greenwood, Justin: Interest Representation in the European Union, New York: Palgrave Macmillan,
      2007, p. 103.
35   Commission of the European Communities: European Governance. A White Paper, Brussels,
      2001, pp. 14–15, http://ec.europa.eu/governance/white_paper/index_en.htm

As mentioned above, the bond between ETUC and the Commission has become stronger under the presidency of Jacques Delors. Comparably speaking, ETUC's closest ties are with the DG Employment and Social Affaires, but it is also well connected with DG Regio and DG Information. The Commission is funding some of ETUC's institutes, such as the European Trade Union Institute for Research, Education and Health and Safety. Whilst some authors consider this liaison advantageous[36], others criticize ETUC as being overly dependent upon DG Employment and Social Affairs, which is eroding its autonomy.[37]

Nonetheless, the European Commission remains an important partner for ETUC, especially since both are ambitious supporters of European integration.

2.4.2.2. European Parliament

The importance of the European Parliament (EP) as a channel of influence for European unions has climbed substantially in light of its increased decision-making competence.

The EP was directly elected in 1979 for the first time. Today, it comprises 785 members. Parliamentarians currently form seven political groups that are linked by political affiliation rather than by nationality. The Single European Act, adopted in 1987, introduced the cooperation procedure, in which the EP may adopt, amend or reject the Council's position within the legislative process. However, at that time, the Council could not be forced to ultimately take the EP's views into consideration. In 1992, the Treaty of Maastricht established the co-decision procedure, which stipulates that neither the Council nor the EP may adopt legislation without the other's consent. The Treaty of Amsterdam (1997) and the Treaty of Nice (2001) both extended the areas of application of the co-decision procedure.

Unions approach the EP primarily through (a) the parliamentarians and (b) the non-party Trade Union Coordination Intergroup, with which ETUC meets monthly. By this means, ETUC has succeeded in tabling its own amendments in the Parliament.[38] In return, ETUC supports the EP in that it 'will be mobilising behind a trade union programme for the next European Parliamentary elections in 2009.'[39]

---

36   Leisnik, P. / van Leemput, J. / Vilrokx, J.: The Challenges to Trade Unions in Europe, Cheltenham: Edward Elgar, 1996.

37   Martin, Andrew / Ross, George: Brave New World of European Labor, New York: Berghahn Books, 1999 and Greenwood, Justin: Interest Representation in the European Union, New York: Palgrave Macmillan, 2007, p. 96 and 111.

38   Greenwood, Justin: Interest Representation in the European Union, New York: Palgrave Macmillan, 2007, p. 104.

39   ETUC: Reform treaty. ETUC Laments a Missed Opportunity to Boost Social Europe, 18 October 2007, http://www.etuc.org/a/4117?var_recherche=reform%20treaty

Despite the close cooperation between ETUC and the European Parliament, which has always strongly supported the progression of 'Social Europe', the fact that the EP is by-passed in the Social Dialogue procedure has generated some tension.[40]

2.4.2.3. European Economic and Social Committee

The European Economic and Social Committee (EESC) was set up by the 1957 Rome Treaties as a consultative institution meant to involve economic and social interest groups in the establishment of the common market. Located in Brussels, it is composed of 344 members that are drawn from economic and social interest groups in Europe. They are nominated by national governments and appointed by the Council of the European Union. This procedure has led to the criticism that the ESC represents neither the breadth of national organized civil society nor transnational organizations. Accordingly, its capacity as a real 'social partner' is widely considered to be limited.[41]

The EESC is divided into three groups – employers, employees and various interests – that cover nine policy sections. The *Employees Group* is composed of members with a background in national trade union organizations, which makes it a useful partner regarding labour interest representation.

Even though the EESC claims that its role has been reinforced by each European Treaty[42], it still possesses advisory capacity only.

2.4.2.4. Committee of the Regions

The Committee of the Regions (CoR) is a forum for political actors 'that provides local and regional authorities with a voice at the heart of the European Union.'[43] It was established in 1994 and also holds advisory capacity only. In the course of the adoption of the Maastricht Treaty, five areas were determined where the European Commission and the Council are obliged to consult the CoR whenever new proposals are made, i.e., the areas of economic and social cohesion, trans-European infrastructure networks, health, education and culture. Just like the Economic and Social Committee, the CoR is composed of 344 persons who are proposed by the member states and appointed by

---

40   Greenwood, Justin: Interest Representation in the European Union, New York: Palgrave Macmillan, 2007, p. 104.
41   Ibid., pp. 41–42 and Leiber, Simone / Falkner, Gerda: Sozialer Dialog der EU und nationale Sozialpartnerschaft. Chronik einer paradoxen Beziehung, in: Karlhofer, Ferdinand / Tàlos, Emmerich (eds): Sozialpartnerschaft, Österreichische und Europäische Perspektiven, Wien, Münster: LIT Verlag, 2005, pp. 159–183, here pp. 160–161.
42   European Economic and Social Committee: Origins, http://www.eesc.europa.eu/organisation/how/index_en.asp, accessed 1 February 2008.
43   The Committee of the Regions: An Introduction, http://www.cor.europa.eu/pages/Presentation Template.aspx?view=folder&id=be53bd69-0089-465e-a173-fc34a8562341&sm=be53bd69-0089-465e-a173-fc34a8562341, accessed 1 February 2008.

the Council. National governments are required to assure that their delegations reflect the national political, geographical and regional / local balance. The Committee comprises several specialist commissions reflecting the areas in which it is consulted.

In terms of inter-institutional cooperation, the CoR has committed itself to consultation with the European Economic and Social Committee: 'to develop political cooperation in the areas of EU policy in which the activities of the social players and regional authorities are complementary'.[44]

However, despite its ambitious aims and its formal consultative powers, the CoR is still judged to have failed to be a significant partner for organized civil society.[45]

2.5. Conclusion

European integration is ongoing and will continue to challenge national unions. While losing members and political influence at the national level, trade unions in the European Union simultaneously have to deal with broadly varying interests regarding a European trade union movement.

Against this background, unions are likely to focus on the national as well as on the European strategy. Trying to solve national problems solely by applying the 'European route' will fail.[46] As long as nation states continue to dominate European politics, there will be an equal number of different national perspectives on European integration.[47] Trade unions have to learn how to pursue their goals on both levels. At the national level, trade unions have 'to defend their political status they achieved in the post war period'[48] in Western Europe, and at the EU level, they must strive to fortify their political influence by broadening their membership and by improving their ability to mobilize workers.

It remains to be seen whether European unions will succeed in overcoming their differences and evolve into a coherent and more influential social partner in EU Governance.

---

44 Committee of the Regions: Resolution of the Committee of the Regions on the Political Objectives of the Committee of the Regions (2006–2008), February 2006, p. 7, http://www.cor.europa.eu/pages/PresentationTemplate.aspx?view=folder&id=f823530f-f568-45a2-ad89-e2b8343a5b7f&sm=f823530f-f568-45a2-ad89-e2b8343a5b7f
45 Greenwood, Justin: Interest Representation in the European Union, New York: Palgrave Macmillan, 2007, p. 41.
46 Mund, Horst / Burmeister, Kai: Gewerkschaften vor der Herausforderung Europa – Nach der EU-Ratspräsidentschaft ist vor der Ratspräsidentschaft, Friedrich-Ebert-Stiftung Internationale Politikanalyse, May 2007, p. 2, http://library.fes.de/pdf-files/id/04473.pdf
47 Streeck, Wolfgang: Gewerkschaften zwischen Nationalstaat und Europäischer Union, Max-Planck-Institut für Gesellschaftsforschung, Working Paper 96/1, 1996, p. 11.
48 Streeck, Wolfgang / Hassel, Anke: Trade Unions as Political Actors, in: Addison, John T. / Schnabel, Claus (eds): International Handbook of Trade Unions, Cheltenham, Northampton: Edward Elgar, 2003, pp. 335–365, here p. 362.

Aleksandra Lis

3. Trade Union Strength in an EU-Wide Comparison

3.1. Introduction

The status quo of labour in Central and Eastern European countries has occupied political scientists and sociologists since the advent of the transition process triggered by the establishment of Solidarność in Poland in 1980. Solidarność's strong political involvement in the transition to a capitalist economy along with its puzzling failure to represent and defend working class interests[1] has led to much speculation about how to most accurately measure the strength of labour in the post-communist context.[2] When trade unions from the post-socialist states joined EU institutions via the eastern enlargement of 2004, the labour issue evolved into a pragmatic question about the trade unions' capacity to act successfully at the EU level.

In this chapter, the strength of trade unions from the old and new member states will be compared based on quantitative measures. These include trade union density and collective bargaining coverage along with the more complex concept of welfare state types as well as figures on trust and public financial support. This quantitative analysis will be used to compare the post-socialist countries under study with the EU average and with certain country groups. This will enable us to assess the extent to which the post-socialist member countries constitute a special case. Data refer to the accession year 2004 in order to describe the initial conditions of trade unions from the new member states when they became active at the EU level. Brief profiles of the main trade unions from the new post-socialist member states which joined the EU in 2004 are given in the appendix to this chapter.

3.2. Trade Union Density and Collective Bargaining Coverage

Classical indicators of trade union strength are union density and collective bargaining coverage. Union density measures the breadth of the trade union movement in a given country. Trade union density is often weighed against employer organization density in order to compare the strength of labour to the strength of capital. Employer organi-

---

1   Ost, David: The Defeat of Solidarity. Anger and Politics in Postcommunist Europe, Ithaca: Cornell University Press, 2006, chapters 1, 5, and 6, pp. 13–37, 121–179.
2   Crowley, Stephen: Explaining Labor Weakness in Post-Communist Europe. Historical Legacies and Comparative Perspective, in: East European Politics and Society, 2004 (Vol. 18), No. 3, pp. 394–429; Ekiert, Grzegorz / Kubik, Jan: Rebellious Civil Society. Popular Protest and Democratic Consolidation in Poland, 1989–1993, Ann Arbor: University Michigan Press, 1999.

zation density is measured in the same way as union density, i.e. by means of assessing its reach within a given country. The respective data are indicated in Table 3-1.

Collective bargaining coverage reflects the willingness of policy-makers to rely on the social partners in the field of economic policy. It is often correlated to union density, but there are nations (e.g. France and most Mediterranean countries) with low degrees of union density but high collective bargaining coverage.

Collective bargaining also differs with respect to its degree of centralization, which encompasses both the level at which bargaining takes place and the way the different levels interact,[3] e.g. whether an establishment is covered by single-employer collective bargaining or multi-employer collective bargaining. Lionel Fulton[4] from the Labour Research Department and the European Trade Union Institute for Research, Education and Health and Safety (ETUI-REHS) differentiates countries according to whether bargaining takes place at the national, industrial or company level or e.g. at two levels simultaneously. In Austria, Slovenia, Portugal, the Netherlands, Greece, Denmark, Italy and Germany, the industrial level plays a key role in negotiations. Malta, the Czech Republic, Poland, the United Kingdom, Bulgaria, Estonia, Hungary, Latvia and Lithuania organize collective bargaining mostly at the company level. There are also a couple of countries that utilize a mixture of levels. In France, Cyprus, Sweden, Slovakia and Romania, collective bargaining takes place both at the industrial and company levels, whereas in Ireland, Spain and Finland, apart from the industrial level, the national level also comes into play, usually in terms of setting the framework for the bargaining process. In Table 3-2 the percentage given for centralization indicates the degree to which collective bargaining takes place on the national level.

Another important indicator for the assessment of the quality of industrial relations in a given country is workplace representation, which possesses a qualitative dimension. According to Lionel Fulton[5], workplace representation varies across the EU and entails representation both through local union bodies and works councils – or similar structures elected by employees. In Austria, Germany, Luxembourg and the Netherlands, workplace representation is provided mainly through works councils that are elected by all employees; there is no legal provision for workplace structures for unions. In eight other nations – Belgium, France, Greece, Hungary, Portugal, Slovakia, Slovenia and Spain – the law allows both union and works council structures to co-exist at the workplace. However, there are major differences between the countries in this group. In some, like Greece and Portugal, works councils exist more in theory

---

3   Fulton, L.: Worker Representation in Europe. Labour Research Department and ETUI-REHS, 2007, http://www.worker-participation.eu/national_industrial_relations/across_europe/collective_bargaining__1 and http://www.worker-participation.eu/national_industrial_relations/across_europe/workplace_representation__1, accessed 4 March 2008.
4   Ibid.
5   Ibid.

than in practice, while in Hungary, Slovakia and Slovenia, the rights and duties of the works council and the local union body overlap to some degree. Spanish works councils undertake collective bargaining and are closely tied to the union, whereas in Belgium and France, the union is clearly the dominant partner. Fulton's analysis further suggests that Bulgaria, Estonia, Ireland and Great Britain could in some ways be seen as fitting into the same pattern. In the past, unions provided the only channel for representation for these countries' labourers, but now elected employee representatives are legally permitted to act alongside the unions. One key difference between this group and countries like Belgium and France is that the legal rights of these elected represent-atives are very limited. In the remaining eleven states – Cyprus, the Czech Republic, Denmark, Finland, Italy, Latvia, Lithuania, Malta, Poland, Romania and Sweden – work-place representation is essentially the domain of the unions (sometimes works coun-cils are an alternative if there is no union presence), although the rights they enjoy vary considerably. Fulton concludes that one common thread running through most of the states is the important role that trade unions play in workplace representation. A union presence is also critical for effective representation at the workplace in those countries without strong legislative support for unions, such as the UK and many of the Central and Eastern Europe states. In these countries, the evidence suggests that without unions, there is little workplace representation – a situation which the recent legislation implementing the EU directive on information and consultation seems unlikely to change. The respective data are given in Table 3-1.

Another common indicator for measuring labour strength is strike activity. This indicator is quite ambiguous and its interpretation largely depends on its context. Crowley states that 'high strike rates might be an indicator of union desperation rather than strength, and conversely, strong unions might not need to strike if they can obtain concessions without industrial action.'[6] The strike activity index (see Table 3-2) is very low for the new EU member states. The data gathered by Crowley show similarly low levels of this indicator.[7] He points out that in order to interpret these low figures as indicators of labour strength in Central and Eastern Europe, one would need to have evidence of concessions obtained without industrial action. However, Crowley argues that such evidence is lacking.

Yet the available evidence suggests just the opposite: over the past decade, there was a sharp decline in real wages throughout the region, and while wages have since risen in many countries, wages are still quite low in comparative terms, even for those countries joining the EU.[8]

---

6   Crowley, Stephen: Explaining Labor Weakness in Post-Communist Europe. Historical Legacies and Comparative Perspective, in: East European Politics and Society, 2004 (Vol. 18), No. 3, pp. 394–429, here p. 404.
7   Ibid., p. 404.
8   Ibid., p. 406.

These categories form the core of established research on welfare state policy and political economy.[9] Figures for EU member states as of the enlargement year 2004 are given in Tables 3-1 and 3-2.

Data presented below in Tables 3-1 and 3-2 indicate some evident trends in the EU member states. In 2004, union density in Europe was generally lower than employer organization density. If we divide the results in Table 3-1 conventionally into high (60–100%), medium (40–59%) and low (1–39%) degrees of density, we can clearly see that with respect to the variable 'trade union density' a majority of EU member states fall into the category 'low degree of density'. These countries are: Austria, the Czech Republic, Estonia, France, Germany, Great Britain, Greece, Hungary, Ireland, Italy, Latvia, Lithuania, the Netherlands, Poland, Portugal, Slovakia and Spain. There are only five countries that could be classified as having a high degree of density: Cyprus, Denmark, Finland, Malta and Sweden. According to the data available for 2004, Belgium, Luxemburg and Spain had a medium degree of density.

Trade union and employer organization density are not necessarily similar in degree. In Estonia, Latvia, Lithuania, Poland and Slovakia, both trade union density and employer organization density are low. On the other hand, the indicators are both high in Malta and Finland. However, most of the countries score high only on one of the indicators. Austria, France, Germany, the Netherlands and Spain exhibit low union density but high employer organization density. Luxemburg and Belgium show medium trade union density and high employer organization density. In contrast, Sweden and Denmark have been found to possess a combination of high trade union density and medium employer organization density.

Workplace representation looks better for trade unions. This indicator is again divided according to the same logic into three categories: high (60–100%), medium (40–59%) and low (1–39%) levels of workplace representation. Only Estonia, Hungary, Latvia, Lithuania, Poland, Portugal and Malta score low on this variable. Austria, Belgium, Denmark, Finland, France, Italy, Netherlands, Slovenia and Sweden all exhibit high percentages of workplace representation. The rest of the countries for which these data were available demonstrate a medium level of workplace representation. Although there are only seven countries with low values for this indicator, it is striking that five of them happen to be new post-communist EU member states, four of which (Estonia,

---

9   Espin-Andersen, G: The Three Worlds of Welfare Capitalism, Cambridge: Polity Press, 1990; Espin-Andersen, G: Social Foundations of Post-Industrial Economies, Oxford, New York: Oxford University Press, 1999; Goodin, R. E. / Heady, B. / Muffels, R. / Dirven, H. J.: The Real Worlds of Welfare Capitalism, Cambridge: Cambridge University Press, 1999; Leibfried, S.: Towards a European Welfare State? On Integrating Poverty Regimes into the European Community, in: Ferge, Z. / Kolberg, J. E. (eds): Social Policy in a Changing Europe, Frankfurt/M., Boulder/CO: Campus, Westview Press, 1992, pp. 235–259; Castles, F. G. / Mitchell, D.: Worlds of Welfare and Families of Nations, in: Castles, F. G. (ed.): Families in Nations. Patterns of public Policy in Western Democracies, Aldershot: Dartmouth, 1993, pp. 93–128.

Latvia, Lithuania and Poland) have high values for all three indicators discussed above. The most obvious conclusion to be drawn from this data set is that the Baltic States make up a group of national economies with very weak organized participation in industrial relations. Other post-communist new EU member states closely follow this group by virtue of their decreasing trade union density and medium employer organization density and workplace representation. The most prominent outlier is Slovenia, which reveals medium trade union and employer organization density and a high level of workplace representation.

Table 3-1:   Main Actors in Industrial Relations

Country	Trade Union Density (%)	Employer Organization Density (%)	Workplace Representation (%)
Austria	33	100	61
Belgium	49	72	66
Cyprus	70*	n.a.	n.a.
Czech Republic	22*	n.a.	n.a.
Denmark	80	52	67
Estonia	14	25	25
Finland	71	70	90
France	8	78	65
Germany	18	63	53
Great Britain	28*	n.a.	n.a.
Greece	20	70	42
Hungary	17	40	36
Ireland	38	n.a.	53
Italy	34	51	66
Latvia	16	25	27
Lithuania	14	20	23
Luxemburg	46	80	58
Malta	63	63	10
Netherlands	25	85	64
Poland	17	20	22
Portugal	17	58	34
Slovakia	30	30	50
Slovenia	44	40	64
Spain	16	72	41
Sweden	77	55	86

Note: * – data refer to 2007
Source: EIRO on-line: Industrial Relations Profiles (Austria, Belgium, Denmark, Estonia, Finland, France, Germany, Greece, Hungary, Ireland, Italy, Latvia, Lithuania, Luxemburg, Malta, Netherlands, Poland, Portugal, Slovakia, Slovenia, Spain, Sweden), May 2004, http://www.eurofound.europa.eu/eiro/date_index. htm, accessed 27 October 2007, data for Cyprus, the Czech Republic and Great Britain were collected from ETUI-REHS, 2007, Cyprus: http://www.worker-participation.eu/national_industrial_relations/countries/ cyprus; the Czech Republic: http://www.worker-participation.eu/national_industrial_relations/countries/ czech_republic; Great Britain: http://www.worker-participation.eu/national_industrial_relations/countries/ united_kingdom, accessed 4 April 2008.

The data shown below in Table 3-2 provide additional information about industrial relations in the EU member states. Most of the listed countries have a high level of collective bargaining coverage (Austria, Belgium, Cyprus, Denmark, Finland, France, Germany, Greece, Italy, the Netherlands, Portugal, Slovenia, Spain, Sweden), whereas the postsocialist member states are characterized by much lower values. Again, Slovenia is an outlier with more similarities to the old EU member states than to the newly acceded Central and Eastern European countries. In a similar vein, according to the previous data set, the Baltic States, the Czech Republic and Poland make up the group with the lowest collective bargaining coverage. They resemble Great Britain in this respect. Hungary, Luxemburg, Malta and Slovakia indicate medium values on this index.

Table 3-2:   Industrial Relations Processes

Country	Collective Bargaining Coverage (%)	Degree of Bargaining Centralization (%)	Strike Activity Index (%)
Austria	98	7	17
Belgium	96	61	n.a.
Cyprus	75*	highly decentralized	n.a.
Czech Republic	15	29	n.a.
Denmark	83	54	19
Estonia	22	25	3
Finland	82	57	8
France	90	17	10
Germany	65	47	1
Great Britain	36	highly decentralized	n.a.
Greece	65	39	n.a.
Hungary	42	26	4
Ireland	n.a.	64	5
Italy	70	34	18
Latvia	20	30	0
Lithuania	15	23	1
Luxemburg	58	33	2
Malta	56	24	6
Netherlands	81	58	1
Poland	35	20	0
Portugal	87	30	4
Slovakia	50	33	0
Slovenia	100	43	3
Spain	81	38	35
Sweden	92	56	3

Note: * – data refer to 2007
Source: see Table 3-1

As mentioned above, collective bargaining process might also vary according to the level of centralization. Only Belgium and Ireland indicate high levels of centralization. Denmark, Finland, Germany, the Netherlands, Slovenia and Sweden all exhibit a medium degree of bargaining centralization. The rest of the countries listed, which include the Baltic States, the Czech Republic, Cyprus, Great Britain, Hungary, Poland and Slovakia, have a low degree of bargaining centralization.

The most disputed indicator, the strike activity index, is relatively low for all the EU member states. For the sake of completeness, the values above 15% are indicative of a high level of strike activity (Austria, Denmark, Italy and Spain), while values below this number fall on the low end of the strike activity index. Some countries, did not report any strike activity in 2004, including Latvia, Poland and Slovakia.

3.3. Types of Welfare States

The type of welfare state is a qualitative indicator that captures the influence of the welfare state's institutional environment on union identity and preference-formation. Marius Busemeyer, Christian Kellermann, Alexander Petring and Andrej Stuchlík (see also their contribution to this book) group the member states into five distinct welfare types: continental, Scandinavian, Anglo-Saxon and Eastern European.

The authors argue that the continental welfare state, which is the model used by the EU core countries (including Austria, France, Germany and the Netherlands), serves as a blueprint for the common European Social Model.[10] This group of countries is characterized by medium trade union density, ranging from 20% to 35%, with France exhibiting an exceptionally low 8%. The collective bargaining coverage in these countries lies above 60%, climbing to almost 100% for Austria.

The other clusters differ from the core type in many respects. A much higher degree of union density and a similar level of collective bargaining coverage, i.e. around 80–90%, characterize the Scandinavian type, including Finland, Sweden and Norway. The Anglo-Saxon pattern is quite different. Both Ireland and the United Kingdom have a low union density, and the UK has low collective bargaining coverage (in this category only data for the UK were available). The Mediterranean type, present in Greece, Spain, Portugal and Italy, is quite similar to the continental type in terms of union density, but possesses a lower degree of collective bargaining coverage.

According to the authors, the Eastern European type of welfare state makes up a distinct category. It is characterized by both a very low level of union density and low collective bargaining coverage. The low figures describing the second dimension differ-

---

10   Busemeyer, Marius / Kellermann, Christian / Petring, Alexander / Stuchlík, Andrej: Overstretching Solidarity? Trade Union's National Perspectives on the European Economic and Social Model, International Policy Analysis, Friedrich Ebert Stiftung, 2007, p. 4.

entiate this type from the continental model and reflect the policy-makers' reluctance to rely on the social partners in drafting social and economic policy.

3.4. Trust and Participation

At the same time, the public's trust in trade unions in the European Union's member states is generally low, as the figures in Table 3-3 indicate. This is particularly evident in the new member states, like the Czech Republic, Latvia and Estonia. Slovenia and Slovakia also score relatively low in this area. On the contrary, Denmark, Finland, Luxemburg and the Netherlands indicate slightly higher levels of trust in trade unions, as do Hungary and Malta. However, the differences between the values for these countries tend to be minor.

Table 3-3:   Trust in Trade Unions (%)

Country	A great deal	Quite a lot	Not very much	Not at all
Austria	4	20	56	20
Belgium	5	32	43	20
Cyprus	n.a.	n.a.	n.a.	n.a.
Czech Republic	3	21	51	25
Denmark	8	41	40	11
Estonia	6	28	45	21
Finland	5	41	45	9
France	4	32	40	25
Germany	4	32	49	15
Great Britain	5	22	50	23
Greece	2	13	48	38
Hungary	12	31	35	23
Ireland	9	32	45	13
Italy	4	26	45	25
Latvia	4	23	45	27
Lithuania	2	30	57	11
Luxemburg	9	43	37	11
Malta	12	36	31	21
Netherlands	5	45	40	10
Poland	6	22	44	29
Portugal	5	34	44	17
Slovakia	5	31	44	20
Slovenia	7	22	47	24
Spain	6	28	45	21
Sweden	6	38	45	12

Source: European Value Survey 1981–2004, http://www.europeanvalues.nl/, accessed 25 January 2008.

In keeping with the relatively low levels of trust, trade unions in every country lost the battle for donations in 2004; citizens preferred to give to other organizations.

Humanitarian organizations in every nation fared better than trade unions. In the Czech Republic, Poland, Hungary, Germany and Spain, people donated more eagerly to church or other religious organizations than to trade unions. Environmental organizations received more financial support than trade unions only in the Czech Republic, Hungary and Germany. Interestingly, however, only German citizens donated more money to political parties than to trade unions, and business / professional / farmer organizations received more contributions than trade unions only in Hungary.

Slovenia is an exception among the new EU member states regarding its citizens' financial contributions to trade union activities – 8.5% of respondents in the European Social Survey 2004 claimed to have donated some money to trade unions in the last twelve months, as can be seen in Table 3-4. In 2004, Czechs gave mainly to humanitarian organizations (7.9%), while Poles and Hungarians favoured religious organizations (4.0% and 2.6%) over trade unions. Slovenia's high level of financial donations to trade unions is exceptional even among the old EU member states, where the contribution to union activities is relatively low (1.0–2.0%).

Table 3-4: Financial Donation to Voluntary Organizations (% of Respondents Who Made Donations Within the Last Twelve Months)

Financial donation	Czech Republic	Poland	Hungary	Slovenia	Germany	Spain
Trade union	0.4	2.0	0.3	8.5	0.7	2.0
Business / profession / farmer organization	0.3	0.5	0.4	2.6	0.7	0.8
Political party	0.3	1.0	0.1	1.8	1.0	0.5
Humanitarian organization etc.	7.9	3.0	1.2	10.0	15.0	5.6
Environmental / peace / animal rights organization	2.5	1.3	0.4	1.0	9.0	1.7
Church or other religious organization	2.3	4.0	2.6	6.3	9.0	3.0

Source: European Social Survey 2004, http://www.europeansocialsurvey.org/, accessed 20 July 2004.

3.5. Conclusion: The Post-Socialist Countries from a Comparative Perspective

According to the data presented here, among the new EU member states with a Communist past, only Slovenia resembles the core EU countries in terms of trade union density (44%) and collective bargaining coverage (100%).

The Baltic States (Estonia, Latvia and Lithuania) make up a sharply distinct group in the EU, since their trade union density and collective bargaining coverage are both very low. In Estonia trade union density is 14% and collective bargaining coverage is

22%; in Latvia the figures are 16% and 20%, respectively, and in Lithuania, they are 14% and 15%. These countries largely follow the pattern of the Anglo-Saxon type of industrial relations, where both trade union density and collective bargaining coverage are very low.

Almost all the new member states with a Communist past show a low degree of bargaining centralization (Estonia 24%, Hungary 26%, Latvia 30%, Lithuania 23%, Poland 20%, Slovakia 33%). This measure is much higher in Slovenia (43%); only six of the old EU member states have higher figures. The strike activity index is very low for all new member states (0–4%) and for most of the old member states. Spain is the only country with a high score on this index (35%). Italy, Denmark and Austria are also quite active (17–20%).

The level of trust in trade unions is low in almost all EU member states. There are slight differences; Denmark, Finland, Luxemburg and the Netherlands, for example, indicate slightly higher levels of trust in trade unions as compared to the new post-communist EU member states. Slovenia maintains its position as an outlier in terms of donating money to trade union organizations; its citizens donate a much higher percentage of money to trade unions than those in any of the other countries examined here, including the newly acceded Central and Eastern European member states.

The data discussed above show the new EU member states from Central and Eastern Europe to be a relatively coherent region with Slovenia as an explicit outlier whose welfare model bears similarities to the continental version. Meanwhile, the Baltic States' systems most closely resemble the Anglo-Saxon model. The remaining post-socialist member states, which joined in 2004 (the Czech Republic, Hungary, Poland and Slovakia) all demonstrate a relatively weak labour scenario characterized by low trade union density, low collective bargaining coverage, a low degree of bargaining centralization and a low level of strike activity.

3.6. Appendix: Main Trade Unions in the Post-Socialist EU Member States (2004)

Country and name of the organization	Year of foundation	Major constituency	Political affiliation
Czech Republic			
Christian Labour confederation / Christian Trade Union Coalition (KOK)	1990	It has about 15,000 members.	Claims to be independent of any parties, movements and any other subjects.

Country and name of the organization	Year of foundation	Major constituency	Political affiliation
Czech-Moravian Confederation of Trade Unions (ČMKOS)	1992	It has about 772,000 members.	Claims to be independent of any parties, movements and any other subjects.
Association of Autonomous Trade Unions (ASO)	1995	It associates 15 independent federations.	Claims to be independent of any parties, movements and any other subjects.
Estonia			
Confederation of Estonian Trade Unions (EAKL)	1990	It is the biggest union in the country, with 18 associated affiliates and about 47,500 members.	Claims to be independent of any parties, movements and any other subjects
Estonian Employees' Unions' Confederation – TALO	1992	It associates 12 independent federations.	Claims to be independent of any parties, movements and any other subjects.
The Confederation of Food Producers and Rural Workers (ETMAKL)	1997	It has about 9,600 members.	Claims to be independent of any parties, movements and any other subjects.
Hungary			
The National Association of Hungarian Trade Unions (MSZOSZ)	1990	It associates about 235,000 members in 37 independent federations.	Strongly associated with the socialist party MSZP.
The Democratic League of Independent Trade Unions (LIGA)	1988	It has about 106,000 members.	Claims to be independent of any parties, movements and any other subjects.

Country and name of the organization	Year of foundation	Major constituency	Political affiliation
The National Federation of Workers' Councils (MOSZ)	1990	It has about 50,000 members.	Claims to be independent of any parties, movements and any other subjects but shares values with the Christian democratic parties.
Forum for the Co-operation of Trade Unions (SZEF)	1990	It has about 446,000 members.	Claims to be independent of any parties, movements and any other subjects.
The Confederation of Unions of Professionals (ÉSZT)	1989	It has about 85,000 members.	Claims to be independent of any parties, movements and any other subjects.
The National Federation of Autonomous Trade Unions (ASZSZ)	1993	It has about 128,000 members.	Claims to be independent of any parties, movements and any other subjects.
Latvia			
The Free Trade Union Confederation of Latvia (LBAS)	1990	It associates 24 independent federations and has about 165,000 members.	Claims to be independent of any parties, movements and any other subjects.
Lithuania			
Lithuanian Trade Union Confederation (LPSK)	2002	It associates 25 independent federations and has about 124,000 members.	Claims to be independent of any parties, movements and any other subjects.
Lithuanian Trade Union 'Solidarumas'	1993	It represents about 25% of union members in 12 independent federations.	Claims to be independent of any parties, movements and any other subjects.

Country and name of the organization	Year of foundation	Major constituency	Political affiliation
Lithuanian Labour Federation	1991	It is the smallest con-federation and rep-resents some 10% of unionized workers.	It has a Christian-democratic orientation.
Poland			
All Poland Alliance of Trade Unions (OPZZ)	1984	It associates 99 inde-pendent federations.	Emerged from the former monopoly socialist confedera-tion and today lean-ing to the social-demo-cratic end of the politi-cal spectrum.
The Independent Self-Governing Trade Union Confederation Solidarity (NSZZ Solidarność)	1980	It associates about 900,000 members in 12,000 committees at the company level.	Initially represented the dissident Christian groups. In the tran-sition period it had a dual role as a party political force with gov-ernment involvement as part of the AWS alliance, Solidarność Electoral Action. The organization fell out of electoral favour in 2000. After this set-back Solidarność with-drew from party polit-ical activity in order to refocus its efforts on directly representing employee interests.
The Trade Unions Forum (FZZ)	2002	It has about 400,000 members.	Established with the explicit strategy of neutrality vis-à-vis political parties.

Country and name of the organization	Year of foundation	Major constituency	Political affiliation
Slovakia			
The Confederation of Trade Unions of the Slovak Republic (KOZ SR)	1990	It associates 38 independent federations.	Associated with the social-democratic SMER party.
The Independent Christian Trade Unions of Slovakia	1993	It associates about 10,000 members in 3 independent federations.	Claims to be independent of any parties, movements and any other subjects.
Slovenia			
Association of Free Trade Unions of Slovenia (ZSSS)	1990	It consists of 20 organizations and has about 370,000 members.	It has a leftist political affiliation.
Neodvisnost, Confederation of New Trade Unions of Slovenia (KNSS)	1990	It consists of 10 organizations and has about 38,000 members.	It has a right wing political affiliation.
The Confederation of Trade Unions of Slovenia PERGAM (PERGAM)	1991	It comprises 8 organizations and has about 87,000 members.	Claims to be independent of any parties, movements and any other subjects.
The Confederation of Trade Unions '90 of Slovenia	1991	It consists of 22 organizations and has about 40,000 members.	Claims to be independent of any parties, movements and any other subjects.

Source: EIRO on-line 2004, http://www.eurofound.europa.eu/eiro/country_index.htm

Brigitte Krech

4. Presence and Visibility of Polish, Czech and Slovak Trade Unions at the EU Level

4.1. Introduction

The political environment of the European Union consists of many thousands of actors: civil servants in the EU institutions, Members of the European Parliament, diplomats at the Permanent Representations to the EU, lobbyists, non-governmental organizations, think tanks, business representatives – as well as representatives of trade unions. Each enlargement wave of the European Community has increased the number of stakeholders.

For trade unions specifically there are six ways to exert influence on political decision-making processes at the EU level: (1) direct consultations with the European Commission, (2) consultations with national representatives in the Council of Ministers, (3) direct consultations with the European Parliament, (4) participation in the Social Dialogue, (5) involvement in the European Economic and Social Committee (EESC), and (6) engagement in transnational umbrella organizations and networks. An office in Brussels is also frequently cited as a channel of influence. While an office as such does not automatically guarantee involvement in decision-making processes, it can facilitate the pursuit of all the avenues listed above.[1]

The importance of representation in Brussels has increased in recent years. 'In Brussels, influence is personal.'[2] To understand the role that trade unions from the post-socialist member states play in EU governance, it is therefore vital to analyse the unions' presence and visibility at the EU level geographically, i.e. in Brussels and to a limited degree also in Strasbourg. In this chapter the four biggest post-socialist member states, i.e. the Czech Republic, Hungary, Poland and Slovakia, will be analysed accordingly.

For the purpose of comparison, three old member countries were added:
- Germany (whose relatively large size results in greater leverage within the decision-making framework in the EU institutions),
- Spain (similar in size to Poland), and
- Finland (due to the general weight of trade unions in Finland).
The structure of the chapter follows the list of channels of influence given above.

---

1   See the chapter by Janna Wolff for a detailed account.
2   See Guéguen, Daniel: European Lobbying, Brussels: Europolitics, 2007, preface.

4.2. European Commission and Council of Ministers

Trade unions from the post-socialist EU member states claim to have very limited access to the European Commission and the Council of Ministers.[3] A major reason for the paucity of direct consultations is that none of the trade unions from the post-socialist member states has an office in Brussels. The responsible trade union members from the new member states tend to travel to Brussels only when they have a concrete appointment there.

The main obstacle to establishing their own offices in Brussels is the perceived high costs. An office with one person plus an assistant costs about 100,000 euros per year to run. Concerning employer representation from the four new member states studied here, there are currently three national employers' representatives based in Brussels – from the Czech Republic (Confederation of Industry and Transport of the Czech Republic – SP ČR, Brussels Office), Hungary (Confederation of Hungarian Employers and Industrialists – MGYOSZ) and Poland (Polish Confederation of Private Employers Lewiatan – PKPP Lewiatan). Of the three old member states named above, all have employer representation based in Brussels.[4]

4.3. European Parliament

The overall impact of the European Parliament (EP) on EU decision-making processes has increased over the years, especially due to the rise in co-decision mechanisms in the legislative procedure. The EP has 785 members, elected every five years. All committee meetings and the mini-sessions take place in Brussels. The plenary sessions take place in Strasbourg.[5]

Though trade unions can obtain access to EP committee hearings, a more direct route to the European Parliament is offered by Members of the European Parliament (MEPs) with a trade union background. As Table 4-1 shows, there are several MEPs with a trade union background from Poland, but only two from Hungary, one from the Czech Republic and none from Slovakia. Of the fifty-four Polish MEPs, twelve have worked for and with unions in their professional career. The substantial presence of Polish trade union activists in the European Parliament is largely due to the strong political engagement of Poland's two major national trade unions, which in the 1990s participated in national parliamentary elections and in the national government. As

---

3   See the results of an interview project presented in part III ('Country Studies') of this volume.
4   See list of national employers' federations in: The European Public Affairs Directory 2008, pp. 114.
5   For further information, see European Parliament: How Parliament is Organised, http://www.europarl.europa.eu/parliament/public/staticDisplay.do?language=EN&id=45, accessed 25 January 2008.

Table 4-2 shows, the Polish case is exceptional even compared to old member states with strong trade unions like Germany or Finland.

Table 4-1:   MEPs from Post-Socialist Member States with a Trade Union Background by Party Affiliation (2004–2009)

Poland	Hungary	Czech Republic	Slovakia
European People's Party: 4 Union for Europe of the Nations: 4 Liberals: 3 Socialists: 1	European People's Party: 1 Socialists: 1	Socialists: 1	None
Total: 12	**Total: 2**	**Total: 1**	**Total: 0**

Source: European Parliament: Your MEPs, http://www.europarl.europa.eu/members.do?language=EN, accessed 25 January 2008.

Table 4-2:   MEPs from Old Member States with a Trade Union Background by Party Affiliation (2004–2009)

Germany	Spain	Finland
Greens/European Free Alliance: 2 Socialists: 1	Socialists: 3	None
Total: 3	**Total: 3**	**Total: 0**

Source: European Parliament: Your MEPs, http://www.europarl.europa.eu/members.do?language=EN, accessed 28 March 2008.

Brief profiles of each MEP with a trade union background from the countries listed in Tables 4-1 and 4-2 are given in the appendix.

4.4.   Social Dialogue

The Social Dialogue, part of the European social model, is defined in the EC Treaty[6] and includes consultations and negotiations by the social partners. At the European level the Social Dialogue consists of the bipartite dialogue (between employers and trade union organizations on the European level) and the tripartite dialogue (between both social partners and public authorities).

The Commission has emphasized that the 'European social dialogue complements the national practices of social dialogue which exist in most Member States.'[7] The

---

6   See Appendix.
7   See European Commission: European Social Dialogue, http://ec.europa.eu/employment_social/social_dialogue/index_en.htm, accessed 15 March 2008.

European Social Dialogue has produced more than 300 joined documents adopted by the European social partners.[8]

Acting through European as well as national associations, trade unions from the new member states are taking part in the Social Dialogue. Because the national Social Dialogues were assessed as weak for most of the candidate countries in the pre-accession period before 2004,[9] Social Dialogue partners from the post-socialist EU member states have taken part in EU-funded projects in order to familiarize themselves with new tasks and objectives.

The EU has mandated the criteria of transparency, accountability and representativeness for all social partners wishing to engage in the Social Dialogue at the EU level.[10]

The Commission has currently undertaken several research projects in order to assess the representativeness of social partners in different employment sectors. To this end, the 'European Foundation for the Improvement of Living and Working Conditions' did a recent study on the representativeness of social partners in the agricultural sector.[11] The projects generally confirm that trade unions from the new member states are legitimate – albeit less visible – partners in the Social Dialogue.

4.5.   European Economic and Social Committee (EESC)

The EESC delivers opinions to the Council, the European Parliament, and the Commission as well as offering an advisory role towards the EU institutions.[12] The EESC, Group II (Employees Group) consists of members from trade union organizations from all twenty-seven EU member states – including confederations and sectoral federations. Group II has 120 members representing more than 90 union organizations; most of

---

8   A database with texts on the Social Dialogue and information on the sector etc. can be found under http://ec.europa.eu/employment_social/dsw/dspMain.do?lang=en, accessed 15 March 2008.

9   See European Commission: Strengthening Social Dialogue in an Enlarged Europe, p. 3, http://ec.europa.eu/employment_social/social_dialogue/docs/sept_04_forum_liaison_en.pdf, accessed 15 March 2008.

10   For details and a critical assessment, see Obradovic, Daniela / Vizcaino, Jose M. Alonso: Good Governance Requirements Concerning the Participation of Interest Groups in EU Consultations, in: Obradovic, Daniela / Pleines, Heiko (eds): The Capacity of Central and East European Interest Groups to Participate in EU Governance, Stuttgart: Ibidem, 2007, pp. 67–107.

11   For the study, see European Foundation for the Improvement of Living and Working Conditions: Representativeness of the Social Partners. Agricultural sector, 2007, http://www.eurofound.europa.eu/docs/eiro/tn0608017s/tn0608017s.pdf. EUROFOUND is an Agency of the European Union set up in 1975 and based in Dublin/Ireland. The Agency aims at contributing to the establishment of better living and working conditions in the EU through comparative research for the European Commission, governments, employers, and trade unions. The Foundation also established the European Monitoring Centre on Change (EMCC) in order to analyse industrial and company change throughout Europe.

12   See European Economic and Social Committee, http://www.eesc.europa.eu/organisation/how/index_en.asp, accessed 25 January 2008.

them are affiliated with the European Trade Union Confederation (ETUC). Poland has seven members in Group II, the Czech Republic and Hungary have four each and Slovakia has three members. The members of the EESC are not permanently based in Brussels; they hold their plenary sessions there.

Table 4-3:   Members of Group II of the EESC from New Member States by Trade Union (2004–2009)

Poland	Czech Republic	Hungary	Slovakia
NSZZ Solidarność: 3	ČMKOS: 4	SZEF-ÉSZT: 1	KOZ SR: 3
OPZZ: 2		EDOSZ: 1	
FZZ: 2		LIGA: 1	
		MOSZ: 1	
Total: 7	**Total: 4**	**Total: 4**	**Total: 3**

Source: EESC. Employees Group (Group II). Members, http://eescmembers.eesc.europa.eu/eescmembers.aspx?critgroup=GRII&culture=en, accessed 25 January 2008.

Table 4-4:   Members of Group II of the EESC from Old Member States by Trade Union (2004–2009)

Germany	Spain	Finland
DGB: 2	ELA: 1	STTK: 1
ver.di (in DGB): 1	UGT: 2	SAK: 1
ver.di: 1	CC.OO.: 3	AKAVA: 1
IG Metall: 1	Fundación Educación y	
IG/BCE: 1	Trabajo: 1	
IG BAU: 1		
Total: 7	**Total: 7**	**Total: 3**

Source: EESC. Employees Group (Group II). Members, http://eescmembers.eesc.europa.eu/eescmembers.aspx?critgroup=GRII&culture=en, accessed 28 March 2008.

4.6.   European Umbrella Organizations

ETUC, the European Trade Union Confederation, is one key stakeholder on European level[13]. ETUC has currently eighty-two member organizations and is affiliated with twelve European industry federations representing sixty million trade unionists on EU level[14]. Countries with several bigger national federations, like Hungary or Poland, can have several ETUC members. The six Hungarian ETUC members are the Autonomous Trade Union Confederation (ASZSZ), the Democratic League of Independent Trade Unions (LIGA), the National Federation of Workers' Councils (MOSZ), the National Confederation of Hungarian Trade Unions (MSZOSZ), the Forum for the Co-operation of Trade Unions (SZEF) and the Confederation of Unions of Professionals (ÉSZT). The

---

13   See http://www.etuc.org/, accessed 25 January 2008.
14   See ETUC: Our Members, http://www.etuc.org/r/13, accessed 25 January 2008.

two Polish member organizations are the Independent and Self-Governing Trade Union 'Solidarność' (NSZZ Solidarność) and the All-Poland Alliance of Trade Unions (OPZZ).

Countries with one dominant national trade union federation have only one ETUC member. The Slovakian member is the Confederation of Trade Unions of the Slovak Republic (KOZ SR). The Czech Republic's the Czech-Moravian Confederation of Trade Unions (ČMKOS) is affiliated with ETUC. However, the number of member organizations does not necessarily reflect a country's strength within the European umbrella organization. Germany, for example, also has only one ETUC member with the German Confederation of Trade Unions (DGB).

A better indicator of influence is representation in the ETUC leadership: the ETUC Secretariat is responsible for relations with European institutions as well as employers' organizations. Józef Niemiec, the Confederal Secretary, is the only member of the Secretariat from a post-socialist member state.[15] Niemiec was a co-founder of NSZZ Solidarność in 1980 and a member of its Works Council at 'Telkom-Telos' in Cracow. His responsibilities at ETUC include: social protection, disabled people, regional policy, economic and social cohesion, internal markets, and services of general interest.

4.7. Conclusion and Future Perspective

This chapter aimed at giving an overview of the current representation of Central European trade unions in Brussels. These groups are currently well represented through European umbrella trade union organizations and in the European Economic and Social Committee, where formal rules determine the number of members. In addition, several MEPs from the post-socialist member states, especially from Poland, have a trade union background. However, the next European Parliament elections in 2009 will pose a challenge for potential MEPs with a trade unionist background, as it is estimated that half of the present deputies will not be re-elected to the European Parliament. However, trade unions from the new member states lack a permanent presence in Brussels and have very limited direct access to the European Commission. Because their activities at the EU level are by and large limited to participation in collective bodies like the EESC or umbrella organizations, their visibility at the EU level is also limited.

Accordingly, the formation of (informal and formal) coalitions is an important tool for enhancing their influence on the EU level. In the future new coalitions with other civil society representatives might be established among trade unions from the new EU member states on topics of common concern (e.g. employment and globalisation; employment patterns with respect to environmental issues, e.g. climate change). However, ETUC, as the major umbrella organization of trade unions, will continue to play an essential role.

---

15   See ETUC: About Us, http://www.etuc.org/a/25, accessed 25 January 2008.

4.8. Appendix

4.8.1. Short Profiles of MEPs With a Trade Union Background, in Alphabetical Order (2004–2009)[16]

4.8.1.1. Czech Republic

Falbr, Richard
- Socialist Group in the European Parliament

Union activities in curriculum vitae:
- Trade union lawyer (1970–1989);
- Chairman of the Bohemian-Moravian Service Workers' Trade Union (1990–1998);
- Vice-Chairman of the Czech and Slovak Confederation of Trade Unions (1990–1994);
- Chairman of the Bohemian-Moravian Confederation of Trade Unions (1994–2002);
- Member of the administration of the International Confederation of Free Trade Unions (1992–2002);
- Member of the Governing Body of the International Labour Organisation (1993–2002);
- Member of the administration of the Trade Union European Confederation (1995–2002).

4.8.1.2. Germany

Horáček, Milan
- Group of the Greens / European Free Alliance

Union activities in curriculum vitae:
- 1965–1967 called up for military service in a penal battalion on a charge of 'political unreliability' in the ČSSR, his country of birth;
- From 1968 in political exile in Germany; worked there as an electrical fitter and on the journal 'Gewerkschafter' (Trade Unionist).

---

16   European Parliament: Your MEP´s, http://www.europarl.europa.eu/members.do?language=EN, accessed 25 January 2008.

Jöns, Karin
- Socialist Group in the European Parliament

Union activities in curriculum vitae:
- Editor affiliated with the Central Executive Committee of the ÖTV (Public Service, Transport and Communications Workers' Union) (1978–1980);
- Member of the United Service Sector Union ver.di (formerly the ÖTV and IG Medien [media workers' union]);
- Member of the Workers' Welfare Association (AWO).

Rühle, Heide
- Group of the Greens / European Free Alliance

Union activities in curriculum vitae:
- Member of the Commercial, Banking and Insurance Workers' Union (HBV).

4.8.1.3. Hungary

Kósáné Kovács, Magda
- Socialist Group in the European Parliament

Union activities in curriculum vitae:
- Chairperson, Higher Education Council, Hungarian Teachers' Union (1977–1980);
- Secretary, Central Board, Hungarian Teachers' Union (1980–1985).

Őry, Csaba
- Group of the European People's Party (Christian Democrats) and European Democrats

Union activities in curriculum vitae:
- Founder and spokesman, Democratic Union of Scientific Workers (since 1988);
- Administrator and vice-chairman (1988–1993);
- Chairman (1994), LIGA trade unions.

4.8.1.4. Poland

Buzek, Jerzy
- Group of the European People's Party (Christian Democrats) and European Democrats

Union activities in curriculum vitae:
- Starting in 1980, Member of the independent, self-governing trade union NSZZ Solidarność;
- Chairman of the First National Congress of Delegates of Solidarność in 1981;
- Active in the Solidarność underground structure after 1981.

Foltyn-Kubicka, Hanna
• Union for Europe of the Nations Group
Union activities in curriculum vitae:
• Member of the independent self-governing trade union NSZZ Solidarność (1980).

Jałowiecki, Stanisław
• Group of the European People's Party (Christian Democrats) and European Democrats
Union activities in curriculum vitae:
• Chairman of the Regional Administration and member of the National Committee of Solidarność (1981–1983).

Janowski, Mieczysław Edmund
• Union for Europe of the Nations Group
Union activities in curriculum vitae:
• Member of the independent self-governing trade union NSZZ Solidarność (since 1980);
• Member of Solidarity Election Action – Social Movement (RS AWS) (1998–2003).

Kułakowski, Jan Jerzy
• Group of the Alliance of Liberals and Democrats for Europe
Union activities in curriculum vitae:
• Member of the General Secretariat of the International Federation of Christian Trade Unions (1954–1957);
• Secretary, General Secretary of the European Organisation of the International Federation of Christian Trade Unions (1974–1976);
• Secretary of the European Trade Union Confederation; General Secretary, World Confederation of Labour (1976–1989).

Lewandowski, Janusz
• Group of the European People's Party (Christian Democrats) and European Democrats
Union activities in curriculum vitae:
• Member of the independent self-governing trade union NSZZ Solidarność (1980–1989).

Onyszkiewicz, Janusz
• Group of the Alliance of Liberals and Democrats for Europe
Union activities in curriculum vitae:
• Press spokesman and officer of the independent, self-governing trade union NSZZ Solidarność (1980–1989).

Pęk, Bogdan
• Union for Europe of the Nations Group
Union activities in curriculum vitae:
• Vice-Chairman of the independent, self-governing trade union NSZZ Solidarność to the Regional Enterprise for the Meat Industry (OPPM) (1980–1984).

Pinior, Józef
• Socialist Group in the European Parliament
Union activities in curriculum vitae:
• Founder and one of the chairmen of the Lower Silesian region of the independent, self-governing trade union NSZZ Solidarność (1980–1989);
• Co-founder of the underground Radio Solidarność in Wrocław. From July 1987, spokesman for 'Polish-Czech Solidarność'. Participant in events organized by the Orange Alternative;
• Stayed in Brazil and Argentina in 1989 at the invitation of the labour organization. Conducted a comparative study into the processes of emergence from undemocratic systems in Southern Europe, Latin America and Central and Eastern Europe.

Roszkowski, Wojciech
• Union for Europe of the Nations Group
Union activities in curriculum vitae:
• Member of the independent self-governing trade union NSZZ Solidarność (1980–1993).

Sonik, Bogusław
• Group of the European People's Party (Christian Democrats) and European Democrats
Union activities in curriculum vitae:
• Founder of the Students' Committee of Solidarność (1977);
• Vice-chairman of the Małopolska Region Administration of Solidarność (1980–1982).

Staniszewska, Grażyna
- Group of the Alliance of Liberals and Democrats for Europe

Union activities in curriculum vitae:
- Member of the administration and Podbeskidzie regional council of the independent, self-governing trade union NSZZ Solidarność (1980–1981);
- Member of the underground authorities of NSZZ Solidarność (1983–1989);
- Member of the underground and subsequently legal National Executive Committee of NSZZ Solidarność (1988–1990).

4.8.1.5. Spain

Ayala Sender, Inés
- Socialist Group in the European Parliament

Union activities in curriculum vitae:
- Coordinator, Provincial Executive Committee of the UGT in Saragossa (1989–1990);
- Social Action Officer, UGT Confederal Executive Committee (1990–1994);
- Member of consultative committees on equality, migration, the environment within the ETUC, ICFTU and TUAC.

Martínez Martínez, Miguel Angel
- Socialist Group in the European Parliament

Union activities in curriculum vitae:
- Responsible for trade union trading at the International Confederation of Free Trade Unions (1973);
- Member of the UGT, Provincial executive committee for Ciudad Real (1980).

Riera Madurell, Teresa
- Socialist Group in the European Parliament

Union activities in curriculum vitae:
- Joined the FETE-UGT teaching trade union in 1980.

4.8.2.   Articles 138 and 139 of the EC Treaty

Both articles refer to the role of the European social dialogue in the process of European integration.[17]

4.8.2.1. Article 138

The Commission shall have the task of promoting the consultation of management and labour at Community level and shall take any relevant measure to facilitate their dialogue by ensuring balanced support for the parties.

To this end, before submitting proposals in the social policy field, the Commission shall consult management and labour on the possible direction of Community action.

If, after such consultation, the Commission considers Community action advisable, it shall consult management and labour on the content of the envisaged proposal. Management and labour shall forward to the Commission an opinion or, where appropriate, a recommendation.

On the occasion of such consultation, management and labour may inform the Commission of their wish to initiate the process provided for in Article 139. The duration of the procedure shall not exceed nine months, unless the management and labour concerned and the Commission decide jointly to extend it.

4.8.2.2. Article 139

Should management and labour so desire, the dialogue between them at Community level may lead to contractual relations, including agreements.

Agreements concluded at Community level shall be implemented either in accordance with the procedures and practices specific to management and labour and the Member States or at the joint request of the signatory parties, by a Council decision on a proposal from the Commission.

---

17   See European Commission: Institutional Recognition of the European Social Dialogue, http://ec.europa.eu/employment_social/social_dialogue/recognition_en.htm, accessed 15 March 2008.

Andrej Stuchlík, Christian Kellermann, Alexander Petring, Marius R. Busemeyer

5. The Positions of Trade Unions Concerning European Economic and Social Policies – an EU-Wide Comparison

5.1. Introduction[1]

The Social Dimension and the European Social Model have become the catchwords of the recent debates on the future of the EU. Some parties felt that the rejected draft of the constitutional treaty contained an excess of neoliberal elements, while others feared the introduction of *'dirigiste'* over-regulation to safeguard national inclinations towards protectionism. The Lisbon Treaty took over many social policy provisions of the former document, including the Charter of Fundamental Rights. However, the actual instrument being used to square the circle is the Lisbon Strategy, revised in 2005, which stipulates that economic competitiveness should foster and sustain the EU's social dimension.

The constitutional process since the Laeken Council has mainly been concerned with the balance of social and economic issues as well as the institutional set-up of the Union and the scope of European political regulation as such; in short, it aims to identify the scope of welfare provision that is possible to sustain at the European level.

Apart from that, we observe another phenomenon that could trigger conflict: member states are not only competing economically within the EU but also in terms of social security and welfare provision. Hence, arguments in favour of further Europeanization will likely meet with growing reluctance the more the process threatens to unravel the affected nations' social legacies.[2]

In this vein, the admittance of former communist societies to the EU since 2004 has made the forecast even gloomier, because the growing heterogeneity among social systems jeopardizes European-wide solidarity. Additionally, the issue of real convergence is impacted by the fact that the new member states, though themselves a heterogeneous group, may nonetheless provide a genuine welfare regime and thereby increase the institutional diversity within the Union.[3]

---

1 This chapter is a revised version of Busemeyer, Marius R. / Kellermann, Christian / Petring, Alexander / Stuchlík, Andrej: Overstretching Solidarity? Trade Union's National Perspectives on the European Economic and Social Model, Bonn: Friedrich-Ebert-Stiftung, International Policy Analysis, September 2007, http://library.fes.de/pdf-files/id/04751.pdf

2 The fierce debate over the country-of-origin-principle as part of the Directive on services (2006/123/EC O.J. L 376/36) is certainly among the more prominent examples.

3 See e.g. McMenamin, Iain: Varieties of Capitalism Democracy. What Difference Does East-Central Europe Make?, in: Journal of Public Policy, 2004 (Vol. 24), No. 3, pp. 259–274.

There are no simple answers; a steady stream of recommendations has been trick-ling in from the complex expert discourse on enhanced growth and social inclusion. At the same time, the national discourse in most member states is both shaped and blurred by concepts like job exportation, tax competition and the migration of low wage employers, who force high-wage employees out of their jobs.

Trade unions saw the current crisis and institutional quarrels of the EU as a chance to promote and realize a more socially balanced European Union. Their economic and social objectives indeed touch upon all relevant fields of the European Social Model, such as wage policy, social policy and liberalization of services. For trade unions in the euro area, the issue of monetary policy is of major importance as well.

However, when it comes to expanding the 'social union' or 'social dimension', trade unions' perceptions differ greatly across Europe. This holds true despite some general but significant consensus aiming to enhance macroeconomic coordination at the European level.[4] That is because unions focus on their national constituencies.

The present chapter deals with policy positions of trade unions on the state and future of the European Economic and Social Model and is based on a series of expert interviews.[5] With regards to the new member states, we will single out Poland, the Czech Republic and Slovakia for closer scrutiny.[6]

Our research revolves around three questions: a) In which areas do the trade unions' interests converge, and on which issues do they exhibit a plurality of positions instead? b) In case of the latter, what accounts for these differences? c) And finally, what is spe-cial about the Eastern European member states?

First, we look at the delegation of competencies to the supranational layer from a theoretical point of view. Apart from the bargaining over the budgetary implications of Europeanization processes, we expect another dimension of potential conflict: the institutional conflict. We assume that the process of building a common European

---

4   Hyman, Richard: Trade Unions and the Politics of the European Social Model, in: Economic and Industrial Democracy, 2005 (Vol. 26), No. 1, pp. 9–40, here p. 10.

5   We conducted more than 100 interviews with trade union and political leaders in seventeen European countries (Austria, the Czech Republic, Denmark, Finland, France, Hungary, Germany, Greece, Ireland, Italy, the Netherlands, Poland, Portugal, Slovakia, Spain, Sweden and the UK) in 2005 and 2006. We collected qualitative survey data on core policy issues of the European Social Model, e.g. macroeconomic policies, social policy and cohesion, the liberalization of serv-ices, and the social dialogue. Questionnaire and replication data is available at http://www.fes. de/ipa/inhalt/ewsm_e.htm. The goal of the project was to gather information about unions' positions at the national rather than the EU level, since we assumed Brussels representatives to be prone to show a 'pro-EU bias'.

6   Interviews with trade unions' confederations in the new member states were conducted in: Poland – All-Poland Alliance of Trade Unions (OPZZ) and Independent and Self-Governing Trade Union Solidarność (NSZZ Solidarność). Czech Republic – Czech-Moravian Confederation of Trade Unions (ČMKOS) and Union of Health and Social Care Professionals (Odborový Svaz Zdravotnictví a Sociální Péče České Republiky – OSZSP). Slovak Republic – Confederation of Trade Unions of the Slovak Republic (KOZ SR).

Economic and Social Model (EESM) privileges some welfare states more than others and that differences in the character of institutional regimes have an impact on the trade union leaders' willingness to subscribe to the idea of a common EESM and hence support further delegation. Because trade unions are, to varying degrees, less involved in governmental policy-making, we expect their preferences to be more pronounced and close to left of centre parties.[7]

The remainder presents our empirical findings, which are grouped according to three sections: (1) economic policy, (2) social policy and (3) tax competition.

5.2. European Integration. Varying Preferences Across Welfare States

The process of European integration over the past decades has led to the development of European structures and organizations in many areas. Although not without tensions, trade unions in Europe have promoted European structures since the 1950s. Since 1973, the European Trade Union Confederation (ETUC) has served as the umbrella organization, consisting of twelve Industry Federations and eighty-one National Trade Union Confederations. Their aim is 'to [...] promote the European Social Model [...] including full employment, social protection, equal opportunities, good quality jobs, social inclusion, and an open and democratic policy-making process that involves citizens fully [...].'[8]

However, neither the existence of a single voice nor the existence of common interests among workers can be taken for granted – at least not in a European Union of twenty-seven member states with different levels of economic development, performances and structures. Regarding the elitist debate on how much of a social dimension the EU should provide, trade unions at the European level often seem to be merely safeguarding existing conditions[9] and defending the status quo.

Research on preference formation vis-à-vis European integration has so far concentrated on voters and parties.[10] It is therefore necessary to think more comprehensively

---

7   Busemeyer, Marius R. / Kellermann, Christian / Petring, Alexander / Stuchlík, Andrej: Europäische Verteilungskonflikte und sozialdemokratische Positionen zum Europäischen Wirtschafts- und Sozialmodell, in: IPG – Internationale Politik und Gesellschaft, No. 4, 2006, pp. 138–156; Busemeyer, Marius R. / Kellermann, Christian / Petring, Alexander / Stuchlík, Andrej: Politische Positionen zum Europäischen Wirtschafts- und Sozialmodell – eine Landkarte der Interessen, Bonn: Friedrich-Ebert-Stiftung, Europäische Politik, August 2006.

8   ETUC: Our Aims, http://www.etuc.org/r/2

9   Hyman, Richard: Trade Unions and the Politics of the European Social Model, in: Economic and Industrial Democracy, 2005 (Vol. 26), No. 1, pp. 9–40, here p. 29.

10 See e.g. Marks, Gary / Steenbergen, Marco R. (eds): European Integration and Political Conflict, Cambridge: Cambridge University Press, 2004; Marks, Gary, et al.: Party Competition and European Integration in East and West, in: Comparative Political Studies, 2006 (Vol. 39), No. 2, pp. 155–175.

about concepts that can explain different and joint positions within the group of trade unions in EU member states.

As can be gleaned from the citation of the ETUC's goals above, European trade unions are supposed to have a common interest in defending the interests of European workers and employees. Consequently, trade unions could be expected to show a relatively great degree of unity in forming positions about certain elements of the EESM. Accordingly, policies that further sustainable economic growth, full employment, the quality of working life, or social inclusion, for instance, should all be supported, while policies that favour 'upper income class interests' should be opposed.

However, a more realistic understanding of trade unions and their positions vis-à-vis the EESM is that while European trade unions display some similarities on the surface, they differ widely with regard to their policy positions. These differences can have various reasons: for instance, many European policies have distributional consequences[11] that might be perceived as being costly for trade unions in rich EU member states (e.g. liberalization of services markets), but beneficial for workers in poorer member states.[12]

In practice, it is hard to predict the distributional consequences of specific EU policies in full. It is therefore difficult for trade union leaders to base policy decisions on the expected distributive consequences of policies. We hypothesise that they instead remain embedded in the national institutional framework of their respective member states. This framework acts as a 'filter' and largely defines their identity and strategies, as well as their relations with and approach to government in general. This is not to say that trade unions would willingly sacrifice the common goal of promoting the collective interests of European workers in favour of narrowly defined national distributive interests. In contrast, all European trade unions want to promote the social and economic advancement of their membership, but the actual translation of membership interests into policy positions depends on the institutional and organizational environment.

Table 5-1 groups EU member states into five distinct clusters according to conventional research on welfare regimes[13] in order to capture country differences along

---

11   Marks, Gary: Conclusion. European Integration and Political Conflict, in: Marks, Gary / Steenbergen, Marco R. (eds): European Integration and Political Conflict, Cambridge: Cambridge University Press, 2004, pp. 235–259.
12   Unsurprisingly, all interview partners in the new member states defended the country-of-origin-principle as conceived in first version of the directive of services.
13   Esping-Andersen, Gøsta: The Three Worlds of Welfare Capitalism, Cambridge: Polity Press, 1990; Esping-Andersen, Gøsta (ed.): Welfare States in Transition, National Adaptations in Global Economies, London: Sage, 1996; Goodin, Robert E. / Headey, Bruce / Muffels, Ruud / Dirven, Henk-Jan: The Real Worlds of Welfare Capitalism, Cambridge: Cambridge University Press, 1999; Leibfried, Stephan: Towards a European Welfare State? On Integrating Poverty Regimes into the European Community, in: Ferge, Zsusza / Kolberg, Jon E. (eds): Social Policy in a Changing Europe, Frankfurt/M., Boulder/CO: Campus, Westview, 1992, pp. 245–279.

three dimensions: *Union density* is a measure of how encompassing the trade union movement is in a given country. *Collective bargaining coverage* is often related to union density, but there are cases (e.g. France and most Mediterranean countries) with low degrees of union density, but high collective bargaining coverage. So in a way, collective bargaining coverage reflects the willingness of policy-makers to rely on the social partners in the field of economic policy. *The type of welfare state* is a qualitative indicator, capturing the influence of the welfare state's institutional environment on the identity and preference-formation of unions.

Table 5-1:   Worlds of Welfare Capitalism and Union Attributes in Selected EU Member States

Country	Welfare type	Union density (%)	Union membership in thousands (2003)	Collective bargaining coverage (%)
Austria	Continental = core European Social Model	36.5	1,151.0*	97.5
France		9.7	1,830.0	92.5
Germany		25.0	7,120.0	68.0
Netherlands		23.2	1,575.2	82.5
Denmark	Scandinavian	74.4	1,710.5	82.5
Finland		76.2	1,495.0	92.5
Sweden		81.1	2,984.2	92.5
Ireland	Anglo-Saxon	38.0	515.7	n. a.
United Kingdom		31.2	6,524.0	32.5
Greece	Mediterranean	27.0	639.0±	n. a.
Italy		34.9	5,327.7	82.5
Spain		14.9	2,196.8	82.5
Portugal		24.3	1,165.0±	82.5
Czech Republic	New member states Eastern European	27.0	1,075.2#	27.5
Poland		14.7	1,500.0#	42.5
Slovak Republic		36.1	700.0	52.5

Note: #2001; *2002; ±2003.

Source: Data for 2001-03: EIRO on-line, http://www.eurofound.europa.eu/eiro/country_index.htm. Data on union membership: Visser, Jelle: Union Membership Statistics in 24 Countries, in: Monthly Labor Review, 2006 (Vol. 129), No. 1, p. 43 f. Data on union density and collective bargaining coverage: OECD: OECD Employment Outlook, 2004.

Because the process of constructing a common EESM[14] impacts differently on welfare states, it also triggers differences in the trade unions' policy preferences: these institutional frameworks shape the trade unions and determine their relative position in the national welfare state and labour market framework. More concretely, we think that the *Continental* welfare state model of the founding member states serves

---

14   For a survey of the literature concerning the EESM and policy proposals see Petring, Alexander / Kellermann, Christian: New Options for a European Economic and Social Policy, Bonn: Friedrich-Ebert-Stiftung, Europäische Politik, October 2005.

as a blueprint or core for a common EESM. To put it differently, political leaders across Europe expect that if something like a common EESM emerged, it would strongly resemble this type of welfare state. As a consequence, trade union leaders evaluate the prospect of a common EESM against the status quo in their own national setting, resulting in 'Euroscepticism' on the one hand (Scandinavia, UK) or tentative support (Mediterranean countries) on the other.

Trade unions in the *Continental* set (Germany, France, the Netherlands, Austria, Italy) have been living with a relatively long corporatist tradition, especially in Germany, the Netherlands and Austria. Even in France, where union density is low, collective bargaining coverage is very high. Therefore, trade unions in these countries have an interest in ongoing European integration and in creating a common standard at a high level in order to eventually safeguard the performance of their own Economic and Social Model. This holds true especially when confronted with the competitive pressures arising from the EU's increasing heterogeneity. At the same time, they have only a slight interest in expanding interstate redistributive funds, as this would worsen their position as net-payers.

In contrast, trade unions in *Anglo-Saxon* as well as *Scandinavian* countries tend to be rather 'Eurosceptic'. At first sight, it might seem rather odd to group Anglo-Saxon and Scandinavian countries together. But these countries can be expected to exhibit a similar degree of union's reluctance regarding Europeanization. First, they have an interest in minimizing interstate redistribution, because as net payers they are involved in financing EU-redistribution (e.g. European Social Funds) to a considerable extent. Second, and more importantly, the creation of a common EESM could potentially undermine the position of trade unions in the respective national welfare state and labour market regime. Scandinavian countries possess a high degree of both union density and collective bargaining coverage, and are comparatively generous welfare states. Therefore, if the creation of a EESM entails some development towards the EU average, trade unions in these countries would have to cope with some downward pressure with regard to social standards.[15] At the same time, trade unions in the Scandinavian countries need at least some sort of EU policy in order to protect national arrangements from increasing competitive pressure from new EU member states.

In the United Kingdom (and to a lesser extent in Ireland), industrial relations are much more decentralized than in other member states. The imposition of one EESM could potentially weaken the flexibility of these labour market arrangements, and thus possibly erode the economy's overall competitiveness.

---

15   This holds true despite the fact that of course member states may introduce or maintain instruments exceeding European minimum standards. Competitive pressure is continuously exerted by EU law. See e.g. ECJ C-438/05, 12-11-2007 International Transport Workers' Federation, Finnish's Seamans Union vs. Viking Line ABP, OÜ Viking Line Eesti.

The situation is somewhat different for trade unions in the *Mediterranean* group. Until very recently, these member states benefited greatly from the interstate redistribution policy (structural and cohesion funds). However, they have a greater affinity to the EESM of the EU core countries. This applies to the Mediterranean states (Spain, Portugal, Greece), which, depending on the development of economic prosperity, manifest a medium degree of decommodification, though comparatively coordinated market economies. Yet, this description also applies to Ireland, which differs from the ideal-typical Anglo-Saxon model by virtue of its expansion of mechanisms for coordinating the market economy (for example, social pacts between employers and trade unions). In this regard, the UK is the only representative of the Anglo-Saxon model that remains a liberal market economy within the EU. Trade unions in the Mediterranean countries can meanwhile hope for improvements in the socio-political situation in their own countries as a result of the expansion of social policy at the EU level and the institutionalization of a common EESM. Because their own national welfare states and production regimes are fairly similar to the Continental welfare state type, trade unions in these countries are expected to be mainly supportive of the creation of further delegation.

Finally, according to the *Eastern European* pattern, trade unions in the new member states are expected to have divergent opinions towards the creation of a common EESM. On the one hand, being the main beneficiaries of interstate redistribution for some time to come, political actors in Poland, the Czech Republic and Slovakia could be expected to welcome this sort of EU social policy. On the other hand, post-communist legacies and recent liberal developments, a comparatively low degree of decommodification, and medium levels of union density and collective bargaining coverage also testify to the fact that these states are relatively remote from the welfare state model of the EU core, or at least are changing more rapidly. As a matter of fact, trade unionism is still in flux in most of Central and Eastern Europe[16]; many observers describe them as 'victims of transformation'.[17] Moreover, union effectiveness varies significantly due to differing rates of membership decline and amounts of political credibility gained during the transition period.[18] These factors also affect their strategies towards European integration as well as their institutional capacity. An additional element that makes their preference formation more intricate is the fact of

---

16   See e.g. Kohl, Heribert / Platzer, Hans-Wolfgang: Arbeitsbeziehungen in Mittelosteuropa, Baden-Baden: Nomos, 2nd edn, 2004.

17   See conference section VI at 'Towards Transnational Trade Union Representation? National Trade Unions and European Integration', Bochum, 6–8 December 2007, http://www.ruhr-uni-bochum.de/iga/isb/isb-hauptframe/forschung/TowardsTransnationalTradeUnion/TowardsTransnationalPapersSectionVI.htm

18   Avdagic, Sabina: State-Labour Relations in East-Central Europe. Explaining Variations in Union Effectiveness, in: Socio-Economic Review, 2005 (Vol. 3), No. 1, pp. 25–53.

accession itself. Before May 2004, policies towards the EU were significantly shaped by 'conditionality' and compliance with the Acquis communautaire.[19]

As a consequence, the establishment of a common EESM along the lines of the Continental welfare state model with respectively high minimum standards could adversely affect their competitive advantage. Hence, the net gain of an interstate redistribution policy must be high enough to compensate for the benefits forfeited due to the (perceived) loss of competitive advantages. *Eastern European* unions face the dilemma between maintaining their competitive edge through low wages and liberal market arrangements on the one hand and their willingness to improve wages and social standards on the other.

In the following section, we will check our theoretical propositions against the survey data.

5.3. The Economy

5.3.1. The Stability and Growth Pact and Monetary Policy

A significant majority of unions agrees that the Stability and Growth Pact (SGP) is a necessary arrangement in Europe and the new member states are no exception here. Nevertheless, trade unions have often criticized the Pact for leaving too little fiscal room to manoeuvre in the case of weak economic growth. Especially the three-per-cent-rule is regarded as being too restrictive and capable of spurring cyclical effects. As one Czech representative put it: 'The criteria are far too restrictive, as CEE countries face special conditions. The SGP should focus on real convergence instead.'

The large majority of the unions in our sample were therefore in favour of a general reform of the SGP-criteria. The revision of the Stability and Growth Pact in 2005[20] was considered by many to be insufficient, since structural reform was not stipulated. According to the majority of unions, different business cycles in Europe, to which the Pact has no answers, are an additional problem. Despite these criticisms, there is no consensus on the use of anti-cyclical measures at the EU level. Among the CEE countries only one Polish trade union federation supported counteractive measures.

Most unions surveyed favoured a differentiated treatment of investments for calculating national deficits, i.e. taking into account the nature of deficit, evaluating debts due to investment – in conformity with the Lisbon Strategy – differently from debts

---

19   Schimmelpfennig, Frank: Starke Anreize, ambivalente Wirkungen. Die Europäisierung Mittel-
        und Osteuropas, in: Leviathan, 2004, (Vol. 32), No. 2, pp. 250–268; Schimmelpfennig, Frank /
        Sedelmeier, Ulrich: Candidate Countries and Conditionality, in: Graziano, Paolo / Vink, Maarten P.
        (eds): Europeanization, Houndsmills, Basingstoke: Palgrave, 2007, pp. 88–101.
20   Essentially an extension of situations where not to apply the excessive deficit procedure (Treaty
        Establishing the European Community [TEC] Art. 104).

for consumption and advocated a stronger focus on structural deficits as the Polish trade union Solidarność has proposed.

Another option is the abolition of the annual percentage target in favour of the sixty-per-cent-rule (level of indebtedness), but only a few unions endorsed this idea. The same was true when structural budget deficits were taken as a reference value, possibly including future pension-system burdens. Interestingly, we found no cleavage between old and new EU member states on this issue.

Regarding monetary policy, most union representatives in our sample favoured an inflation goal higher than two per cent or at least demanded a symmetric interpretation of the goal. However, nearly half of the unions had no clear position on this technical issue, calling instead for a rather general democratization / politicization of monetary policy.

Trade unions commonly criticize the monetary policy of the European Central Bank (ECB) as being too narrowly focused on the price level[21]; however, no clear picture of ECB criticism emerged and even among the set of new member states, opinions were widespread. Notably, trade unions' federations in the Czech Republic tend to fear that the ECB's inflation target will dampen growth potential.

A majority agreed, however, that wage and monetary policies should be coordinated in order to help boost employment. Both targets should be understood as complementary target variables. It is striking then that the vast majority of interviewed union representatives opposed a stronger focus of monetary policy on growth and employment. Interestingly, on this issue, trade unions in Poland, the Czech Republic and Slovakia are more 'left' than their Western partners. As to be expected regarding the real convergence process, they unanimously support a mandate revision that takes employment or regional disparities into account.

5.3.2.   Wage Coordination, Employment Policies and the Lisbon Strategy

5.3.2.1.   Wage Policy

As of today, wage policy remains one of the most important *national* tools of adjustment, whereby monetary and fiscal policy are being Europeanized or significantly curbed. Thus, the trade unions' main goal is to prevent 'competitive disinflation' and to initiate a productivity-growth-oriented wage policy.[22] There are also more far-reaching

---

21   Arestis, Philip / Mosler, Warren: Makroökonomische Politik im Euroraum. Eine kritische Betrachtung, in: WSI-Mitteilungen, 2005, No. 12, pp. 675–681.

22   Cf. The 'Doorn Declaration' 1998. For more information see Marginson, Paul / Schulten, Thorsten: The Europeanisation of Collective Bargaining, in: EIRO – European Industrial Relations Observatory on-line, 28 July 1999, http://www.eurofound.europa.eu/eiro/1999/07/study/tn9907201s.htm

forms of coordination taking place in the European Metalworkers' Federation, which strives to prevent wage dumping exchanging information and reaching agreement on targets and to avoid inflationary tendencies by means of wage settlements.[23]

However, and for quite different reasons, the majority of unions are against an EU-wide coordination of wage policies. Here we found a clear clustering of policy preferences matching our theoretical observations outlined above for the EU-15, but the picture is less clear-cut for the new member states.

As expected, there was fierce opposition against a common EU wage policy from Scandinavian and Anglo-Saxon countries. Trade union leaders in the Scandinavian countries fear that collective wage bargaining at the EU level will undermine their ability and power in national-level wage bargaining, resulting in downward pressure on wages or limited flexibility to coordinate wages across economic sectors. UK trade unions, in contrast, are more concerned with maintaining the flexibility of decentralized wage bargaining, not only out of concerns for competitiveness, but also in the interest of preserving the influence of local trade unions. In the same vein, we found that Czechs trade unions were opposed to enhanced coordination: 'If at all, this would be something for the Eurogroup, but today economic differences are far too great', said a Czech representative. However, Slovak and Polish unionists were less pessimistic.

In contrast, union leaders in Mediterranean countries supported stronger coordination of wage agreements. Some unions have sceptical views on coordination, but are at least in favour of stronger consultations and the exchange of information. We explain the positive attitude of union representatives in Mediterranean countries by their openness towards coordination and collective wage bargaining and that EU social policy initiatives can actually help to strengthen the modestly strong position of trade unions within national arrangements.

Since the beginning of the 1990s, trade unions have changed their agenda, moving away from their initial aim to develop and foster uniform wage rates in Europe.[24] Still, the crucial level for wage negotiations remains the nation state. Furthermore, at the core of such negotiations are pattern-setting collective bargaining agreements, in which wage agreements are generally binding. However, when asked about their preferred level of wage agreement, some union representatives (in France, Portugal, Greece, the Czech Republic and Slovakia) said that they favoured an EU-wide sectoral solution. One Greek trade unionist envisaged a system using an EU-15 average with special convergence programmes for the new member states. In contrast, union

23   Schroeder, Wolfgang / Weinert, Rainer: Europäische Tarifpolitik. Ein neues Politikfeld?, in: Schroeder, Wolfgang / Weßels, Bernhard (eds): Die Gewerkschaften in Politik und Gesellschaft der Bundesrepublik Deutschland. Ein Handbuch, Wiesbaden: Westdeutscher Verlag, 2003, pp. 567–589, http://cms.uni-kassel.de/uploads/media/Europ_ische_Tarifpolitik_Schroeder-Weinert_Gewerkschaftsbuch.pdf

24   Ibid., p. 577.

representatives in the United Kingdom prefer wage bargaining to stay on the company rather than on the national level.

Apart from bargaining matters, a demand for the introduction of a European minimum wage has been raised.[25] While there is a minimum wage in many EU countries, some trade unions regarded this as a threat to their bargaining autonomy. This is especially the case in Sweden, where representatives fear minimum wages will generate an 'income policy', thereby weakening their political stance. The Danish representatives' position was equally critical, but they acknowledged that a very low minimum wage might be helpful to the new member states; they were divided on this issue. While Polish representatives argued in favour of more EU competencies, the Czech and Slovak trade unions regarded any European solution as utopian or at least unfeasible.

Mediterranean countries generally supported minimum wages on a country-specific basis; only two Greek unions preferred a genuinely harmonized EU-wide minimum wage.

Regarding wage policy, we found evidence that supports our general claim: The welfare state 'outliers' – Scandinavians on the one hand and the UK on the other – are more sceptical towards further delegation. Unionists in Scandinavian countries are against EU-wide wage policies or collective wage bargaining at the EU level and against the imposition of a common minimum wage (at most on a very low level out of solidarity with unions in the new member states). The British opposition is rooted in different concerns: these unionists want to maintain the flexibility of local wage bargaining. With reservations, trade unions in Mediterranean countries are more supportive, because they hope for upward pressure on wages; in addition, their national institutional framework is more amenable towards coordinated solutions.

5.3.2.2. Macroeconomic Governance

Economic coordination and macroeconomic governance within the EU is founded upon a complex set of rules and procedures (cf. Art. 99 TEC). It comprises a variety of surveillance tools, from deficit monitoring to the European Employment Strategy (EES)[26], the Open Method of Coordination (OMC) and the Macroeconomic Dialogue[27]. Despite including all affected stakeholders, the latter has so far failed to deliver substantial results.

---

25 See for instance Schulten, Thorsten et al. (eds): Thesen für eine europäische Mindestlohnpolitik, Düsseldorf: Hans-Böckler-Stiftung, 15 April 2005, http://www.boeckler.de/pdf/wsi_2005_thesen_ mindlohn_de.pdf and Zitzler, Jana: Plea for a European Minimum Wage, Bonn: Friedrich-Ebert-Stiftung, International Policy Analysis, April 2007, http://library.fes.de/pdf-files/id/04144.pdf

26 Added as Art. 125–130 TEC in Amsterdam, the coordination of employment policies was referred to as 'Luxembourg process', before it became part of the Lisbon strategy.

27 A German-French initiative which was launched in June 1999 during the Cologne summit.

Usually, the rationale for enhanced European macroeconomic governance is the claim that national economic governance will eventually become less effective due to Europeanization and globalisation. Hence, we asked: 'Do you think that macroeconomic policy is less efficient without some form of coordination?' Though many Continental unions concurred, all of the Scandinavian unions felt that national economic policy is still an effective instrument; the majority held no clear-cut position. The same was true for the new member states. In most cases they did not have a position or said that nowadays 'the ECB's taking care of business cycles anyway'.

The European Employment Strategy has recently been incorporated into the Lisbon Strategy. The halftime revision of the Lisbon agenda was followed by the streamlining of both procedures in spring 2005.[28] The policy goals associated with employment are: reducing unemployment, increasing employment rates, increasing women's employment rates, reducing youth and long-term unemployment, creating better jobs, improving training, extending child care, etc. This is also reflected in the general positions towards the Lisbon Strategy of the unions across Europe. However, many unions criticize the strong focus on competitiveness as being too 'neoliberal'.

Most European unions assess the impact of the EES in their countries to be rather small, while the Open Method of Coordination is increasingly being recognized as an important EES instrument. However, in new member states, the EES faces another obstacle, which is the lack of institutional absorption capacity. As one Polish representative put it:

> In Poland there is no employment policy compatible with the EES; it works rather in opposition to it, as an excluding strategy. Each year bigger and bigger professional groups are being excluded (due to outsourcing, restructurings, and so on). Instead of a pro-employment policy, we have an exclusionary one.

Still, many delegates favour an even stronger coordination of employment policies, with again the exception of Scandinavian unions. Among the new member states in our sample, Slovak and Polish unionists would like to see at least a better mix of EES with the Social Dialogue, while in the view of the Czech-Moravian Confederation of Trade Unions (ČMKOS), Europeanization would not be beneficial, because the disparities 'even among the eastern European countries' remain too high.

To a relatively high degree, unionists share common perceptions regarding for instance the issue of macroeconomic governance. They support the general goals of the Lisbon Strategy but criticize much of its actual implementation. In contrast to wage policies, this area is more distant from the unions' day-to-day activities. When institu-

---

28   Commission of the European Communities: Working Together for Growth and Jobs. A New Start for the Lisbon Strategy, COM 2005/24, 2005, http://ec.europa.eu/growthandjobs/pdf/COM2005_024_en.pdf

tional conflicts are set aside, we find a stronger convergence of policy positions, but consensus remains only at an abstract level.

5.4. Social Policy

Regarding EU social policy, there are demands mainly from left to centre parties to strengthen social components alongside the development of market freedoms. They also underscore the necessity of safeguarding the welfare states from the negative external effects of the internal market. As could be expected, this general stance is widely shared by the unions. Moving from problem perception to palpable propositions, the picture changes. All new member states agree upon the need to 'strengthen the social dimension' but at the same time conclude that due to the EU's enlargement in 2004, this aim has become increasingly unrealistic (e.g. Slovakia's Confederation of Trade Unions – KOZ SR).

When measured in terms of the Esping-Andersen typology of social democratic, liberal and conservative welfare states, no convergence of welfare states towards an EESM can be discerned over the 1990s.[29] Most unions in the sample viewed the persistent heterogeneity of welfare states as the major obstacle to enhancing the EU's social competencies. Accordingly, the majority rejected the idea of a single social model in Europe.[30] Opposition to that idea comes mainly from Scandinavian but surprisingly also from Continental and Mediterranean unions. Five unions in our sample expressed the view that a single social model is not only unrealistic, but also undesirable.

In fact, the majority considered the EESM to be more of a blueprint rather than a viable political agenda. According to that perspective, unions should strive to see that EU directives are transposed into national law in a socially acceptable way.

The generally high degree of scepticism with regard to the establishment of a common EESM, which is variously viewed by leaders as undesirable or impracticable, shows that the notion of institutional conflicts and the trade unions' fear of encroachment of EU policies that might endanger their hard-won positions on the national level are very real. At the same time, almost all union leaders opined that the social dimension of the European Union should be strengthened.

As a consequence of this general dilemma, political leaders tend to consider the OMC as a panacea, because it provides some (soft) coordination of policies, but basically has no immediate consequences for national policy-making. And the OMC is appealing to most unions, too, if only due to its lack of hard constraints. However, the

---

29   Petring, Alexander: New Labour im Vergleich. Konvergenz oder Divergenz in der europäischen Sozialdemokratie?, in: Berg, Sebastian / Kaiser, André (eds): New Labour und die Modernisierung Großbritanniens, Augsburg: Wißner, 2006, pp. 301–337.

30   Question No. 29: 'Is there a single European Social Model to be aimed at and how should it look like?'

new member states stand out in that none of them has developed a firm position regarding the OMC.

5.4.1.   The Social Dialogue

The 'Dialogue with the social partners is one of the pillars of the European Social Model, although freedom of association and wage bargaining autonomy are still the prerogatives of member states.'[31] The Commission can 'develop the dialogue between the social partners at the European level, which could, if the two sides consider it desirable, lead to relations based on agreement' (Art. 138 TEC). Alongside the Social Dialogue at the macro level, a number of branch committees have been set up in the EU since 1998.[32]

As a central institution of the EESM, the Social Dialogue was generally assessed positively by the unions in our sample. In addition, the very concept, i.e. policy coordination in corporatist institutions, is largely supported. Therefore, almost all unions called (and unanimously those from Poland, the Czech Republic and Slovakia) for a stronger role for social partners in EU policy-making in general.

However, the picture is much fuzzier in terms of an assessment of the actual results of the dialogue so far. Positive and negative assessments were given in equal measure: while the majority of Scandinavian and Mediterranean unions in the survey were not satisfied with the Social Dialogue's results thus far, the Anglo-Saxon and Continental countries reported a more positive experience. Unions in Eastern Europe in particular gave a positive assessment of the results of the EU Social Dialogue so far, though again, the interplay with national governments remains crucial. As one Slovakian delegate put it: 'In the last three years the Slovak government badly neglected the process.'

In general, however, the trade union leaders we spoke to were more sceptical than leaders of social democratic parties about the results of the dialogue.[33]

The well-known clustering of policy positions was most discernible when union leaders were asked how to strengthen the role of the social partners at the EU level. For the most part, participants agreed that the most pressing problem is as follows: because corporatist institutions have to be built anew at the EU level and EU institutions (like the Commission) are either unwilling or not powerful enough to enforce the employers' commitment to these corporatist institutions, employers can basically veto

---

31   Petring, Alexander / Kellermann, Christian: New Options for a European Economic and Social Policy, Bonn: Friedrich-Ebert-Stiftung, Europäische Politik, October 2005, p. 6.

32   Moreover, formal EU recognition of the social partners' right to negotiate framework agreements at the European level, they have signed cross-sectoral European framework agreements, which have been implemented as directives.

33   See Busemeyer, Marius R. / Kellermann, Christian / Petring, Alexander / Stuchlík, Andrej: Perspectives on the European Economic and Social Model: Distributional and Institutional Conflicts, in: International Journal of Public Policy, 2008 (Vol. 3), No. 1/2, pp. 39–57.

or block the establishment of a comprehensive Social Dialogue. As one Danish interview partner observed, employers' associations also lack the organizational capacity to enforce jointly decided policies on the national level; therefore, the general feasibility of a comprehensive Social Dialogue is questionable. Some union leaders (e.g. in Spain and Greece) explicitly criticized the EU Commission for not doing enough to promote the Social Dialogue and for using the employers' opposition as an 'excuse for doing nothing', whereas one partner in Poland put it differently: 'Ironically: Every time the Commission wants to play a stronger role it's easier for social partners to come up with an agreement. Yes, it might be useful, but it should be avoided whenever possible.'

In sum, concerning the Social Dialogue, we found that the trade unions' policy positions tended to cluster along the lines suggested by the welfare type model presented above. On an abstract level, policy positions on the need for an extended Social Dialogue were relatively convergent and coherent. But when the union leaders were asked *how* this goal ought to be achieved, their policy positions started to diverge and largely reflected the relative position of the respective union within the national institutional framework. Strong unions are less enthusiastic about taking the 'supranational' route by further institutionalizing the role of the social partners at the EU level and utilizing the Commission to put more pressure on employers.

Unions from countries with strong traditions of social partnership emphasized that the process of European integration must not be allowed to endanger the internal workings and integrity of national institutions, but at the same time touted social partnership as an effective policy instrument that ought to be used more extensively (e.g. in Austria).

In contrast, countries with weak traditions of social partnership (e.g. Greece) were more supportive of strengthening the EU level, because they felt this would also strengthen their role in the national arena.

5.4.2.   European Works Councils

The directive on European works councils was adopted in 1994 to promote the Social Dialogue at the enterprise level. These entities, which are primarily designed for information dissemination and consultation, have so far been established in approx. 40% of the enterprises that fall under the jurisdiction of the directive.[34] Via their consultations with the trade unions, European works councils can make an important contribution to transnational coordination. Of course, the Europeanization of collective bargain-

---

34   Lecher, Wolfgang / Platzer, Hans-Wolfgang: Europäische Betriebsräte, in: Schroeder, Wolfgang / Weßels, Bernhard (eds): Die Gewerkschaften in Politik und Gesellschaft der Bundesrepublik Deutschland. Ein Handbuch, Wiesbaden: Westdeutscher Verlag, 2003, pp. 588–613.

ing policy is still regarded by many with scepticism. European works councils[35] could play a vital role in Europe-wide sectoral collective agreements. The networking, coordination and demarcation of tasks between trade unions and European works councils, however, remain unsatisfactory.[36] Therefore, most unions in our sample were in favour of a stronger coordination of strategies and policies with the European works councils. The same holds true for the new members, with the noticeable exception of the Czech Republic, whose unions prefer to maintain the status quo.

5.5. Tax Competition

At present, the tax policy of the European Union predominantly pertains to the rates of indirect taxes (such as VAT and consumption taxes) as part of the common market harmonization.[37] As the community budget is partly financed from VAT income, the contributive burden ought to be fairly distributed by means of harmonization among all EU members.

Apart from that, tax provisions must not hinder free movement of capital within the community. Indeed, cross-border competition in corporate taxation has intensified since the eastward enlargement brought about a slew of low-tax states (e.g. Estonia, Slovakia) into the fold. Trade unions claim that such a competition may become harmful: the example of Ireland has shown that low tax rates on corporate profits and corporation taxes can contribute to accelerated economic growth – sometimes at the expense of other EU member states, since corporations tend to report parts of their value added in such low-tax countries.

This phenomenon was also observed by a large majority of the unions in our sample – they also spoke of harmful tax competition in the EU, although some unions tend to take a rather dim view of competition itself. Furthermore, they see the enhanced tax competition as a product of the eastern enlargement. 'Enlargement aggravates the problem because the new member states possess a very lean (and liberal) state, despite their communist past', commented a French unionist. Of course, one would expect unionists from the new member states to offer a different perspective. In fact, they unanimously agreed that there is indeed tax competition going on, but they were split on the issue of whether it is also detrimental. Czech unions approved, but Polish interview partners said that the competition had already existed before the enlargement and has not been aggravated.

---

35   At present, 1258 agreements are in place. The Database on European Works Councils Agreements, http://www.ewcdb.org/list_agreements.php

36   Lecher, Wolfgang / Platzer, Hans-Wolfgang: Europäische Betriebsräte, in: Schroeder, Wolfgang / Weßels, Bernhard (eds): Die Gewerkschaften in Politik und Gesellschaft der Bundesrepublik Deutschland. Ein Handbuch, Wiesbaden: Westdeutscher Verlag, 2003, pp. 588–613.

37   Petring, Alexander / Kellermann, Christian: New Options for a European Economic and Social Policy, Bonn: Friedrich-Ebert-Stiftung, Europäische Politik, October 2005, p. 8.

In the long run, it is argued, pressure will grow to reduce tax rates in the countries concerned so that in the end, income from corporate taxation will tend towards zero and 'free riders' will profit from a high level of infrastructure.[38] So far, the EU has only achieved the enactment of a 'code of conduct' which is supposed to ensure that no competition-distorting tax benefits are introduced.[39]

The introduction of a European minimum tax for companies also found strong support among the unions in our sample. Most support issued from unions in the Mediterranean region, but there was no significant regional pattern within the entire group of unions against this proposal.

In order to accelerate the integration of the single market, the EU has taken a number of measures to coordinate and adapt taxation systems. The requirement of unanimity in the Council of Ministers has once more proved a hindrance in this respect. Taxation policy is therefore bucking the trend towards an ever closer union.[40] Most of the unions in our sample in fact voiced support for exchanging the requirement of unanimity in the Council of Ministers for majority rule. Interestingly, this aspect found no consensus within social democratic parties.[41]

5.6. Conclusion

Our survey revealed a number of interesting findings concerning trade unions' positions on various issues. Obviously, if the unions' perceptions of problems do not jibe, then the chances of achieving consensus on political measures are virtually nil. If there is agreement on the general problem, however, it should be much easier to reach consensus on corrective measures. Our findings demonstrated the degree of consistency and preference formation among unions in the European Union. We also examined the influence of the respective national welfare structures, which helps to explain the variety of positions towards Europeanization.

We found that European trade unions held relatively coherent and converging policy positions on general issues on an abstract level, i.e. the 'general perception' (see Table 5-2) as well as on issues that either affect European workers in different countries similarly or on which trade unions have relatively little influence (e.g. monetary and fiscal policies). The same holds true for unions from the new member states.

---

38   Jarass, Lorenz / Obermair, Gustav M.: Vorschlag für ein zukünftiges EU-Steuersystem, mimeo, 2005.

39   The EU is not aiming at the development of uniform tax rates or minimum tax rates, although an EU basis for assessment for corporate taxation is to be worked out by 2008.

40   Genschel, Philipp: Steuerharmonisierung und Steuerwettbewerb in der Europäischen Union, Frankfurt/M.: Campus, 2002.

41   Busemeyer, Marius R. / Kellermann, Christian / Petring, Alexander / Stuchlík, Andrej: Perspectives on the European Economic and Social Model. Distributional and Institutional Conflicts, in: International Journal of Public Policy, 2008 (Vol. 3), No. 1/2, pp. 39–57.

Regarding the SGP and its necessary reform, unionists from Poland, the Czech Republic and Slovakia share the majoritarian attitude. However, the new member states are less prone to change the ECB mandate in order to focus on growth targets, and they clearly deviate from the majority of unions on this issue.

Regarding the 'general perception', trade unions in general were supportive of the promotion of the Social Dialogue and the strengthening of the social dimension, but were unable to formulate more concrete proposals. Unsurprisingly, the unions' policy positions diversified when the issues were concretised. Unions were also largely supportive of the general European macroeconomic framework (ECB, Stability and Growth Pact), but advocated reform.

In fact, the three new member states fit well into the general picture and revealed split opinions in exactly the same areas as the majority of trade unions across the European Union.

Table 5-2:   Trade Unions' Positions on the EESM – *General Perception*

	Fiscal policy	Monetary policy	Wage policy	Macro-economic coordina-tion	Social policy		Tax competi-tion
General percep-tion	SGP is nec-essary Reform of SGP-criteria necessary	*Does the ECB a good job?*	*Coordi-nation of wages*	Macro-economic coordina-tion is nec-essary	Stronger social dimen-sion pref-erable	No threat: 'social tourism' EU-Migra-tion no problem	Existing tax com-petition
New mem-ber states	Consensus with majority	PL: divided SK: yes CZ: no	PL: divided SK: yes CZ: no	Consensus with majority	Consensus with majority	Consensus with majority	Consensus with majority

Note: non-consensual positions are in italics. Source: own compilation

This trend changed slightly when we focused on concrete reform initiatives and policy proposals (see Table 5-3).

Taxation as such is another consensual issue: most unions think that minimum company taxation would be a desirable reform option. There is also widespread agreement that majority rule should be introduced in the Council of Ministers regarding taxation. However, enhancing the competencies of the Commission is not an option shared by a clear majority. Many unions attributed their reluctance to such a solution to the current Commission's (perceived) neoliberal orientation and not to a general dislike for this proposal. In particular, the Scandinavian unions expressed fear of a downward adjustment of their national tax rates. The experiences in the different welfare worlds (including their related systems of industrial relations) with the Commission are quite diverse. By contrast, unions in Poland, the Czech Republic and Slovakia would even like to see an enhanced role for the Commission, as they are less hostile towards its (perceived) neoliberal orientation.

Table 5-3:   Trade Unions' Positions on the EESM – *Policy Proposals*

	Fiscal policy	Monetary policy	Wage policy	Macro-economic coordination	Social policy		Tax competition
Actual policy proposals	Stronger focus on Investments vs. consumption	ECB should put a stronger focus on growth (real convergence)	*Introduction of minimum wages (at least some EU competence)*	Coordination of wages Coordination of employment policies	OMC useful for social policy	*Single social model*	Minimum taxation Majority rule *Taxation competencies for Commission*
New member states	Consensus with majority	PL: no position SK: yes CZ: yes	PL: yes SK: no CZ: no	PL: divided SK: yes CZ: no	No position	PL: against SK: yes CZ: yes	PL: yes SK: yes CZ: yes

Note: non-consensual positions are in italics. Source: own compilation

Divergence of policy positions occurred on issues that are crucial to the unions' day-to-day activities. We found evidence for the clustering of policy positions that reflects the respective position in the national welfare state and labour market arrangements. For example, in the realm of social policy, we found only little agreement on specific initiatives. While most unions agree to use the OMC to develop a stronger social dimension, there is no consensus on further steps or no clear position at all in the new member states.

Positions on the minimum wage vary significantly, too: Mediterranean and Polish unions support the introduction of a minimum wage, while especially Scandinavian as well as Slovak and Czech unions oppose the establishment of a minimum wage. Obviously, Scandinavian countries, with their encompassing unions and universal welfare systems, associate this notion with a downsizing of their collective bargaining system. Meanwhile, the new member states are divided on this issue.

While unions in Mediterranean and new member countries consider many EU directives tantamount to upgrading standards, Continental and especially Scandinavian unions perceive liberalization as a threat to their institutional settings of corporate governance and industrial relations.

To sum up, there is a significant degree of consensus and agreement among European trade unions in key political areas. However, there are also many issues where national differences prevail and prevent a concerted strategy. Trade unions in Europe act in different national arenas, they have varying resources, and their scope of influence is by no means identical. As those national settings cannot be harmonized – let alone homogenized – over night, a search for more differentiated measures might be a solution in many areas. However, there are also some issues – e.g. the potential coordination of wage policies – where disagreement remains constitutive.

Katarzyna Gajewska

6. Polish Trade Unions for the European Cause. The Case of the EU Directive on Services in the Internal Market

6.1. Introduction

In January 2004 the European Commission worked out a proposal for a Directive on Services in the internal market, or what became commonly known as the Services Directive or the Bolkestein Directive,[1] that provides a single market for services within the member states of the European Union (EU).[2] The first draft of the Services Directive argued for extensive liberalization and proposed several important changes in the EU services market. The explicit aim was to remove any barriers to the expansion of the internal market in services and to guarantee the expansion of cross-border services in different EU member states.

The draft directive provoked intense debate in the European Parliament (EP). The key point of discussion was the proposal of the 'country of origin principle' which declares that companies can offer services throughout the EU provided they follow the laws of their home countries. Supporters of the proposal, economic liberals, agued that a free service market would help to increase employment and productivity. But critics who sought to protect the continent's social model said that it would damage working conditions in richer EU member states and would lead to competition between workers and to job losses because the low-cost service suppliers from Eastern Europe would undercut their rivals from Western Europe. Consequently, the standards regarding the price and quality of service or the qualifications of the workers could be diminished or lost completely. This in turn could hasten the downward spiral of wages, taxes and social security inside the EU member states. The harmonization principle preferred by the old member states obliged the firms to abide by the host country's domestic law. This was seen by the new member states as Western protectionist practice against the Eastern states. This perception was confirmed by a report from Evelyne Gebhardt, member of the Socialist Group (Party of European Socialists –PES) in the EP, who said that the 'impression has been given that this draft is intended to set the interest of the fifteen "old" member states against those of the ten "new"

---

1   The directive was drafted under the leadership of the former European Commissioner for the Internal Market Frits Bolkestein and has been popularly referred to by his name.
2   Directive 2006/123/EC of the European Parliament and of the Council of 12 December 2006 on services in the internal market, for more information see http://eur-lex.europa.eu/LexUriServ/ LexUriServ.do?uri=CELEX:32006L0123:EN:NOT

ones that joined us in May 2004.[3] The directive was seen in general as defining the shape of European integration, namely whether the free market or social standards would take priority.

On 16 February 2006 the European Parliament plenary worked out a compromise which reformulated some important articles of the Directive. The main changes were: to uphold the fundamental rights to collective bargaining and action; and to abolish the 'country of origin principle', while enabling EU member states to exercise better supervision and apply rules to protect the public interest.[4] The Directive on Services in the Internal Market was finally approved by the European Parliament on 12 December 2006. EU member states have to adopt the Directive by the end of 2009.

The long-lasting debate in the European Parliament was accompanied by mass protests by the trade unions of several EU member countries. In November 2004 the European Trade Union Confederation (ETUC) issued a statement to the EU Council calling for a more balanced approach to protecting public services and social welfare. In addition, demonstrations were announced by many organizations, including ETUC, the Association for the Taxation of Financial Transactions for the Aid of Citizens (ATTAC) and the European Social Forum. On 19 March 2005 over 75,000 people marched in Brussels to demonstrate their opposition to the Directive. The crowd consisted primarily of working people and trade unionists from Belgium, France, Germany, Italy and the Netherlands. The two main Polish trade union confederations, the Independent Self-Governing Trade Union Solidarność (NSZZ Solidarność) and the All-Poland Alliance of Trade Unions (OPZZ) supported the Western trade unions. 14 February 2006 the second big demonstration on the issue took place in Strasbourg, where about 30,000 people, mostly from trade unions from nearly every country in the EU-25, took part. The Polish mining and teaching unions were main participants in the demonstration, but not the only ones. There were also local initiatives against the Service Directive. There were 130 people protesting in Warsaw this day, including mainly the representatives of ATTAC, and anarcho-syndicalist and leftist movements (parties which are not in Parliament). Anarchists, ATTAC Polska and the Greens also protested in Olsztyn, Wrocław and Katowice.[5] Additionally, Miners' Trade Unions, the Free Trade Union August 80 (Wolny Związek Zawodowy – WZZ Sierpień 80) and the All-Poland Unemployed Union (Ogólnopolski Związek Bezrobotnych – OPZ) signed a petition of protest against the liberal directive.[6] Moreover, there was a counter-dem-

---

3   Evelyne Gebhardt, 14 February 2006 during a debate in the European Parliament.
4   Redžepagić, Srđan: European Social Model vs Directive Bolkestein, in: Panoeconomicus, 2006, No. 1, pp. 65–77, here p. 73.
5   Niklewicz, Konrad / Kuźmicz, Maciej: Wolne usługi nie dla nas?, in: Gazeta Wyborcza, 10 February 2006.
6   Ciszewski, Piotr: Spór wokół Bolkensteina, in: Trybuna, 11 February 2006.

onstration of pro-capitalist groups in favour of a liberal version (information from a website stopbolkestein.org.pl).

The motives and participation of the Polish trade unions in the demonstrations against the Service Directive is the main subject of this chapter. The lack of mobilization among national constituencies is identified as a cause for the failure of the Social Dialogue at the EU level.[7] However, the decision on the Service Directive was accompanied by a successful mobilization. The commitment of Polish trade unions can be interpreted as a sign of their solidarity with trade unions in the West. From the concept of competitive solidarity, we would assume that the workers from the new member states would have opposing interests to their Western counterparts regarding the EU directive, and we would expect them to prefer the 'country of origin principle' over the 'harmonization principle'. Ebbinghaus and Visser[8] define the high labour standards as not being in the interest of labourers in poorer countries. Low working standards would help them to decrease unemployment and labour over-supply, which are the factors that weaken trade union strength. Given the wage differences in the EU, Eastern workers could still earn much more abroad than at home even if they accept wages lower than those paid to Western workers. The competitive cost advantage would also contribute to the economic success of the local markets.

This case study should be read against the background of other studies on Polish trade unions. The issue here is not only the different economic interests formulated by the political elites. The trade unions in Poland surprised Western scholars with their pro-market attitude after the fall of Communism, which has been explained in terms of Poland's legacies. Ost's ethnographic study[9] provides the most in-depth analysis of this phenomenon. Crowley[10] and Meardi[11] have made similar contributions. The latter one draws on the scenario of the increasing divide between Eastern and Western workers.

---

7   Hyman, Richard: Changing Trade Union Identities and Strategies, in: Hyman, Richard / Ferner, Anthony (eds): New Frontiers in European Industrial Relations, Oxford: Blackwell, 1994, pp. 108–139, here p. 135.

8   Ebbinghaus, Bernhard / Visser, Jelle: European Labor and Transnational Solidarity. Challenges, Pathways, and Barriers, Mannheimer Zentrum für Europäische Sozialforschung (MZES), Mannheim, 1996, p. 5.

9   Ost, David: The Defeat of Solidarity. Anger and Politics in Postcommunist Europe, Ithaca: Cornell University Press, 2006.

10   Crowley, Stephen: Explaining Labor Weakness in Post-Communist Europe. Historical Legacies and Comparative Perspective, in: East European Politics and Societies, 2004 (Vol. 18), No. 3, pp. 394–429.

11   Meardi, Guglielmo: Trade Union Activists, East and West. Comparison in Multinational Companies. Aldershot: Ashgate, 2000; Meardi, Guglielmo: Trojan Horse for the Americanization of Europe? Polish Industrial Relations Toward the EU, in: European Journal of Industrial Relations, 2002 (Vol. 8), No. 1, pp. 77–99.

6.2. The Polish Public Debate

The Polish government under Prime Minister Kazimierz Marcinkiewicz aimed at maintaining the 'country of origin principle' and a liberal version of the Directive. Minister of Economy Piotr Woźniak argued that an open market for services would be advantageous for Poland because it is better to have 450 million potential clients in the European Union than only 38 million in Poland.[12] Jarosław Pietras, the Polish Minister on European Affairs at that time, told Eurobserver on 2 February that the liberalization of services would confirm the full presence of new member states in the EU by removing barriers in the common market. It would also prevent the marginalization of migrants from new member states and keep them from being pushed into the shadow economy. He instructed a group of over twenty Polish Members of the European Parliament (MEPs) to vote for the liberal version of the Directive.[13] Polish MEPs from the central-liberal party Civic Platform (Platforma Obywatelska – PO), the right party Law and Justice (Prawo i Sprawiedliwość – PiS), the national ultraconservative party League of Polish Families (Liga Polskich Rodzin – LPR) and the populist party Self-Defence of the Republic of Poland (Samoobrona Rzeczpospolitej Polskiej – SRP) voted against the changes in the liberal version.[14] Konrad Szymański from Law and Justice found the amendments additionally less attractive because they had been drafted by German politicians.[15] Bronisław Geremek of the Democratic Party (Partia Demokratyczna-demokraci.pl) and Dariusz Rosati of the left Social Democracy of Poland (Socjaldemokracja Polska – SdPl) were the only Polish MEPs not supporting the original liberal version. At the national level there was also nearly complete consensus on the liberal version. Even the leader of Social Democracy of Poland, Marek Borowski, was in favour.[16] Only the Green party (Zieloni 2004), which is not represented in parliament, was against the 'country of origin principle'.[17]

The seven most important associations of employers and entrepreneurs from Lower Silesia signed a common statement on this issue. They demanded a liberal version that would make them competitive on the common market.[18] Similarly, the Polish Confederation of Private Employers Lewiatan (PKPP Lewiatan), was in favour of the

---

12   Kuźmicz, Maciej: Spór rządu ze związkami o dyrektywę usługową, in: Gazeta Wyborcza, 15 March 2006.
13   Rettman, Andrew: Old Europe Hypocritical on Services, Polish Minister Says, in: euobserver. com, 3 February 2006.
14   Niklewicz, Konrad: Rozwodniona dyrektywa usługowa też daje korzyści, in: Gazeta Wyborcza, 17 February 2006.
15   Niklewicz, Konrad: PE przyjął dyrektywę usługową, in: Gazeta Wyborcza, 16 February 2006.
16   Ciszewski, Piotr: Spór wokół Bolkensteina, in: Trybuna, 11 February 2006.
17   Niklewicz, Konrad / Kuźmicz, Maciej: Wolne usługi nie dla nas?, in: Gazeta Wyborcza, 10 February 2006.
18   PAP [Polish Press Agency]: OPZZ przeciwko unijnej dyrektywie usługowej, in: Onet.pl Wiadomości, 13 February 2006.

liberal version.[19] The final version of the Service Directive, in which the 'country of origin' clause had been stricken, was negatively received by employers. The newspaper 'Rzeczpospolita' quoted two employers, a vice directorate of a firm and a co-owner of a consulting-educational firm, as saying that the competitiveness of Polish firms would be diminished and that expansion into the West no longer made much sense.[20]

That the issue clearly divided European public and societies along national lines is best illustrated by the inner party negotiations within the Party of European Socialists. The representatives of the ten 'new' countries within the Socialist party took a different stance from the rest. The Polish group within the PES actively participated in the formulation of a stance vis-à-vis the party's voting. It promoted a potentially wide range of services covered by the directive, the 'country of origin principle', and the removal of administrative barriers for posted workers. Dariusz Rosati, the Polish MEP in the PES group, found the arguments of the left-wing parties populist and spoke out in favour of the 'country of origin principle'. He criticized the draft proposed by Evelyne Gebhardt for trying to undermine free competition. He also supported extending the range of services covered by the Directive, such as water or energy supply or postal services.[21] In his view, the broad interpretation of the term 'services of general interest' could endanger the compromise. It could, for instance, enable France to prevent the liberalization altogether.[22] In his article commenting on the issue in the newspaper 'Rzeczpospolita', Rosati claimed that the whole debate around the Directive was manipulated by Western politicians. The 'country of origin principle' should not have sparked fears about social dumping, because it does not address labour laws; labour law issues are regulated in the EU Posted Workers Directive 96/71/EC.[23] He therefore felt that the whole fracas concerning the directive had been based on misunderstandings. He found it deplorable that the Polish trade unions had let themselves be sucked into this 'game'. MEPs from Poland and other new member states managed to block a rule allowing protectionist practices justified by social or consumer policy.[24]

---

19   Niklewicz, Konrad / Kuźmicz, Maciej: Wolne usługi nie dla nas?, in: Gazeta Wyborcza, 10 February 2006.
20   Słojewska, Anna: Europa otwarta dla naszych fachowców, in: Rzeczpospolita, 16 November 2006.
21   Rosati, Dariusz: Przed głosowaniem nad projektem dyrektywy usługowej w Parlamencie, Website of Dariusz Rosati, 10 February 2006, http://www.rosati.pl/index.php?option=com_content&task=view&id=138&Itemid=50
22   Niklewicz, Konrad: Zagrożenia nowej dyrektywy usługowej, in: Gazeta Wyborcza, 3 September 2006.
23   Directive 96/71/EC of the European Parliament and of the Council of 16 December 1996 concerning the posting of workers in the framework of the provision of services, for more information see: http://eur-lex.europa.eu/LexUriServ/LexUriServ.do?uri=CELEX:31996L0071:EN:HTML
24   Rosati, Dariusz: Dyrektywa usługowa – Konkurencja, choć niedoskonała, in: Rzeczpospolita, 27 February 2006.

The Minister of Economy, Piotr Woźniak, who tried to enforce the changes after the first reading in the European Parliament, also criticized the Polish trade unions. He wondered why the trade unions were against a directive that could help Polish firms. He interpreted their stance as misguided, claiming that they 'falsely understood solidarity with the trade unions from Germany and France'. The Vice-Minister of Economy, Marcin Korolec, pointed out that the trade unions mostly represented big companies, whereas the Service Directive concerned small and mid-sized enterprises. The discussions with the trade unions did not budge either side from its position. Attempts by the trade unions to lobby the government to withdraw from endorsing the 'country of origin principle' were fruitless; the Polish government announced that it would not change its position.[25]

A content analysis of the Polish press[26] shows that the liberal version of the Service Directive was promoted in all major newspapers. 'Gazeta Wyborcza', presented the liberal version of the Directive as reflecting national interests. Konrad Niklewicz, the main – and in fact only – reporter on the issue in this newspaper, consistently supported the liberal version before the vote in Parliament and after the European Commission had prepared a new Service Directive at the end of March 2005. 'Rzeczpospolita' represented the firms' point of view, which is to be expected given its focus on a managerial readership. 'Gazeta Wyborcza' also saw eye to eye with the firms on this issue and trumpeted their possible gains from the Directive. The newspaper points out that the real winner in the battle would be the 'Polish plumber', which is shorthand for the self-employed service providers and professionals wanting to work abroad. Consequently, the national 'we' in this issue was composed of the firms wishing to expand their supply market or post or subcontract their workers, and the workers themselves wanting to work abroad. This interest coalition was represented by the Polish government. The higher environmental and social standards in Western countries were seen as an obstacle. The goal of the Polish government was to become more competitive on the Western market by exploiting the lower standards in Poland. The other two sides of the triangle consisted of Western workers, who wanted to maintain their high labour standards and pursue protectionist strategies, and Polish trade unions, which were perceived by the government as acting against the national interest, and therefore as the black sheep of the family. The way the rift on the Service Directive was portrayed in 'Gazeta Wyborcza' resembles the conceptualisation of competitive solidar-

---

25   Kuźmicz, Maciej: Spór rządu ze związkami o dyrektywę usługową, in: Gazeta Wyborcza, 15 March 2006.

26   The analysis is based on the press articles from the centre-right newspaper 'Rzeczpospolita', the centre-left newspaper 'Gazeta Wyborcza', the leftist newspaper 'Trybuna' that sympathises with the trade unions, and information from the online portal prepared by the Polish Press Agency (PAP).

ity described by Streeck.[27] The cleavage was said to be clearly along national lines, or more precisely, between old and new member states. National interests are derived from the countries' economic features and are common to workers and firms. Workers from the East and West are in competition with each other. Only 'Trybuna', a smaller newspaper close to the trade unions, illustrated the issue in a different way, namely as a conflict of interests between the firms and especially between multinational corporations and employees in service sectors. The former want to undermine the social standards of work and exploit the workers, and the latter want to maintain or raise standards.

6.3. Bringing European Issues to the National Level of Polish Trade Unions

The European trade union movement was intensely involved in the Directive; ETUC, European industry federations and national-level trade unions all were active in the debate. The Service Directive became an issue for the trade unions at the end of 2004. No real differences between the countries emerged, but there were squabbles among the branches. For instance, the academicians' trade union in Sweden saw potential problems with the Directive, but also recognized certain advantages at the beginning. The construction trade unions found the Directive problematic. Generally, there were no differences across national lines, although the high-wage countries like Germany had a stronger interest in this issue.

The Eastern trade unions, such as those from Poland and Estonia, recognized the economic advantages of the liberal Service Directive for their countries, but also detected certain risks. An unregulated service sector is disadvantageous. Competition with lower wages would make it difficult to increase the wages of affiliated members in the long run. The trade unions from the mentioned countries were convinced of this from the beginning. The Eastern trade unions supported the stance of their Western counterparts, but there was not as much engagement from their side. This disparity can be explained by the much lower risk for the low-wage countries; furthermore, the public debate had a different character. The political parties, even the social democratic ones, were in favour of the liberal version. Polish and Hungarian trade unions were summoned by their governments to explain why they had taken part in the demonstration on 19 March 2005 against the national interest.[28]

The existing structures of trade union organization and communication channels were deployed for the organization of the demonstration. The organization of the

---

27 Streeck, Wolfgang: Competitive Solidarity. Rethinking the 'European Social Model', Max-Planck-Institut für Gesellschaftsforschung Working Paper 99/8, 1999.
28 Interview with Thorben Albrecht, DGB Department of International and European Trade Union Policy, 24 March 2006, Berlin.

demonstration was proposed by the General Secretary of the ETUC; affiliates voted to participate in it at the Executive Committee meeting in December 2005. The ETUC sent an invitation to its national affiliates. It was further disseminated to the lower organizational levels, such as branch unions.

The presence of a Polish representative in the European structures might also have helped in the organization. Józef Niemiec, the former Secretary of NSZZ Solidarność and since 2003 the ETUC General Secretary, received a leaflet from the Green Party in the European Parliament and forwarded it to the NSZZ Solidarność Foreign Affairs Department with the annotation that it was more or less in line with the ETUC stance and should be further passed along. The Foreign Affairs Department forwarded it to the Press Department of NSZZ Solidarność. The national media presented a different picture and therefore, there were many discussions and questions from the trade unionists as to why the trade union was against the liberal version of the Service Directive.[29] The national levels of NSZZ Solidarność and OPZZ represented the stance negotiated in the ETUC and presented the issue in a communication to the lower organizational levels. They did not engage much in the mobilization itself, leaving that task to the branch and regional levels.

The ETUC also invited the OPZZ International Affairs and European Integration Department to take part in the demonstration, arguing that it would be good to join forces. The invitation was forwarded to ninety branch federations; meanwhile, OPZZ organized an internal debate on the issue. The International Affairs and European Integration Department sent the Polish translation of the service draft to its ninety branch / sectoral federations to obtain their feedback. The branches sent back their comments or amendments, and based on these, OPZZ formulated its stance. Their official position was communicated in a letter by the French General Confederation of Labour (CGT) General Secretary Bernard Thibault and OPZZ leader Jan Guz. Most concerned were the Polish Teachers' Union (Związek Nauczycielstwa Polskiego – ZNP), which felt threatened by the inclusion of the public services in the Directive, and the Trade Union of Miners (ZZG) which expressed general concerns about labour rights and standards. The national level seems to have had a rather passive role in the mobilization. It instead disseminated the information and formulated a stance based on the branches' feedback. The fact that OPZZ's teacher and miner branches decided to take part is explained by Ostrowski with the available resources for such undertakings. These two federations have the most members and were most affected by the issue. The national level had the financial resources to take part, but funds were

---

29   Interview with Marta Pióro, Press Department NSZZ Solidarność, 22 June 2006, phone.

not earmarked for this purpose. The costs of participation in the demonstration were covered by the budget from branch member contributions.[30]

The trade unions obtained information on the issue not only via the national level, but also from their European Industry Federations. The representative of the NSZZ Solidarność Secretariat of Food Industry Workers stressed that neither the European Federation of Trade Unions in Food, Agriculture and Tourism Sectors (EFFAT) nor anyone else had tried to convince the trade union to take part. EFFAT had simply provided information on the planned action; the choice was left to the trade union. If the trade union was interested, it received further information from the organizers regarding the practical details. The Trade Union of Miners obtained materials from OPZZ's national branch and found further information on the Internet. The contacts with foreign trade unions did not have a direct impact on participation. Besides the material from OPZZ, the Polish Teachers' Union also received information on the issue from the Education International and European Trade Union Committee for Education (ETUCE). This entity invited the trade union to take part in the demonstration. The Education Section of NSZZ Solidarność also received information and an invitation through this channel. The following quote illustrates how the decision to participate was framed by the ETUCE. Participation was seen as a symbol of the unity of the European trade union movement and represented an important opportunity for the trade unions to have a say on the EU directive:

> [...] and it was signalled to us that there are powers in Europe that would like this com- mercialisation to apply to education also. And it was signalled to us that if the trade unions showed ... a certain unity, i.e. that they are against liberalisation, then it would be easier for the negotiators at the European level to change the final version of the directive.[31]

The German Confederation of Trade Unions (DGB), engaged in the mobilization of Eastern trade unions as well. There were discussions with the trade unions from low-wage countries, but this cannot be called lobbying. There were several meetings between Western and Eastern trade unions in which the Service Directive was discussed. For instance, on 4 December 2004, there was a conference in Vienna entitled 'Freedom of services = future of services?'[32] that was attended by representatives from the United Services Union in Germany (Vereinte Dienstleistungsgewerkschaft – ver.di), NSZZ Solidarność, the Czech-Moravian Confederation of Trade Unions (ČMKOS) and the Austrian Federation of Trade Unions (Österreichischer Gewerkschaftsbund – ÖGB). During the conference on the Constitutional Treaty from 21 to 22 October 2005

---

30   Interview with Piotr Ostrowski, OPZZ Department for International and European Affairs, 22 June 2006, phone.

31   Interview with Stefan Kubowski, leader of NSZZ Solidarność Education Section, 12 February 2007, Gdańsk.

32   III DLZ conference 'Dienstleistungsfreiheit = Dienstleistungszukunft?', for more information see http://www.dienstleistungszukunft.de/chemnitz/Frame_komplett.html

in Děčín, there was a discussion block between the German Confederation of Trade Unions and ČMKOS on the Service Directive. There was also a two-day conference on the issue from 26 to 27 October 2005 in Frankfurt (Oder) entitled 'Public services in the EU – chances and limits of the competition',[33] which was organized by the Interregional Trade Union Council Viadrina and by DGB and NSZZ Solidarność.

6.4. Explaining Participation of Polish Trade Unions in Terms of Organizational Belonging

The account given above illustrates that the decision to participate was made in the context of intensive interaction within the European trade union movement. The framing of the motivation also confirms that membership in European organizations and relations with Western trade unions were of crucial importance for participation. In the following I will describe the mobilization process of branch trade unions, including the mining branch of OPZZ, the Trade Union of Miners and two teachers' trade unions, one belonging to OPZZ, and the Education Section NSZZ Solidarność. In addition to the participants in the February 2006 demonstration, I also included in my survey a branch trade union that took part in the March 2005 demonstration, also against the Service Directive, the NSZZ Solidarność Secretariat of Food Industry Workers. This trade union has extensive experience in participating in European demonstrations. They have stressed the identification with the European or international trade union organizing structures. This finding is relevant for the assessment of the international organizational structures' impact on the trade unions.[34]

For instance, a respondent from the NSZZ Solidarność Secretariat of Food Industry Workers answered the question of why they had participated in the demonstration by stating that the Secretariat had been a member of EFFAT since 1996. Participation was thus considered obligatory. He reiterated this sentiment by saying: 'If we belong to an organization, then we should feel like a family'. In his view, affiliates should sup-

---

33 Conference, Öffentliche Dienstleistungen in der EU – Chancen und Grenzen des Wettbewerbs', for more information see http://www.eu.dgb.de/article/articleview/3904/1/210/

34 NSZZ Solidarność was incorporated into the international contacts before the collapse of the regime. In 1986, it was the only East European trade union to join the International Confederation of Free Trade Unions and World Confederation of Labour. In 1991, it gained observer status in the ETUC and become an affiliate in 1995 (Einbock, Joanna: Case Study. The Activities of Polish Trade Unions at the EU Level, in: Pleines, Heiko [ed.]: Participation of Civil Society in New Modes of Governance. The Case of the New EU Member States, Part 3: Involvement at the EU Level, Bremen: Forschungsstelle Osteuropa, 2006, pp. 79–86, here p. 82). The OPZZ applied for membership in 1998 and hoped to be accepted in December 2001 during the ETUC Congress. However, the request was refused due to the conflict with NSZZ Solidarność about the assets of the trade union from the Communist period.

port their representatives at the European level if needed.[35] The interviewee from the mining trade union, ZZG, also explained that his branch wanted to belong to and establish its presence in the European trade union movement.[36] Participation in the demonstration was consistent with this aim.

ZZG also indicated that its membership in OPZZ and the European Mine, Chemical and Energy Workers' Federation (EMCEF) had led to its participation in the demonstration. The Education Section NSZZ Solidarność also cited its affiliation with the respective European branch federation, the European Trade Union Committee for Education, as a factor in its decision. It was informed about the possible impact of the Directive by the organization. ZNP did not refer to its various memberships at first but instead stressed the importance of the issue itself. Nevertheless, its membership in the European Industry Federation, ETUCE and the Education International is generally significant. Later in the interview, active engagement in these structures was stated to be a priority. Although it was not made explicit, we can see that the ZNP's decision to participate in the demonstration was influenced by its interest in the European federation.

Over and above the specificity of the Service Directive, the ZNP saw that there are general common interests which unite trade unions across national borders. The idea of catching up with the West by promoting lower standards was considered to be against the principles of trade unionism; ZNP representatives cited the idea of solidarity in European trade unionism. They believe that showing the unity that exists among the trade unions is advantageous. They espouse the concept of strength in numbers; one can only be effective by acting together. The motivation for showing solidarity with other trade unions was also repeated a number of times by the National Education Section of NSZZ Solidarność. The president stressed the importance of promoting an 'awareness that we are together so that in case something bad is happening in the European Parliament against education, like this directive, we will be able to defend ourselves.'[37]

6.5. Establishing Position within the European Trade Union Movement

The interviewees revealed that their participation in the demonstrations was not solely motivated by the 'obligation of membership' in the organizational structures,

---

35 Interview with Mirosław Nowicki, Leader of NSZZ Solidarność Secretariat of Food Industry Workers, 6 November 2006, Warsaw.
36 Interview with Wacław Czerkawski, Deputy Leader of Miners' Trade Union, ZZG, 2 November 2006, Katowice.
37 Interview with Stefan Kubowski, leader of NSZZ Solidarność Education Section, 12 February 2007, Gdańsk.

but was seen as a way of cementing their organizations' relationship with the other trade unions. This is exemplified by the mining trade union's explanation of its participation. The participation of ZZG was conceived as a form of 'showing presence' and becoming a constitutive part of the European labour movement. Protest is one of the forms of cooperation, and they wanted to show that their trade union was ready to participate and not just be a passive observer. The importance of being noticed was also mentioned by the National Education Section NSZZ Solidarność:

> At least from the reports from those that were there, I saw that the West European unions were pleased that Solidarność had shown up, so we were also happy that Europe [the trade unions] had seen us, that we are still strong [...] that we will gather, come and form an important group when needed.[38]

Participation was seen as a way of showing that the trade unions abroad could count on them. This sentiment was echoed by all the trade unions. There is an implicit expectation of reciprocity in it. My interviewee felt that it would be possible to recruit allies from abroad to help solve national problems.

Similarly, the leader of the NSZZ Solidarność Secretariat of Food Industry Workers stressed the importance of showing interest in European issues and supporting Western trade unions. It was also a matter of prestige. He was even more specific about the rewards: by means of active participation, the trade union wanted to establish itself within the European trade union representative structures in order to have better access to information as well as a say in organizational decision-making. This engagement simultaneously enhances the defence of workers' interests and elevates the prestige of the trade union.[39]

The ZNP Coordinator of International Cooperation and Educational Projects also considered active involvement in European-level activities to be important. She pointed out that the engagement pays off: it is not the size of the trade union but rather the extent of its engagement that secures participation in decision-making. By taking part in demonstrations, they wanted to show that they are a reliable partner and ready to engage in European affairs.[40]

6.6.   Europeanization of Polish Trade Unions

The above analysis illustrated that while Polish trade unions participated in the European demonstration to protest the Service Directive and its impact, there is also more at stake. The trade unions derive their motivation by virtue of belonging to trade union

---

38   Interview with Stefan Kubowski, leader of NSZZ Solidarność Education Section, 12 February 2007, Gdańsk.
39   Interview with Mirosław Nowicki, Leader of NSZZ Solidarność Secretariat of Food Industry Workers, 6 November 2006, Warsaw.
40   Interview with Dorota Obida, Polish Teachers' Trade Union, ZNP, Coordinator of International Cooperation and Educational Projects, 6 November 2006, Warsaw.

organizations. Active involvement is seen as advantageous for the quality of their membership. They are interested in reciprocal relations with the other trade unions and expect exchanges in the future. Solidarity with Western trade unions is a way of pursuing the individual interests of the trade unions. Although the attitudes and convictions that led the trade unions to participate were internalised or became internalised in the process of interacting with other trade unions, one can see a further impact of the actual commitment to the protest against the Service Directive.

Although my interviewees would argue that the awareness of common interests or the perception of the impact of the directive was shared, their participation might have strengthened the existing relationships and have had a top-down impact on Polish trade unions.

For instance, the trade unions in the education sector recognize that educators face similar problems in all countries. They have observed this through their participation in transnational networks and exchanges. The commercialisation of education revealed itself to be a problem in all European countries. The National Education Section of NSZZ Solidarność stresses that the Service Directive was against their general interests, which happened to be common with those of the West European trade unions:

> Most important for us was to prevent education from becoming almost entirely privatised; that was always our will. With or without a European directive, with or without a call from ETUCE, we would want to fight against complete privatisation [...]. The motivation was ours, we have thought it through, nobody needed to explain it to us [...]. We were happy that the ETUCE, the European partner, was on the same page.[41]

The European trade union organizations do not necessarily change the general attitudes of the local trade unions. Their convictions are based not only on the process of socialization but also if not foremost on their experiences at the national level. Therefore, one should not interpret the participation in the demonstrations as resulting in changed attitudes but rather as a way of strengthening relationships through the pursuit of collective goals. This event might have reinforced the feeling of being 'in the same boat', which could have further implications for improving the trade unions' capacity when acting at the European level.

The commitment to collective action might also have had an impact on the lower levels of the trade unions. It sparked off intensive discussions on the European issues and helped to define the attitude towards European integration. For instance, the decision to participate was explained in the trade union press to members. The articles showed the benefits of solidarity with the West and explained how workers might be

---

41   Interview with Stefan Kubowski, leader of NSZZ Solidarność Education Section, 12 February 2007, Gdańsk.

affected by a European issue. The National Education Section of NSZZ Solidarność saw the experience of demonstrating abroad as having advantages for the trade union:

> For us [...], when my people see that others accept them, that it is important, then in Poland they start to like each other more and value that they are in a trade union, and [...] are able to defend something.[42]

In other words, he associates the feeling of having performed well and receiving positive feedback from the other trade unions with better identification with the trade union at home.

The participation in the 14 February 2006 demonstration in Strasbourg, although extraordinary, was rather limited in the context of the Polish trade union movement as a whole: only three sectors took part. This does not mean that the cause was not supported by the others. Organizational membership and participation in European decision-making does not necessarily lead to more active participation in demonstrations, which I am going to illustrate with the example of the construction branch trade union. Its leadership shared the opposition towards the 'country of origin principle' with their Western counterparts, but did not participate in the demonstration.

The interviewee from construction trade union, Budowlani, saw the fate of Polish and Western workers as intertwined: if Polish workers destroy labour standards abroad through social dumping, there will be no chance of establishing higher standards in Poland.[43] Similarly, his trade union perceives a common interest with the Western trade unions. Another important factor for the trade union was identifying with and seeing itself as part of the broader structure of trade unionism. Although his trade union apparently saw eye to eye on the Service Directive issue with the unions that participated in the demonstration, it did not see a need to engage in this kind of activism.

Instead the interviewee stressed that best strategy for influencing European politics is lobbying and engaging in the Social Dialogue at the European level. The interviewee praised the latter form of access to decision-making as effective. His trade union has not attempted to lobby Polish MEPs in the European Parliament. The interviewee described MEPs as so difficult to influence that even their own parties cannot do it. Furthermore, he said, there was no need to take action, because the European structures informed and consulted the trade union about the issue and therefore represented their stance on it. The non-participation was instead explained in terms of a different perception of opportunities for influence in the EU.[44]

---

42 Interview with Stefan Kubowski, leader of NSZZ Solidarność Education Section, 12 February 2007, Gdańsk.
43 Interview with Jakub Kus, construction trade union, ZZ 'Budowlani' Trade Union Secretary, 6 November 2006, Warsaw.
44 Interview with Jakub Kus, construction trade union, ZZ 'Budowlani' Trade Union Secretary, 6 November 2006, Warsaw.

Belonging to the international structures of trade union representation plays an important role for Polish trade unions. However, this embedment can also be a reason for non-participation: representation is delegated. Other factors, like the common platform of trade unionism and seeing engagement as a form of 'earning' mutuality from other trade unions, also played a role. These general convictions do not matter when there is a conflict or no opportunity to formulate common interests, however.

6.7. Conclusions

It is clear from the above that the reasoning promoted by the Polish media and politicians resembled the theoretical conceptualisation on competitive solidarity.[45] However, one could observe mobilization and engagement on the side of Polish trade unions that was contrary to the 'national interest'. This counters the prediction of competitive solidarity among the trade unions. It is also evidence of gradual change in the Polish trade unions, which have been transformed from enthusiasts for capitalism into critics of competition between workers. The institutional structure of European trade unionism, with its different levels of organization, was revealed to have the potential to mobilize workers at the European level. There is interaction and information exchange across borders and between the levels of trade union structures, from the European to the local branch levels. Polish trade unions are also incorporated in these communication channels.

The case study illustrated that organizational belonging or the perceived self-interest in strengthening relationships with Western trade unions is capable of nudging Polish counterparts towards 'European action' or solidarity. The trade unions share values and attitudes (at least at the top level) and are keen on deepening their relationship with Western trade unions. This goes counter to the predictions of scholars who based their research on the attitudes found after the collapse of Communism. It turns out that Poland's later experience with capitalism and its exchanges with other trade unions have contributed to learning over time. Therefore, the conclusions regarding a European divide between East and West are not only disproved by concrete examples, but are also less and less probable given the tendencies towards liberalization and tightening of ties between trade unions. Tentatively, one can assume that Europeanization in the top-down direction is also likely to continue to intensify if and when similar future events occur. The divide is rather vivid at the level of intergovernmental negotiations, but this schism has largely been caused by the politicians and media rather than by civil society.

---

45 Streeck, Wolfgang: Competitive Solidarity. Rethinking the 'European Social Model', Max-Planck-Institut für Gesellschaftsforschung Working Paper 99/8, 1999.

The example of non-participation indicated that identification with the institutional structures and awareness of general common interests is not enough. Lobbying is seen to be a more effective tool and scepticism about the impact of the demonstrations has been expressed. A representative of the construction trade union explained his organization's lack of action as being due to the limited opportunities to effect change at the national level or the futility of lobbying Polish MEPs. In addition, membership in European umbrella organizations can also be an excuse for not mobilizing one's own resources for European issues (in this case, the Service Directive).

Part III. Country Studies

Heiko Pleines

7. Trade Unions from Post-Socialist Member States in EU Governance. An Introduction

7.1. Introduction

This part of the book presents the results of the research project 'Already arrived in Brussels? Representation of the Interests of Trade Unions of the New Member States at the EU Level', which examined the integration of trade unions from the new member states at the EU level. The project, which received financial support from the Otto Brenner Foundation, was conducted by the Research Centre for East European Studies at the University of Bremen in collaboration with the Sociological Institute of the Czech Academy of Sciences, the Sociological Institute of the Slovak Academy of Sciences and the Koszalin Institute of Comparative European Studies. Brigitte Krech was responsible for conducting the interviews in Brussels.

Three of the larger new member states, Poland, the Czech Republic and Slovakia, were chosen for the empirical analysis. Taken together, these countries have a greater number of trade unions, and their trade unions also possess different organizational structures. In each of the three countries, national umbrella organizations as well as strong individual trade unions were selected for analysis. To ensure comparability, national umbrella organizations as well as the branch unions for the metal and mining industries were selected for each of the countries. The trade union studies thereby include the strongest trade unions in the largest post-socialist EU member states and thus represent a best case scenario with respect to influence potential. The trade union studies were thus consciously selected as cases of maximum influence potential rather than as representative of the new member states. This is due to the prevailing assumption of weak representation of trade unions from the new member states on the EU level. If even the strongest trade unions fail to gain traction on the EU level, then the assumption will have been validated.

This chapter gives an introduction into the project topic while the following three chapters present more detailed country studies. The project results are summarized in a comparative perspective in the concluding chapter.

7.2. The Trade Unions in the Countries under Review

State-run trade unions existed in all three project countries during the socialist period. In Poland, however, an independent opposition trade union, the Independent and Self-Governing Trade Union Solidarność (NSZZ Solidarność), had already been established by the beginning of the 1980s. In 1989 it became a central actor in the regime change. Union leader Lech Wałęsa became the state president, with Solidarność forming the government. The formerly socialist trade union All-Poland Alliance of Trade Unions (OPZZ) also managed to survive the regime change. Both trade unions were active in the political system until 2001. OPZZ participated in the government from 1993 to 1997; Solidarność took the helm again from 1997 to 2001. Both trade unions lost public support over the course of the 1990s, however, and saw their membership numbers dwindle dramatically. In reaction to the politicization of the two large trade unions, the Trade Unions Forum (FZZ) was established in 2002 as a third national umbrella organization with the explicit objective of maintaining political neutrality. In large part due to defections from OPZZ, the FZZ quickly attained national importance. It currently represents 20% of all Polish trade union members, while OPZZ and Solidarność each have a share of around one-third.[1]

Whereas a plurality of trade unions took root in Poland, in the Czech Republic and Slovakia the successor organizations of the socialist trade union federation of Czechoslovakia remained dominant. In the Czech Republic, the Czech-Moravian Confederation of Trade Unions (ČMKOS) represents more than two-thirds of the nation's trade union members. The second largest trade union, the Association of Independent Trade Unions (ASO), represents around 20%. Trailing in third place is the trade union for cultural workers, the Confederation of Arts and Culture (KUK), with around 5%. The total number of trade union members has halved since the mid-1990s.[2]

In Slovakia, the successor organization to the socialist trade union is called Confederation of Trade Unions of the Slovak Republic (KOZ SR) and represents more than 90% of the country's trade union members. The other trade unions are thus irrelevant on the national scene. The Slovakian trade unions' membership erosion was

---

1   Tholen, Jochen: Labour Relations in Central Europe. The Impact of Multinationals' Money, Aldershot: Ashgate, 2007, pp. 27–33; Towalski, Rafał: EIRO. 2004 Annual Review for Poland, Brussels, 2005, http://www.eurofound.europa.eu/eiro/2005/01/feature/pl0501104f.htm. More detailed: Ost, David: The Defeat of Solidarity. Anger and Politics in Postcommunist Europe, Ithaca: Cornell University Press, 2005; Deppe, Rainer / Tatur, Melanie: Rekonstitution und Marginalisierung. Transformationsprozesse und Gewerkschaften in Ungarn und Polen, Frankfurt/M., 2002, pp. 94–134, 221–248; Pańków, Włodzimierz / Gąciarz, Barbara: Industrial Relations in Poland. From Social Partnership to Enlightened Paternalism?, in: Blazyca, George / Rapacki, Ryszard (eds): Poland into the New Millennium, Cheltenham: Edward Elgar, 2001, pp. 72–90.
2   Tholen, Jochen: Labour Relations in Central Europe. The Impact of Multinationals' Money, Aldershot: Ashgate, 2007, pp. 27–33; Hála, Jaroslav / Kroupa, Aleš: EIRO. 2004 Annual Review for Czech Republic, Brussels, 2005, http://www.eurofound.europa.eu/eiro/2005/01/feature/cz0501103f.htm. More detailed: Pollert, Anna: Labor and Trade Unions in the Czech Republic, 1989–2000, in: Crowley, Stephen / Ost, David (eds): Workers after Workers' States. Labor and Politics in Postcommunist Eastern Europe, Lanham: Rowman & Littlefield, 2001, pp. 13–36; Myant, Martin / Smith, Simon: Czech Trade Unions in Comparative Perspective, in: European Journal of Industrial Relations, 1999 (Vol. 5), No. 3, pp. 265–285.

fairly limited compared to their counterparts in Poland and the Czech Republic. As a result, Slovakia enjoys a relatively high degree of trade union organization.[3]

In addition to the national umbrella organizations, branch federations for the metal and mining industries will be included in this analysis. They are among the strongest in terms of membership and influence in all three countries under review. For Poland, the respective branch federations of OPZZ were selected, i.e. the Federation of Metalworkers' Trade Unions ('Metalowcy')[4] and the Trade Union of Miners (ZZG). For the Czech Republic, the relevant organizations are the industry associations in ČMKOS, i.e. the Czech Metalworkers' Federation KOVO (OS KOVO) and the Union of Workers in Mines, Geology and Oil Industry (OS PHGN). In Slovakia, the associations selected for the analysis are part of the KOZ, i.e. the Slovak Metalworkers' Federation KOVO (OZ KOVO) and the Union of Workers in Mines, Geology and Oil Industry (OZ PBGN).

Because collective bargaining is centralized to a limited degree rare in all three countries, the trade unions are frequently primarily active at the company level, where they negotiate for individual wage agreements. The national coordination of the trade unions and the incorporation of the industry associations in national umbrella organizations are therefore relatively loose. As the following table for the year of the countries' accession to the EU shows, collective bargaining coverage, especially in Poland and the Czech Republic, is far below the EU average.[5]

Table 7-1:   Strength of Trade Unions: Membership Figures and Collective Bargaining Coverage (2004) (%)

	Poland	Czech Republic	Slovakia	EU average
Trade union density	17	22	30	25
Collective bargaining coverage	35	35	50	66
Degree of bargaining centralization	20	27	33	34

Source: EIRO, http://www.eurofound.europa.eu/eiro/country_index.htm

At the beginning of the 1990s, committees bringing together trade unions, employer organizations and state actors in economic and social policy were formed in all three countries. Given that these committees had a primarily advisory function, however,

---

3   Tholen, Jochen: Labour Relations in Central Europe. The Impact of Multinationals' Money, Aldershot: Ashgate, 2007, pp. 27–33; Cziria, Ludovít: EIRO. 2004 Annual Review for Slovakia, Brussels, 2005, http://www.eurofound.europa.eu/eiro/2005/01/feature/sk0501101f.htm. More detailed: Čambáliková, Monika: Industrial Relations and Social Dialogue. Actors, Strategies and Challenges in the SR, in: Labour, Industrial Relations and Social Bargaining, Prague, 2000, pp. 83–94; Myant, Martin / Slocock, Brian / Smith, Simon: Tripartism in the Czech and Slovak Republics, in: Europe-Asia Studies, 2000 (Vol. 52), No. 4, pp. 723–739.
4   www.federacja-metalowcy.org.pl
5   See for example: Tholen, Jochen: Labour Relations in Central Europe. The Impact of Multinationals' Money, Aldershot: Ashgate, 2007, pp. 27–33.

this so-called tripartite approach provided the trade unions with very limited opportunities for influence.

The tripartite commission founded in Poland in 1994 currently includes the three
major trade union federations and four employer federations. There is considerable
political strife among the trade unions. At the end of the 1990s, when Solidarność was
part of the government, the national tripartite negotiations broke down. Individual
issues were resolved, however, and settlements were regularly reached at the branch
level.

By 1990 the Czech Republic had already established a tripartite committee with
the Council for Economic and Social Agreement. With the exception of a crisis phase
in the second half of the 1990s triggered by the uncooperative behaviour of Václav
Klaus' laissez-faire government, negotiations were conducted consensually as a rule. In
Slovakia, meanwhile, the tripartite committee founded in erstwhile Czechoslovakia fell
apart in 1997 due to the government's intractable behaviour. It did not regroup until
a change of government in 1999. After that, however, settlements were only reached
in exceptional circumstances.

In short, Polish, Czech and Slovakian tripartite relations have been described as
conflict-oriented, consensus-oriented and gridlocked, respectively.[6] However, one element that all three tripartite committees share is that they hardly provide the trade
unions with any real influence potential on national policy.[7] The trade unions in the

---

6   Tholen, Jochen: Labour Relations in Central Europe. The Impact of Multinationals' Money,
     Aldershot: Ashgate, 2007, p. 28.
7   This assessment is shared by e.g.: Ost, David: After Postcommunism. Legacies and the Future
     of Unions in Eastern Europe, in: Phelan, Craig (ed.): The Future of Organised Labour. Global
     Perspectives, Oxford: Peter Lang, 2006, pp. 305–331; Mansfeldová, Zdenka: Case Study. Czech
     Labour and Capital Interest Representation. The Social Dialogue at the National and EU Level,
     in: Working Papers of the Research Centre for East European Studies, No. 67, 2005, pp. 40–50;
     Matthes, Claudia-Yvette / Terletzki, Peggy: Tripartite Bargaining and its Impact on Stabilisation
     Policy in Central and Eastern Europe, in: International Journal of Comparative Labour Law and
     Industrial Relations, 2005 (Vol. 21), No. 3, pp. 369–403; Kohl, Heribert / Platzer, Hans-Wolfgang:
     Arbeitsbeziehungen in Mittelosteuropa. Transformation und Integration. Die acht neuen
     EU-Mitgliedsländer im Vergleich, 2nd edn, Baden-Baden: Nomos, 2004; Mailand; Mikkel / Due,
     Jesper: Social Dialogue in Central and Eastern Europe. Present State and Future Development, in:
     European Journal of Industrial Relations, 2004 (Vol. 10), No. 2, pp. 179–197; Deppe, Rainer / Tatur,
     Melanie: Rekonstitution und Marginalisierung. Transformationsprozesse und Gewerkschaften in
     Ungarn und Polen, Frankfurt/M.: Campus, 2002, pp. 228–234; Čambáliková, Monika: Tripartismus
     in der Slowakei – Leere Struktur oder außerparlamentarische Form der Interessenvertretung?, in:
     Zeitschrift für Gemeinwirtschaft, 2001 (Vol. 38), No. 6, pp. 27–46; Casale, Giuseppe: Experiences
     of Tripartite Relations in Central and Eastern European Countries, in: International Journal of
     Comparative Labour Law and Industrial Relations, 2000 (Vol. 16), No. 2, pp. 129–142; Cox, Terry
     M. / Mason, Robert: Interest Groups and the Development of Tripartism in East Central Europe,
     in: European Journal of Industrial Relations, 2000 (Vol. 6), No. 3, pp. 325–347; Myant, Martin /
     Slocock, Brian / Smith, Simon: Tripartism in the Czech and Slovak Republics, in: Europe-Asia
     Studies, 2000 (Vol. 52), No. 4, pp. 723–739; Kurtan, Sandor: Gewerkschaften und Tripartismus
     im ostmitteleuropäischen Systemwechsel, in: Merkel, Wolfgang / Sandschneider, Eberhard
     (eds): Systemwechsel 4. Die Rolle von Verbänden in Transformationsprozessen, Opladen:

post-socialist EU member states are therefore described as weak in terms of their organizational abilities, their role in wage negotiations and their political influence.[8]

Prior to the accession of the post-socialist nations to the EU, the European Commission initiated a series of measures intended to prepare civil society organizations from the future member states for engagement at the EU level. The overwhelming majority of trade union representatives interviewed for this project reported having received support in preparation for trade union work in the EU before their countries joined the EU in 2004.[9] They cited the provision of information, training and support in international networking as important measures.[10] Overall, the support provided by the EU was described as at least satisfactory by the great majority of respondents.[11]

In retrospect, however, only half of the trade union representatives felt that their trade union had been well-prepared for their work at the EU level in 2004. Only 4% of the respondents held the opposite view, and the remainder expressed mixed feelings.[12] Three-quarters of the trade union representatives reported an improvement in their ability to work at the EU level after the first three years of EU membership.[13] The vast majority of trade union representatives from the new member states thus do not perceive themselves as incapable of coping with the challenge of engagement at the EU level.

7.3.   Examining Engagement on the EU Level. The Project Design

In the following country studies the role of trade unions from post-socialist member states in EU governance will be investigated from two angles. First, the actual (and not merely formal) inclusion of trade unions from the new member states in decision-making processes on the EU level is concerned. Second, the country studies also encompass the Europeanization of trade unions from the post-socialist member states.

Leske+Budrich, 1999, pp. 115–135; Ost, David: Illusory Corporatism in Eastern Europe. Tripartism in the Service of Neoliberalism, in: Sisyphus, 1998, pp. 167–177; Mansfeldová, Zdenka: Sociální partnerství v České republice, in: Brokl, Lubomír et al. (eds): Reprezentace zájmů v politickém systému České republiky, Prague: SLON, 1997, pp. 99–150; Reutter, Werner: Tripartism without Corporatism. Trade Unions in Eastern and Central Europe, in: Agh, Attila / Ilonszki, Gabriella (eds): Parliaments and Organized Interests. The Second Steps, Budapest: Hungarian Centre of Democracy Studies, 1996, pp. 59–78; Orenstein, Mitchell: The Czech Tripartite Council and its Contribution to Social Peace, in: ibid., pp. 173–189.

8   Systematic comparative analyses on this subject are offered by e.g.: Vanhuysse, Pieter: Workers without Powers. Agency, Legacies and Labour Decline in East European Varieties of Capitalism, in: Czech Sociological Review, 2007 (Vol. 43), No. 3, pp. 459–522; Crowley, Stephen: Explaining Labor Weakness in Post-Communist Europe, in: East European Politics and Society, 2004 (Vol. 18), No. 3, pp. 394–429.

9   Project Questionnaire, Summer 2007, Question Q6.

10   Project Questionnaire, Summer 2007, Question Q7.

11   Project Questionnaire, Summer 2007, Question Q8.

12   Project Questionnaire, Summer 2007, Question Q9.

13   Project Questionnaire, Summer 2007, Question Q10.

The country studies are first of all based on the interviews conducted as part of the research project in summer 2007. They included a survey with forty-three questions as well as semi-structured interviews.[14] More than forty trade union representatives, over ten employer representatives and about twenty policy experts and consultants were questioned for the project. A list of respondents and a documentation of interview results is included in the appendix.

Among the trade unions and employer associations, leading members were selected whose area of responsibility includes their organization's relations with the EU (department heads or board members). To obtain a representative statement on the organizations' position, at least two representatives were interviewed per organization where possible. This measure was meant to ensure that the testimony was not influenced by the personal preferences of a dissenter within the organization.

Because all of the representatives interviewed hold leadership positions with respect to their organization's relations on the EU level (sometimes in a department for international relations), they are particularly well-informed about the interview topic. At the same time, it must be assumed that they generally rank the EU's importance above that of other trade union representatives.

In the following country studies the answers to some of the key questions from the guided interviews are reproduced as quotes. As many respondents insisted on anonymity, the interviewees are designated by abbreviations that identify country (CZ: Czech Republic, PL: Poland, SK: Slovakia) and group (Gn: trade unionists of the new member states, An: employers of the new member states, Ex: experts).

---

14   The survey was designed by Heiko Pleines and then critiqued by the project partners, members of the project advisory committee and other experts. The final German-language version of the survey was translated into the other four interview languages (English, Polish, Slovakian and Czech). The translations were then reviewed and emended by means of a back translation by native speakers. The interviews with the representatives were conducted in person by the partner institutions. The completed questionnaires and the recorded guided interviews are being centrally archived at the Research Centre for East European Studies at the University of Bremen.

Joanna Einbock

8.   Polish Trade Unions in EU Governance

8.1.   Trade Unions in Poland

The legal framework for the operation of Polish trade unions after the fall of the communist regime was set by the Trade Union Act of May 1991. Since the 1980s, the Polish trade union movement has been dominated by two major organizations: the Independent and Self-Governing Trade Union Solidarność (NSZZ Solidarność) and the All-Poland Alliance of Trade Unions (OPZZ). Yet another trade union federation, the Trade Unions Forum (FZZ), entered the national arena in 2002.

8.1.1.   Development of Trade Unions in Poland

NSZZ Solidarność emerged from the massive social movement against the communist regime in the 1980s and was the first independent labour union established in a country in the Soviet bloc. The trade union was forged during worker protests and official-ised in the Gdańsk Accords of August 1980. With Lech Wałęsa at the helm, estimated seven million supporters joined the union. Dissolved under martial law in December 1981, Solidarność continued to function as an underground organization and was finally legalized again in 1989 as a result of roundtable negotiations between the communist government and the Solidarność-led opposition. In the same year, Solidarność formed part of Poland's first non-communist government and became the main backer of a tough reform programme designed to bring about economic and political transfor-mation. Nowadays the union consists of around 14,000 local organizations in thirty-four regions. The local entities are organized into national branch sections, forming six-teen secretariats. NSZZ Solidarność is predominant in industry and major enterprises in Poland. It is estimated that it currently has around 900,000 members.[1]

The martial law imposed in 1981 outlawed all trade unions in Poland, but in October 1982 an act was passed that allowed the re-establishment of politically con-forming unions. The All-Poland Alliance of Trade Unions was founded in November 1984 in accordance with this act as a confederation of over 100 autonomous branch organizations. In the first years of its existence, OPZZ attracted over 5.5 million work-ers. It now consists of nearly ninety national federations and trade unions grouped into nine branches. Its regional structure corresponds to the administrative division of the country into voivodships (provinces) and districts. According to its own estimations, the OPZZ currently boasts 800,000 members. The education and healthcare sectors

---

1   For further information visit www.solidarnosc.org.pl

are eminently represented by OPZZ.[2] Two branch trade union organizations included in this analysis, i.e. the Federation of Metalworkers' Trade Unions ('Metalowcy')[3] and the Trade Union of Miners in Poland (ZZG),[4] are also affiliates of OPZZ.

The third largest Polish trade union federation, the Trade Unions Forum, was established in April 2002. It currently has nearly sixty affiliates and about 400,000 members. It is divided into eight branch and sixteen regional sections. FZZ is comparatively well grounded in the public administration and healthcare sectors. Its affiliates are mainly small trade unions that were previously independent or formerly affiliated with OPZZ.[5]

One of the distinguishing characteristics of the Polish trade union movement is its extreme pluralism, which took root during the transformation period. This feature led to the sustained fragmentation of trade unions and raised doubts about their representativeness, especially at the enterprise level. In the early 1990s, about 230 nationally operating and between 2,000–2,500 locally or regionally operating autonomous trade unions were registered. Polish trade unions in the 1990s also saw a continuous decline in trade union membership as well as in the level of unionization in enterprises, especially in the private sector. In the early 1980s, the trade union density in Poland was roughly 80%. A precipitous decline began in 1993, with unionization levels falling by more than 50% within ten years. The latest surveys of the Polish Public Opinion Research Centre (CBOS) show that in 2006 only 6% of Polish citizens, or 14% of all employees, declared membership in a trade union. Only 32% of the respondents reported the presence of trade unions in their place of employment. The decline was primarily caused by the absorption of the workforce into the private sector, rising unemployment levels and the general climate of distrust towards trade unions. Since privatisation, trade unions have not managed to gain ground in the private sector, which consists mainly of small and medium enterprises (SMEs). Nearly 80% of employees currently work in this sector, but merely 5% of SME employees are covered by collective bargaining agreements.

Thus, in spite of the significant role played by the Polish trade union movement during the historic processes of transformation in Poland, the position of Polish trade unions eroded dramatically over the next twenty years. The phenomenon of declining unionization has occurred to varying degrees in most other EU member states as well, but the level of trade union density in Poland has become one of the lowest in the EU.

---

2   For further information visit www.opzz.org.pl
3   For further information visit www.federacja-metalowcy.org.pl
4   For further information visit www.zzg.org.pl
5   For further information visit www.fzz.org.pl

8.1.2. Assessment of the Role of Trade Unions in National Politics

The trade union movement in Poland was also negatively affected by its high degree of political engagement. For a long time, there was no clear border between the trade unions' political and trade union activities. The two largest trade union organizations traditionally belonged to two politically opposite blocks. OPZZ was for a long time closely connected to the left-wing block, i.e. the Democratic Left Alliance (Sojusz Lewicy Demokratycznej – SLD). NSZZ Solidarność was involved with the Solidarność Electoral Alliance Akcja Wyborcza Solidarność – AWS), which ultimately became part of the Polish governments in the 1990s. Numerous representatives of both trade unions also held seats in the Polish Parliament. To some extent, this degree of engagement was a result of the weakness of the political parties in Poland. The trade unions seized the opportunity to fill the vacuum, but ended up damaging their credibility as representatives of employees' interests. The Polish trade unions' political influence was hence dependent on their connection to the political parties, changes in governing coalitions and the election results. Since 2001, Polish trade unions have forsaken direct political engagement and have concentrated on other activities, such as participation in the Social Dialogue.

The current mechanisms and institutions of the tripartite dialogue between trade unions, employer organizations and the Polish government developed in the early 1990s in the aftermath of a wave of strikes and social conflicts triggered by the economic transformation and the privatisation of state-run enterprises. At this point, the government recognized the necessity of involving the social partners in the decision-making processes concerning social and economic reforms. The Pact on state-owned Enterprises in Transition of February 1993 helped to institutionalize the Social Dialogue in Poland. The Pact was signed by the government, Solidarność, OPZZ, seven national branch trade unions and the Confederation of Polish Employers (KPP), which, as the only existing employers' organization, united mainly state-owned enterprises. In February 1994 the Polish Council of Ministers established the Tripartite Commission for Social and Economic Affairs (hereafter abbreviated as the Tripartite Commission) as a consultative tripartite body. As the main instrument of the Social Dialogue, the Tripartite Commission was initially strong and acted as the primary forum for wage negotiations. Its role declined considerably after 1997, however. New statutory provisions regulating the Tripartite Commission became necessary to maintain the institutionalized dialogue between the social partners. In July 2001 the Polish parliament passed an act establishing a new legal framework for the Tripartite Commission. The act placed particularly strong emphasis on the active participation of the social partners in socio-economic decision-making processes. The Commission's competences involve negotiations on wages and social benefits, tax liabilities, the draft budget, and other issues important for social stability. The chairman and members of the Tripartite

Commission are appointed by the prime minister according to the recommendations of the employee and employer organizations, local self-government, the president of the National Bank of Poland and the president of the Central Statistical Office. In addition, a minimum of 300,000 members was introduced as the criterion of representativeness. The Confederation of Polish Employers, the Polish Confederation of Private Employers (PKPP), the Business Centre Club (BCC) and the Polish Craft Association (ZRP) are currently represented in the Commission. On the trade unions' side, NSZZ Solidarność, OPZZ and the Trade Unions Forum all have representatives in this body. Tripartite Commission meetings can be also attended by representatives of local government, the president of the National Bank of Poland and the president of the Central Statistical Office; these individuals may act as advisors. The new act has also widened the Social Dialogue in Poland to include the local and sectoral levels, but the centralized form of consultation continues to predominate.

Although the new regulations of the Social Dialogue and the withdrawal of the trade unions from active political involvement boosted the image of the new Tripartite Commission, the Social Dialogue in Poland has nonetheless remained weak and has been marginalised for the last few years. The discrepancies among social partners or even between trade unions represented in this body constitute the major obstacle to reaching agreements. This was especially visible during the negotiations on a social pact in 2003, when Solidarność refused to sign the agreement because it feared a loss of influence and mistrusted the government.[6] Intensive negotiations on a new social pact were conducted in 2007 but have not yet been concluded. In general the social partners seem to prefer to bypass the Tripartite Commission and achieve bilateral agreements with the government. This was clearly the case in August 2007, when NSZZ Solidarność concluded a separate agreement with the government on raising the minimum wage for 2008 as well as on a pension scheme for early retirement after the social partners failed to come to a joint decision. This recent incident caused additional tension among the social partners. The position of the Social Dialogue and the culture of negotiations in Poland can thus be described as weak.

8.2. Representation of Polish Trade Unions at the EU Level

8.2.1. Preparations for EU Membership

All trade union representatives who participated in the study confirmed the receipt of some support prior to Poland's accession to the EU in 2004. This support was aimed at preparing the trade unions for their future activities at the EU level. The support

---

6   Gardawski, Juliusz: Evolution of Social Dialogue in Poland, in: Eaton, Adrienne E. (ed.): Proceedings of the 56th Annual Meeting, Industrial Relations Research Association, 2004, pp. 122–132.

mainly consisted of training courses and seminars for union employees, invitations to international conferences, access to international contacts and networks as well as the supply of information. However, the forms and sources of support received varied to a striking degree. In most cases, the interviewees stressed that the help seldom came directly from EU institutions or European umbrella organizations, but much more frequently from partnering trade unions from the 'old' EU member states.

NSZZ Solidarność seemed to be in the most favourable situation prior to Poland's EU accession. As a pioneer of the free trade union movement in Eastern Europe, it was recognized by international bodies early on. It managed to establish various institutionalized and non-institutionalized contacts with its European and international counterparts even before the break-down of the communist regime in Poland. At the EU level, NSZZ Solidarność gained observer status in 1991 at the European Trade Union Confederation (ETUC) and became its affiliate just four years later in 1995. Thanks to this affiliation, NSZZ Solidarność became involved in various activities of interest representation at the EU level. ETUC also supplied grants for training courses, projects and attendance at international conferences. All of these activities helped NSZZ Solidarność to prepare itself effectively for the future challenges it would face as a member of the EU.

The situation looked much different for OPZZ, which had not belonged to any European or international trade union organization for a long time after it officially left the World Federation of Trade Unions (WFTU) in 1991. At its fourth Congress in May 1998, OPZZ set cooperation with ETUC as one of its priorities, and in December of the same year, OPZZ applied for membership. Regarding new admissions, however, ETUC seeks the views of its existing affiliates. The tensions between NSZZ Solidarność and OPZZ seemed to pose a significant obstacle. OPZZ was not slated to become a member of ETUC until March 2006. Nevertheless, the federation had already cultivated tight bilateral relations with trade unions from East and West European countries alike. Given the federated structure of OPZZ, it would be necessary to have a closer look at its member trade unions in order to assess the amount of support received. For example, representatives of the metalworkers' trade union, 'Metalowcy', explicitly cited the support it received from the German trade union IG Metall as the most valuable preparation for becoming active at the EU level. The miners' union, ZZG, also reported positive experiences in bilateral contacts, including staff exchanges and training courses.

The Trade Unions Forum, which was established only in 2002, found itself in a comparable situation. Its affiliates used individual contacts with European partners to prepare themselves for supranational activities. As a federation, however, FZZ stressed the cooperation with the German civil servants' trade union (Deutscher Beamtenbund – DBB), and its membership in the European Confederation of Independent Trade Unions (CESI) as the most valuable pre-accession preparation.

The European Economic and Social Committee (EESC) also played an important role in preparing the Polish trade unions for participation in the European Social
Dialogue. It had maintained relations with Polish interest groups even prior to the EU
eastern enlargement. In 1997 the Polish Committee for European Integration established a joint committee with the EESC. Aimed at increasing the involvement of the
social partners in the negotiation process, the committee's structure mirrored the
EESC's. NSZZ Solidarność and OPZZ belonged to this committee from the very beginning.

Polish representatives also cited their participation in the European Works Councils
(EWC) as an additional form of preparation. Their engagement with the EWC had
started long before the legislation implementing the European Works Council Directive
(94/45/EC) came into force in Poland when it joined the EU in May 2004. Polish workforce representatives have been sitting on the EWCs of various foreign-based multinational concerns since 1997. According to estimates provided by NSZZ Solidarność, prior
to Poland's EU accession there were over seventy multinationals with EWCs operating in Poland. Trade union activists have been the dominant group among Polish representatives on these EWCs, and nearly 50% of all Polish representatives were members of NSZZ Solidarność. The experience they gained from participating in negotiations at this supranational level was viewed as good preparation for continued trade
union interest representation at the EU level.[7]

Given the Polish trade unions' weak finances and lack of experience in the European
affairs, the support they received was generally assessed as helpful. However, some
respondents suggested that more support was needed to compensate for existing
deficits. Furthermore, only the half of the respondents (mainly those from the large
federations) had the impression that in 2004 their organization was well prepared for
the new circumstances and tasks associated with Poland's EU membership. Although
all respondents noticed considerable improvements after more than three years of EU
membership, they also stressed that Polish trade unions are still on a learning curve.

8.2.2.   Channels of Influence

National interest groups can use various strategies to represent their interests at the
EU level. Greenwood elaborated on the available channels as follows:

> The multi-level character of European policy process means that actors seeking to par-
> ticipate in European public affairs therefore have a number of so-called 'routes' of influ-
> ence. At its most simple level, the 'national route' refers to the use of national contacts and
> national governments to influence EU decision-making, whereas the 'European route', or

---

7   On the role of European Work Councils in the three countries under study, see: Tholen, Jochen:
     Labour Relations in Central Europe. The Impact of Multinationals' Money, Aldershot: Ashgate,
     2007.

the 'Brussels strategy', involves seeking to exert influence by representation direct to the European institutions themselves.[8]

Interest groups using the so-called 'European route' can further choose between direct and indirect interest representation. The European Commission and European Parliament offer interest groups access to direct consultations. Besides traditional forms of direct consultation, the European Commission has also developed new modes of governance based on e.g. voluntary agreements, voluntary commitment and codes of best practices. Consultations with national representatives in the Council of Ministers constitute a further avenue for exerting influence.

Interviews with the representatives of Polish trade unions revealed that direct consultations with EU institutions play a minor role in their interest representation at the EU level. Consultations with the European Commission and the Parliament take place indirectly, i.e. solely via European umbrella organizations (such as ETUC). Numerous respondents stressed that they thus frequently use personal contacts to Polish members of the European Parliament and representatives in European committees to present their opinion or receive information. These personal contacts play an important role. For the time being, however, Polish trade unions generally remain weak and too inexperienced in lobbying at the EU level to fully exploit the existing channels of influence. They therefore mainly try to exert influence via the EU Social Dialogue and European umbrella organizations.

The European Economic and Social Committee is the leading actor in the European Social Dialogue. Made up of social partners and other representatives of civil society, this consultative body serves as the main platform for the Polish trade unions to voice their opinion and exercise influence on EU decision-making process. Upon Poland's accession to the EU in May 2004, the Polish government gained the right to nominate twenty-one members for appointment by the Council of the European Union for a renewable four-year term of office. NSZZ Solidarność, OPZZ and the Trade Unions Forum are represented within the employees' groups (see Table 8-1 overleaf).

Although the representatives of the Polish trade union federations are frequently present in Brussels, none of them has an office or a permanent representative there. Direct representation in Brussels is generally viewed by the trade unions as important and helpful, but financially out of reach. The interviews revealed also that Polish trade unions hardly ever represent their interests at the EU level alone. Interest representation in cooperation with trade unions from other EU countries is also restricted to singular cases as necessary. The interviewees stressed that common problems are best solved via European umbrella organizations. As already mentioned, membership in

---

8   Greenwood, Justin: Interest Representation in the European Union, London: Palgrave Macmillan, 2003, pp. 32 f.

these organizations constitutes a further focus of the Polish trade unions' engagement at the EU level.

Table 8-1: Polish Trade Union Representatives to the EESC 2006–2010

Federation	Representative	Position	Section of EESC*
OPZZ	Rożycki, Stanisław	Vice President of the Federation of Unions of Polish Higher Education and Science Teachers	ECO, TEN
	Jasiński, Tomasz	Senior Specialist in International Co-operation and European Integration	REX, SOC
NZSS Solidarność	Krzaklewski, Marian	Member of the National Commission	ECO, TEN, CCMI
	Adamczyk, Andrzej	International Secretary	INT, REX
	Sobon-Bartkiewicz, Katarzyna	Expert in European Integration	SOC
Trade Unions Forum (FZZ)	Szynaka, Edmund	Chief of the Expert Team	REX, SOC
	Siewierski, Wiesław	President of FZZ, Vice President of the Polish Tripartite Commission for Social and Economic Affairs	ECO, TEN

Source: http://eescmembers.eesc.europa.eu

* ECO = Economic and Social Cohesion; TEN = Transport, Energy, Infrastructure and the Information Society; REX = External Relations; SOC = Employment, Social Affairs and Citizenship; CCMI = Consultative Commission on Industrial Change; NAT = Agriculture, Rural Development and the Environment; INT = Single Market, Production and Consumption

NSZZ Solidarność has been a member of ETUC since the 1990s and nearly all of its national branch sections and secretariats are affiliated with European industry federations. OPZZ became a member of ETUC in 2006. In many European industry federations, membership of the national trade union federation in ETUC is a precondition for a national branch federation to become a member. For this reason, the OPZZ's affiliate metalworkers' union, 'Metalowcy', could not obtain the status of a full member in the European Metalworkers' Federation until December 2006. The Trade Union of Miners in Poland has been a member of the European Mine, Chemical and Energy Workers' Federation since 2004. Thirteen of OPZZ's member organizations are now affiliated with European industry federations. The Trade Unions Forum has also gained access to the European arena via its affiliation with CESI. Two of FZZ's members are also members in European industry federations (see Table 8-2).

Table 8-2: Affiliations of NSZZ Solidarność, OPZZ and FZZ to the European Trade Union Federations

European Industry Federations	Branch structures and secretariats of NSZZ Solidarność	Affiliates of OPZZ	Affiliate of FZZ
EMCEF (European Mine, Chemical and Energy Workers Federation)	Chemical Workers' Secretariat; Energy and Miners' Secretariat	Trade Union of Miners in Poland (ZZG w Polsce); Federation of Oil and Gas Industry Workers' Unions (FZZGNiG); Federation of Chemical, Glass and Ceramic Industry Workers Unions in Poland (FZZPCSIC)	Trade Unions Alliance KADRA
UNIEUROPA (Union Network International Europe)	Commercial, Clerical and Professional Employees' Secretariat; National Section of Trade Workers	Trade Union of Graphic Industry Workers (ZZPPP); Federation of Trade Unions of Culture and Arts Workers (FZZ PKiS)	
ETUCE (European Trade Union Committee for Education)	National Section of Education; National Section of Science	Polish Teachers' Union (ZNP)	
EFFAT (European Federation of Trade Unions in Food, Agriculture and Tourism Sectors)	Food Workers' Secretariat; Rural Workers' Secretariat;	Trade Unions Federation of the Food Industry Employees (FZKS)	
ECF-IUF (European Committee of Food, Catering and Allied Workers' Unions within the IUF)	Food Workers' Secretariat		
ETUF-TCL (European Trade Union Federation – Textiles, Clothing and Leather)	Textile Workers' Secretariat	Federation of Independent and Self-Governing Trade Unions of Light Industry (Federacja NSZZ Przemysłu Lekkiego)	
EMF (European Metalworkers' Federation)	Metalworkers' Secretariat	Trade Unions Federation 'Metalowcy'	

European Industry Federations	Branch structures and secretariats of NSZZ Solidarność	Affiliates of OPZZ	Affiliate of FZZ
ETF (European Transport Workers' Federation)	National Maritime Section; National Section of Port Workers; National Section of Railway Workers	Federation of Trade Unions of Seamen and Fishers (FZZMiR); Trade Union of Aviation Workers (ZZ Personelu Latającego i Pokładowego)	Federation of Trade Unions of Polish Railway Workers (FZZ PKP)
EPSU (European Federation of Public Service Unions)	Health Protection Secretariat; Public Service Employees' Secretariat;	Trade Union Federation of Municipal and Local Economy Employees in Poland (Federacja ZZPGKiT)	
EFBWW (European Federation of Building and Woodworkers)		Trade Union of Building Workers 'Budowlani'	
EUROCADRES (Council of European Professional and Managerial Staff)	National Section of Science		
FERPA (European Federation of Retired and Older People)	Secretariat of Pensioners		

Source: Based on the author's own research; the list is not necessarily complete.

Polish trade unions generally assess their membership in and joint activities with European umbrella organizations in a positive light. Access to relevant information and the exchange of experiences were described as the chief advantages of these activities. As the Polish representatives see it, joint interest representation and participation in the European Social Dialogue enable Polish employees to voice their concerns and also provide a way to influence relevant EU policies. Underscoring the significance of NSZZ Solidarność's membership in ETUC, Andrzej Matla from the International Department of NSZZ Solidarność once stated: 'Being represented in ETUC means that our voice has influence on the shape of the European Social Dialogue.'[9]

OPZZ on the other hand counts the direct access to relevant information among the most significant benefits of their membership in ETUC. A representative of OPZZ provided the following example:

---

9   Tygodnik Solidarność, 2005, No. 35 (884).

When the Polish government wanted to change the European directive on weekly work-ing hours without consulting us, we found out about it – among other things – thanks to our participation in the European Trade Union Confederation and we had a chance to present our own opinion. The result was that the government's action without consult-ing the public could be hindered.[10]

Despite the initial uncertainties and fears concerning the financial costs of membership in a European federation, Andrzej Chwiluk, the president of the Trade Union of Miners in Poland (ZZG), also considered the accession of his union to the EMCEF in June 2004 as a turning point. The membership opened up new possibilities for the union, allow-ing it to exert influence on European legislative processes as well as access information and documents to which only the Polish government had previously had access.[11]

8.2.3. Satisfaction with Role at the EU Level

The respondents assessed the overall influence of the trade unions at the EU level com-pared to other interest groups from average to relatively great. However, this assess-ment was heavily dependent on which interest group was taken as the reference point. For example, the majority of trade union representatives viewed employers and business organizations active at the EU level as more influential than trade unions. In contrast, the influence potential of non-governmental organizations (NGOs) was esti-mated as being much smaller. Opinions were also mixed regarding the changes in the position and influence of European trade unions over the last few years. Whereas some respondents stressed the well-established position of the trade unions as part-ners in the European Social Dialogue, others spoke of the multiple global challenges that trade unions currently face. One of the main concerns is the decreasing member-ship rates in trade unions nearly all over Europe. Recent neo-liberal tendencies in the EU are also viewed with alarm, because these could benefit employers and business organizations at the trade unions' expense. The trade unions are ambivalent towards the employers' associations active at the EU level; depending on the situation and area of interest, they are viewed as constructive partners or opponents that some-times block important decisions or actions.

Regarding the position and potential of the Polish trade unions, 50% the respond-ents rated their influence at the EU level as weaker than at the national level; 30% saw no difference. The large Polish federations stressed that at the national level they are social partners represented in the Tripartite Commission and are consulted on mat-ters of socio-economic development in the country, whereas at the EU level they are just one of many trade unions. On the other hand, if the joint interest representation with European umbrella organizations was taken into consideration, they rated their

---

10   Project interview, Summer 2007 (PL-Gn04).
11   Przegląd Wydarzeń Związkowych, 2005, No. 1 (125), p. 11.

influence potential considerably higher. Also the institution of the European Social Dialogue and its impact on the decision-making processes is seen as much more effective than the Social Dialog at the national level. Nearly all respondents were convinced that the engagement of their trade unions provides an important contribution to the unions' interest representation at the EU level. In an interview, Andrzej Malta from NSZZ Solidarność pointed out:

> Through our contribution to the policy of the European Trade Union Confederation (ETUC) we exert significant influence on the shape of some directives. For example, concerning the Directive on Services in the Internal Market, Solidarność was one of the organizations that gave its opinion on the Directive as it was being prepared.[12]

Considering that Polish trade unions have only limited financial and human resources as well as little experience in European level activities, the respondents' satisfaction with the role their union plays at the EU level was considerably high. At the same time, the respondents underscored the weaknesses of Polish trade unions and of the challenges they face.

8.3.   Europeanization of Polish Trade Unions

The next focus of the present analysis is on the attitudes of Polish trade unions towards the EU and its policies as well as on the impact of the EU on the Polish trade union movement. This impact stems in part from the implementation of European directives and regulations in Poland but also includes the effects of networking, mutual support and the transfer of 'European values'.

The incorporation of European issues into the federations' work programmes may be viewed as the first indicator of their Europeanization. In its current Programme Resolutions, adopted at the Fifteenth National Congress of Delegates held in Warsaw in September 2002[13], NSZZ Solidarność stresses its understanding of the EU not merely as a treaty or constitutional commonwealth, but as an entity based on a common European identity consisting of shared roots, heritage and values, including Christian traditions. The Resolutions also underlined the necessity of increasing international cooperation, including the exchange of experience, information and expertise, and further developing joint programmes with trade unions from other EU member states and EU-level trade union organizations, especially with ETUC. NSZZ Solidarność has set active participation in the European Social Dialogue through ETUC and the European industry federations as one of its priorities. The strengthening of the European social model, including the common policy on employment, working conditions and social protection, is among the most important issues. NSZZ Solidarność formulated its aims

---

12   Project interview, Summer 2007 (PL-Gn01).
13   See http://www.solidarnosc.org.pl/dokumenty/xv_kzd/u_prog.htm

also in the Resolution of the Sixteenth National Congress of Delegates on International Cooperation. Chief among these are obtaining constitutional guarantees in the EU for the right to organize cross-border trade unions and negotiate cross-border collective agreements. The federation also wants to implement the social model based on the Social Dialogue, improve its access to information, participate in consultations and exercise co-decision-making power on the European level. The Resolution also called for the democratization of EU institutions through the strengthening of the role of representative bodies, more transparency in decision-making processes and the limitation of the unanimity principle to constitutional matters.[14] With respect to Polish affairs, the Resolution contained a provision to broaden the mandate of the European Social Charter in Poland, especially to include the right to fair remuneration.[15] These objectives were reintroduced at the Twentieth National Congress of Delegates in September 2006.[16]

OPZZ dealt with similar issues and challenges during its last few terms of office. In the preamble of the work programme for the 2002–2006 period, adopted during the fifth Congress of OPZZ in Spala in May 2002, OPZZ stressed its commitment to Poland's integration into the EU and confirmed the objectives of the previous programme, which had identified integration into the EU as Poland's highest priority. OPZZ also exhorted the Polish government to align Polish employment and social laws with the standards of the European Social Charter and the EU Directives. In light of growing globalisation and industrial integration, OPZZ also emphasized the necessity of cooperating with international trade union movements to establish a stable social model. The commitment to the idea of a 'social Europe' plays an important role in this context, a goal that can be reached, according to OPZZ, through close cooperation with European trade unions and social organizations as well as through bilateral partnerships with trade unions from other countries. Stepping up Polish trade unions' active participation in the EU Social Dialogue is one of OPZZ's major priorities. In the current work programme for the 2006–2010 period, adopted at the OPZZ's Sixth Congress in May 2006, Poland's accession to the EU was lauded as the government's major success. At the European level, the programme aims, among other objectives, to tighten cooperation with the European social partners (especially with ETUC), influence the decision-making processes in the EU through active participation in the EESC and raise support for the European Social Model and the European Work Councils. The programme also underscores the necessity for active participation in European projects.[17]

---

14   See http://www.solidarnosc.org.pl/dokumenty/xvi_kzd/uchw.htm, accessed 25 August 2007.
15   Ibid.
16   See http://www.solidarnosc.org.pl/dokumenty/xx/dokumenty/uchw.htm, accessed 25 August 2007.
17   See Program Ogólnopolskiego Porozumienia Związków Zawodowych na lata 2006–2010, Warsaw, 2006, http://opzz.org.pl/assets/File/vi_kongres/Program_i_Uchwaly_VI_Kongres.pdf

In its work programme adopted at its Second Congress in April 2006, the Trade Unions Forum also expressed support for Poland's further integration into the EU, including the adoption of European regulations concerning social standards at the national level. At the same time, the Forum stressed Poland's need to participate in the international Social Dialogue.[18]

This short overview of resolutions and programmes shows that Poland's EU membership and the adoption of European social standards are important to Polish trade unions. The unions' previous aims, orientations and modes of action have all been challenged by the new political constellation resulting from Poland's accession to the EU. The entire trade union movement has thus been forced to work out new approaches, undertake structural changes and place greater focus on activities at the international and European levels. After more than three years of EU membership, Poland's trade unions are convinced that both EU regulations as well as their own engagement at the EU level have had a significant impact on the Polish trade union movement. All respondents noted the increasing importance of the EU, the widening of its competences in the fields relevant to their interests and its impact on the work of national trade unions. The EU was generally assessed as equally important or even slightly more important than national politics. Furthermore, 40% of the respondents evaluated the impact of the EU on national policy as sufficient, whereas 60% were of the opinion that this impact ought to be even stronger. Accordingly, the trade union activists firmly believe that it is necessary to be active both at the national and European levels. The vast majority of the respondents stated that interest representation at the EU level is at least as important as – and concerning some issues, even slightly more important than – at the national level.

Referring to the significance of the EU, the representatives of the Polish trade unions explained that EU legislation and socio-economic standards often better protect the interests of Polish workers and employees than national policies. The EU frequently provides backing for the position of trade unions in their negotiations with the Polish government and employers' organizations. Thus, in Poland, the trade unions are often the driving force behind quick and proper implementation of EU legislation. All of the trade union representatives interviewed also stated that they often use the EU and its legislation as arguments to justify or support their activities at the national level. To this end, they most frequently cite legal frameworks, such as the European Labour Market Regulations, European Minimum Wage Policy, European Retirement Policy, the European Information and Consultation Directive, European Working Time Directive and European professional qualification directives. The respondents stressed, however, that they only use EU policy in their argumentation when it dovetails with

---

18   See Forum Związków Zawodowych: Deklaracja Programowa, http://www.fzz.org.pl/serwis2/index.php?option=com_content&task=view&id=61&Itemid=86, accessed 25 August 2007.

their own convictions and that they never attempt to shift the responsibility to the EU. A representative of OPZZ explained:

> This is not an argument: 'The EU wants it this way.' We speak out whenever regulations implemented in Poland go in the wrong direction or stray from the European standards. But we don't do it the way it was done during the negotiations, when it was said: 'Now we have to conduct very hard reforms because the EU demands it.' At that moment, support for the EU dropped among some groups. 'We have to do it because the EU wants it' is not an argument.[19]

Romuald Wojtkowiak, the president of the metal workers' union 'Metalowcy' emphasized his own internalisation of some arguments based on European standards: 'I may even not notice that I use the European Union or European directives [as arguments] in a discussion if to me something is self-evident and I already act this way.'[20]

Polish trade unions also view the model of the Social Dialogue at the EU level as a desirable standard for the national level. Janusz Śniadek, president of the National Committee of NSZZ Solidarność, stated shortly after Poland's EU accession:

> The experiences of the European dialogue became an inspiration for social partners in Poland even before its EU accession. Now we have gained not only real influence on the course of this dialogue, but we also benefit from its achievements. We are convinced that the quality and the intensity of the Social Dialogue at the European level directly influence the course of the dialogue at the national level.[21]

It was frequently stressed in the interviews that thanks to Poland's EU membership, Polish trade unions have gained additional ground for interest representation. Participation in the European Social Dialogue or membership in European umbrella organizations has been especially valuable. However, these bodies not only represent trade unions in dealings with European institutions or help to exert influence on European decision-making processes but also support their members in their claims at the national level (for example via information provision or joint protest actions). This kind of mutual support and solidarity is also expected from the new members. Bogdan Kaczmarek, the vice-president of 'Metalowcy', elaborated this issue as follows:

> Signing the declaration of accession to the Metalworkers' Federation, we have pledged to support the activities of the Federation for the benefit of other trade unions in other countries. In some ways, these actions are part of our statutory obligation. Hence, when there are protest actions somewhere we back them. Of course, sometimes it is inconvenient for us, because when manufacturing is going to be shifted from France to Poland, we should be glad and not block it. Sometimes philosophy and diplomacy are necessary to reconcile these interests.[22]

This statement suggests that Europeanization has led to a transition in the priorities and that the loyalty towards the common interests of the European trade union

---

19 Project interview, Summer 2007 (PL-Gn04).
20 Project interview, Summer 2007 (PL-Gn08).
21 Tygodnik Solidarność, 2005, No. 35 (884).
22 Project interview, Summer 2007 (PL-Gn07).

movement may even trump national interests. The participation of representatives of Polish trade unions in joint protest actions against the so-called Bolkestein Directive was an example of this phenomenon.

Polish trade unions are also participating in joint projects initiated by the EU or European foundations related to socio-economic issues. Numerous projects with Polish participation have for example been financed by the European Social Fund (ESF) as part of the European EQUAL initiative for employment and social inclusion. These activities contribute to further mutual understanding and facilitate the valuable exchange of experience. However, the Polish respondents pointed out that Polish trade unionists will need additional language and professional training if they are to fully benefit from such joint activities.

8.4. Summary

European legislative and normative standards are increasingly shaping the European trade union movement; as participants in this movement, Polish trade unions are adapting their activities accordingly. They currently perceive the EU as an important arena for the effective representation and promotion of European and national interests. However, due to poor financial resources, lack of lobbying expertise at the EU level and sometimes even language barriers, Polish trade unions are not using all available channels and strategies of interest representation to the full extent. The fragmentation and frictions within the Polish trade union movement itself constitute additional obstacles. Being aware of these deficits, Polish trade unions seek the support of European umbrella organizations and view them as valuable partners. The interviews underscored their belief that membership in these organizations helps them to effectively represent the interests of Polish workers and employees as well as to exert influence on the decision-making processes in the EU. Their presence at the EU level also provides them with direct access to valuable information. Moreover, EU legislation and the Social Dialogue at the EU level provide the trade unions with valuable examples and arguments to bolster their dealings with the Polish government. Polish trade unions in fact often see themselves as supervisors of the adequate implementation of European directives and standards at the national level. Finally, the participation of Polish representatives in various European bodies and the mutual exchange taking place there serve to Europeanize the Polish trade unions, which forces them to adopt the European culture of negotiations, adjust their priorities and look for common solutions.

Zdenka Mansfeldová

9. Czech Trade Unions in EU Governance

9.1. Trade Unions in the Czech Republic

Modern trade unions were reborn in Czechoslovakia after the disintegration of the Revolutionary Trade Union Movement (Revoluční odborové hnutí – ROH) at the beginning of the 1990s. Several trade union confederations were established at that time, including the Czech and Slovak Confederation of Trade Unions. The Czech section of this entity, called the Czech-Moravian Confederation of Trade Unions (ČMKOS), continued its operations after the split of the Czech and Slovak federations in 1993. ČMKOS became the central successor and took over all of the former organization's members and assets. ČMKOS is still the dominant trade union federation and comprises approximately 70% of all trade union members nationwide. At the same time, the Confederation of Arts and Culture (KUK), the Christian Trade Union Coalition (KOK), and the Trade Union Association of Bohemia, Moravia and Silesia (OS ČMS) emerged, followed in 1995 by the Association of Independent Trade Unions (ASO), which was founded by organizations that had left ČMKOS. Besides the confederations mentioned above, there are a number of unaffiliated trade unions and associations that have either been independent from their very establishment or have left some of the confederations, particularly ČMKOS.[1]

A plurality of trade union confederations and the freedom to choose to join one or remain independent are central features of free trade union association and democratic development. In the Czech Republic, trade unions initially experienced a rapid boom in members, followed by slow and steady erosion. All confederations and trade unions have had to cope with a diminishing membership base. Generally, the decline has been caused by transfers of entire trade unions from one confederation to another as well as by the wide-ranging privatization that took place during the 1990s. In addition, the fragmentation or merging of trade union associations has also occurred, but these phenomena are relatively rare. Trade unions have had to adapt to the environment of a market economy, adjust to new kinds of jobs and seek new strategies in their dealings with employers and their own members.

---

1   Kroupa, Aleš / Hála, Jaroslav / Mansfeldová, Zdenka / Kux, Jaroslav / Vašková, Renáta / Pleskot, Igor: Rozvoj sociálního dialogu v ČR, Praha: VÚPSV, 2002; Vašková, Renáta / Kroupa, Aleš / Hála, Jaroslav: Možnosti a bariéry členství v odborech, in: Mansfeldová, Zdenka / Kroupa, Aleš (eds): Participace a zájmové organizace v České republice, Praha: Sociologické nakladatelství SLON, 2005, pp. 129–158, here pp. 129–130.

The Social Dialogue, especially at the national level, represents new territory for the trade unions. In the Czech Republic, the Social Dialogue and its institutionalized form – the Council of Economic and Social Agreement (RHSD) – were established at the beginning of the 1990s. Initially, the RHSD was established as a national tripartite body in the Czech-Slovak Federation; since 1993, it has been the sole national tripartite body in the Czech Republic.[2] All three partners have been involved in the RHSD right from the start: the State, represented by the government; employers, represented by the Confederation of Industry and Transport of the Czech Republic (SP ČR) and the Confederation of Employers' and Entrepreneurs' Associations (KZPS); and employees, represented by trade unions (the strongest trade unions are the Czech-Moravian Confederation of Trade Unions and the Association of Independent Trade Unions [ASO]). At the beginning, employers were represented solely by the Confederation of Employers' and Entrepreneurs' Associations of the Czech Republic (hereafter Confederation). This was a powerful umbrella organization for a time, but its membership base dwindled over the next few years and thus it lost its prominent position. In 1995, the largest of its members – the Confederation of Industry and Transport of the Czech Republic, left the Confederation. Since the mid-1990s, two peak organizations, KZPS and SP ČR, have been members of the employers' delegation in the tripartite body. The Confederation is weaker today, but nonetheless still brings a lot of utility to its members. The two employer organizations participating in the tripartite negotiations, especially SP ČR, represent almost all of the country's large employers.

The name of the tripartite council, along with its statutes, underwent several changes during the 1990s, but its formal role and legal position in the political system have not changed significantly since its foundation. The issues covered by the tripartite's consultations are enumerated in its statutes and concern not only social and economic questions directly connected to industrial relations, but also economic policy, public service and, more recently, the position of the Czech Republic within the EU. The Czech tripartite is not vested with the legal authority to enforce decisions; the RHSD's role is strictly consultative.

Whether or not the tripartite should be subject to legal regulation and whether its general agreements should be legally binding was discussed during the initial

---

2   Mansfeldová, Zdenka: Sociální partnerství v České republice, in: Brokl, L. (ed.): Reprezentace zájmů v politickém systému České republiky, Praha: SLON, 1997, pp. 99–150; Mansfeldová, Zdenka: Case Study. Czech Labour and Capital Interest Representation. The Social Dialogue at the National and EU Level, in: Pleines, Heiko (ed.): Participation of Civil Society in New Modes of Governance. The Case of the New EU Member States, Part 1: The State of Civil Society, Bremen: Forschungsstelle Osteuropa an der Universität Bremen, 2005, pp. 40–50; Mansfeldová, Zdenka: Sociální dialog a jeho budoucnost, in: Mansfeldová, Zdenka / Kroupa, Aleš (eds): Participace a zájmové organizace v České republice, Praha: Sociologické nakladatelství SLON, 2005, pp. 105–128; Kroupa, Aleš / Hála, Jaroslav / Mansfeldová, Zdenka / Kux, Jaroslav / Vašková, Renáta / Pleskot, Igor: Rozvoj sociálního dialogu v ČR, Praha: VÚPSV, 2002.

deliberations about the tripartite and was still unresolved at the time of its establishment. In the end, these ideas were abandoned, which means that neither the creation of tripartite bodies nor the agenda and manner of their functioning are defined by law or regulated in the Czech Republic. The tripartite instead depends on the principle of good will and gentlemen's agreements among social partners and government representatives. The idea of legal regulation was supported by the trade unions, whereas the employers and government representatives did not want the body's output to be legally binding. The idea was briefly revived in the second half of the 1990s but since then has been removed from the agenda. After more than fifteen years of tripartite activity and general Social Dialogue, a number of mechanisms to ensure social consensus have been introduced. With respect to personnel, the trade union and employer organizations are usually headed by individuals with extensive experience with the Social Dialogue and representation of trade unions' and employers' interests at different levels. This was confirmed in the interviews carried out as part of this project.

A total of ten interviews were conducted with representatives of trade union umbrella organizations; three representatives of employer organizations and five experts on these issues were also interviewed. The representatives of the trade unions were highly experienced top officials. 60% of these were decision-makers in their respective organizations. The remaining 40% were respondents able to form a decision-making majority and thus have significant influence on what decisions are adopted. All of the interviewees were long-time trade unionists, with the length of membership ranging from 17 to 44 years, for an average of 31.6 years. Three trade union umbrella organizations were represented in the interviews: ČMKOS, ASO and KUK.

9.1.1. The Czech-Moravian Confederation of Trade Unions (ČMKOS)

The Czech-Moravian Confederation of Trade Unions (ČMKOS) is, with thirty-three trade unions, the largest trade union confederation. It is an important social partner in tripartite negotiations in the framework of the Council of Economic and Social Agreement of the Czech Republic. ČMKOS works in the regions of the Czech Republic through Regional Councils of Trade Unions (RROS) and Regional Offices for Legal Assistance (RPP). It is a member of the International Trade Union Confederation (ITUC), the European Trade Union Confederation (ETUC), and the Trade Union Advisory Committee to the OECD (TUAC).[3]

---

3   International Trade Union Confederation (ITUC), http://www.ituc-csi.org/, European Trade Union Confederation (ETUC), http://www.etuc.org/ and Trade Union Advisory Committee to the OECD (TUAC), http://www.tuac.org. See http://www.cmkos.cz/homepage

9.1.2. The Association of Independent Trade Unions (ASO)

The Association of Independent Trade Unions (ASO) is the second largest trade union confederation in the Czech Republic. It was established in 1995 and today associates fifteen trade unions with a total of about 200,000 members. In cooperation with ČMKOS, it has represented trade unions on the Council for Economic and Social Agreement since 2000. It has replaced the Confederation of Arts and Culture (KUK), which, due to its declining membership, ceased to meet the criteria of representativeness set for the tripartite.

9.1.3. Confederation of Arts and Culture (KUK)

After the collapse of the socialist trade unions in February 1990, cultural workers' trade unions formed their own confederation, which grouped together seventeen autonomous trade unions in 1996. In 2001, the number of affiliated trade unions fell to fourteen. KUK members strongly advocate the principle of professional association, whereby the individual interests of various professions are on equal footing with trade union interests. According to leading KUK representatives, 90,000 members were registered in its member trade unions in 2001.[4]

Of our respondents, seven trade unionists came from ČMKOS, four of whom were direct representatives of the confederation; the remaining three were members of leading trade unions: Czech Metalworkers' Federation KOVO (OS KOVO), and Union of Workers in Mines, Geology and Oil Industry (OS PHGN).[5] Czech Metalworkers' Federation KOVO is the largest trade union in ČMKOS. It has been a member of the European Metalworkers' Federation (EMF) since November 1991, and the International Metalworkers' Federation (IMF) since May 1991. It is represented on the EMF Executive Committee and working groups. Since 1995, OS KOVO's chairman has been an EMF vice-chairman (for the Visegrád Countries).

The Union of Workers in Mines, Geology and Oil Industry is a member of the European Mine, Chemical and Energy Workers' Federation (EMCEF) and International Federation of Chemical, Energy, Mine and General Workers' Unions (ICEM). Two respondents, both from ČMKOS, were members of the European Economic and Social Committee, Group II.

---

4   Kroupa, Aleš / Hála, Jaroslav / Mansfeldová, Zdenka / Kux, Jaroslav / Vašková, Renáta / Pleskot, Igor: Rozvoj sociálního dialogu v ČR, Praha: VÚPSV, 2002.
5   Cf. Czech Metalworkers' Federation KOVO, http://www.oskovo.cz/HTM/index1.htm; Union of Workers in Mines, Geology and Oil Industry, http://osphgn.cmkos.cz

9.2. Representation of Czech trade unions at the EU level

Development of sufficient capacities and qualified personnel in national organizations were the key prerequisites for representation of trade union interests at the EU level. According to Pleines and Obradovic,

> three major prerequisites determine the capacity of civil society organizations to successfully engage in EU governance. The first is a general ability to engage in political decision-making processes. The second is the capacity to engage at the EU level and the third is the fulfilment of EU eligibility criteria regulating access to different consultation processes in EU governance.[6]

Mailand and Due identify similar prerequisites for operating at the national level and participating in the European Social Dialogues. According to them, the success of Social Dialogue depends on the fulfilment of the basic conditions below:

- First, the parties involved must be sufficiently independent of each other.
- Second, it is essential that all parties involved have sufficient organizational capacity and legitimacy to act on behalf of the constituency they represent.
- Third, it is important that the distribution of power between the participants is not too uneven. There has to be some degree of balance.
- Fourth, the participants must show a willingness to cooperate and acknowledge the legitimacy of the other parties' interests.[7]

The incorporation of Czech trade unions and employer associations into the European sphere began as early as the mid-1990s.[8] In particular, its institutional shape was defined in the late 1990s. In 1996, ČMKOS initiated the establishment of the European Integration Team (EIT) as an independent structure comprising representatives of ČMKOS and other trade unions. The Team was founded at the suggestion of ČMKOS and the European Trade Union Confederation. Until 2004, the EIT looked after the preparations for the Czech Republic's accession to the EU. Its task was to disseminate information on European integration and to draft ČMKOS opinions on individual relevant issues related to European integration. After 1 May 2004, the EIT's mission was developed and transformed. Its tasks now include ensuring that trade unions are consulted as a social partner in the drafting of any significant actions and documents

---

6   Obradovic, Daniela / Pleines, Heiko: The Capacity of Civil Society Organisations to Participate in EU Multi-Level Governance. An Analytical Framework, in: Obradovic, Daniela / Pleines, Heiko (eds): The Capacity of Central and East European Interest Groups to Participate in EU Governance, Stuttgart: Ibidem, 2007, pp. 13–23, here p. 19.

7   Mailand, Mikkel / Due, Jesper: Social Dialogue in Central and Eastern Europe: Present State and Future Development, in: European Journal of Industrial Relations, 2004 (Vol. 10), No. 2, pp. 179–197, here p. 183.

8   Mansfeldová, Zdenka: Case Study. Czech Trade Unions and Employers' Associations on the Way to Multi-Level Dialogue, in: Pleines, Heiko (ed.): Participation of Civil Society in New Modes of Governance. The Case of the New EU Member States, Part 3: Involvement at the EU Level. Arbeitspapiere und Materialien No. 76, Bremen: Forschungsstelle Osteuropa an der Universität Bremen, 2006, pp. 66–78.

related to the Czech Republic's position with the EU, and coordinating ČMKOS' representation in national structures connected to the EU and EU bodies in which social partners play a role.

Another important body is the Working Team for European Integration (Pracovní tým pro evropskou integraci – PTEI RHSD), which has operated since 1998 within the Council for Economic and Social Agreement. The Team has seven representatives apiece from the State, trade unions and employers. The Chamber of Commerce and Agrarian Chamber are also represented in the Team, although according to a different principle.[9] The PTEI RHSD is a platform for information sharing and consulting concerning important issues of the Czech Republic's activities within the EU. The Team's conclusions are presented at plenary sessions of the RHSD. All of ČMKOS's representatives on the tripartite team are members of the EIT ČMKOS.

In the pre-accession period, membership in the Committee for European Integration, set up by the Ministry of Foreign Affairs, was also important. At the same time, departments were created at several ministries dealing with European integration and contributing to the preparation of directives. Trade unions have tried to cooperate with some of them, and this system of participation is another channel for promoting the trade unions' interests.

The training and resources offered in this period, however, were not the only preparation the trade unions received for their future activities at the EU level. Nearly all respondents confirmed that the EU assisted trade unions with getting ready for their new responsibilities before 1 May 2004. This assistance primarily consisted of information dissemination, training and workshops for trade union officials, and introduction into international networks. Only about a fourth of it was in the form of financial assistance, and this was mostly disbursed indirectly as part of twinning projects. It can be concluded from the feedback given in the interviews that trade unions deemed the transfer of know-how, arrangement of international contacts and introduction into networks as the most valuable forms of assistance; see Table 9-1.

Table 9-1:   EU Assistance in the Pre-Accession Period as Seen by Trade Union
Representatives and Experts (%)

	Trade Unions	Experts
Financial support	30	80
Training or seminars	90	80
Organisation of international contacts and networks	70	20
Supply of information	90	80
Other	20	40
No answer	10	20

Source: Project Questionnaire, Summer 2007, Question Q7 (documented in the appendix).

---

9   Neither the Chamber of Commerce nor the Agrarian Chamber is a member of the RHSD. The Working Team is a platform for consulting and harmonizing positions with other representatives of employer associations.

The representatives of the trade unions asserted that the Czech trade unions were well prepared (70%) for working at the European level at the time of accession to the EU. With respect to the post-accession situation, half of the respondents commented that only positive changes have occurred.

Trade unionists make use of various channels to exercise their influence within the EU. Czech trade unions primarily focus on participation in the European Social Dialogue (90%) and membership in ETUC or one of European industrial unions (80%). Other channels include the European Economic and Social Committee (EESC) (50%) and direct consulting with the European Commission,[10] while direct consulting with the European Parliament is not as common (40%), and consulting with the members of the Council of Ministers is rather exceptional (20%). Representatives also mentioned the European Foundation for the Improvement of Living and Working Conditions Dublin (Eurofound), the European Agency for Safety and Health at Work in Bilbao, and the Luxemburg Advisory Committee on Safety, Hygiene and Health Protection at Work as other channels for exercising influence and seeking support.

Trade unions do not always act on their own: they also join forces with other unions through European umbrella organizations, institutions (e.g. ETUC) or in cooperation with trade unions from other countries, and they generally appreciate such cooperation. Czech trade unions are also members of other associations and bodies that can serve as additional 'pathways' of influence. First and foremost, these include the European Confederation of Worker Cooperatives of the European Union (CECOP); EMCEF; the European Transport Workers' Federation (ETF); the International Labour Organization (ILO); and the European Federation of Trade Unions in Food, Agriculture and Tourism Sectors (EFFAT). However, despite the benefits membership in these entities confer, not all trade union associations can afford the related expenses. The financial demands of such cooperation were mentioned in various contexts as a very serious problem.

It was suggested that a sub-committee for Eastern Europe, headquartered in Eastern Europe (Prague, Bratislava), i.e. elsewhere than in Brussels, ought to be established in order to cut the costs of representation. A 'branch office' located further east would be closer and cheaper for trade unions from the region. As one representative put it, '[B]eing represented in Brussels is very expensive and basically impossible for some trade union associations.'[11] The sub-committee would then act as the representative body in Brussels.

Trade unions are usually satisfied with their operations at the national level (90%), while being more critical of their activities at the European level (only 60% expressed

---

10 Trade unions give the highest preference to cooperation with individual EU Commissioners and Members of the European Parliament, Project interview, Summer 2007 (Cz-Gn05).
11 Project interview, Summer 2007 (Cz-Gn01).

feelings of satisfaction). Insufficient financial resources might account for some of the dissatisfaction at the European level; activity is more expensive there. Trade union representatives expect that the importance of supranational representation and policy-making will grow, and they fear that they do not have what it takes to keep up. In this context some self-criticism was voiced about lacking the necessary language skills to act at the European level. Even though the respondents claimed to have mastered 2.4 foreign languages on average[12] – not bad compared with the language skills of Czech elites[13] – it must be taken into account that the respondents were the top executives of Czech trade unions and therefore had had extensive international skills. These respondents have been members of different groups and boards at the European level for a long time, but they cannot occupy all positions that come open. A higher number of well-qualified trade union representatives are needed who would be able to work on different EU boards.

Better funding and language skills are just part of the equation. To improve the representation of their interests at the EU, trade unionists need to examine their own work more closely, respond more flexibly to changing conditions and make adjustments to some deeply ingrained work processes. One of the experts summarized what trade unions should do:

1. It is necessary to start making use of what is not usually made use of [in trade unions], that is self-criticism. Trade unions criticize others, but not themselves. The causes of diminished influence and possible failures must be addressed with self-criticism.

2. Trade unions need to be made more attractive for young people. Rigid mechanisms need to be made more flexible.

3. At a time when the media rule, people must be hired who are able to succinctly, clearly and comprehensibly say what needs to be said.

4. A team of experts on a par with the government's or employers' experts should be created. Of course, this would be costly.

5. Trade unions should remain non-partisan. They should communicate with all political parties but not form alliances with any of them. The minute one allies with a political party, that's the end of it.[14]

---

12 The respondents from among the experts were found to have mastered 1.6 foreign languages on average, and the representatives of employer organizations claimed to know an average of five languages. The most prevalent languages are English (70%) and Russian (60%).

13 There are similarities with the results of other projects. In the 6 FP-project INTUNE – Integrated and United. A Quest for Citizenship in an 'ever closer Europe' (CIT3-CT-2005-513421), we found out that Members of Parliament in the Czech Republic had mastered an average of 1.8 foreign languages, while economic elites were proficient in 1.9 foreign languages, see Mansfeldová, Zdenka / Stašková, Barbora: Výzkum politických a ekonomických elit v České republice. Research report, Prague: Sociologický ústav AV ČR, September 2007, p. 10.

14 Project interview, Summer 2007 (Cz-Ex01).

Trade unions interact with their social partners (employer associations) both at the national and European levels. As it turns out, employer organizations and trade unions share some common interests. When asked about cooperation between trade unions and other Czech social partners, employer organizations in particular, at the EU level, the respondents talked of regular and continuous cooperation; see Table 9-2.

Table 9-2: Evaluation of Interaction with the Social Partners (%)

	Trade unions	Employers	Experts
A constructive partner	60	33	20
An opponent that blocks decisions	20	33	20
One competitor among many	-	-	40
Don't know	10	-	10
No answer	10	33	10

Source: Project Questionnaire, Summer 2007, Question Q28 (documented in the appendix).

Despite a number of critical comments concerning specific decision-making situations, the prevailing sentiment among the trade unionists was that employers are a constructive partner for cooperation at the EU level.

> It depends on each case. It happens that employers refuse to push through some decisions that were previously agreed on, and that is certainly not a very constructive approach. But in other matters that are close to their agenda and where the interests of both parties overlap, there I can say they are constructive. They only articulate their position and we articulate ours. So, employers can be constructive partners, but every year it takes longer and longer for us to find a common viewpoint.[15]

> They are a very strong partner. They are not always a constructive partner, but we cannot say that they block the Social Dialogue. But the negotiation with employer associations is not at all easy.[16]

The employers were slightly more critical of their social partners on this issue. However, they too view the trade unions both as constructive partners and opponents at times.

9.3. Europeanization of Czech Trade Unions

With respect to the Europeanization of Czech trade unions, it should be examined whether and to what extent the Social Dialogue, and especially its most important aspect, i.e. collective bargaining in individual industries, leads the trade unions to embrace important European issues. Are EU regulations or agreements between European social partners implemented, and more generally, are the outputs of the European Social Dialogue transferred to the Czech environment? Another important

---

15 Project interview, Summer 2007 (Cz-Gn07).
16 Project interview, Summer 2007 (Cz-Gn08).

question is whether the Czech social partners have been able to create conditions in their Social Dialogue that would enable such transfers to occur.

A possible approach to examining and explaining the integration strategies of the member states is suggested in the work of Simon Hix and Klaus Götz[17], who see European integration as a process that necessarily results in Europeanization. They contend that European integration has had two types of consequences that are mutually interlinked. On the one hand, certain capacities were delegated from the national bodies to EU institutions, which has resulted in some binding political decisions. This in turn has restricted the decision-making and manoeuvring space of national actors. On the other hand, a higher level of governance was created, which enables local actors to overcome certain national barriers, promote their interests at a higher level and even veto certain policies. In this way, they can make use of the greatest advantage they have against national competitors, i.e. better access to information and to the proceedings of EU bodies.

Our research showed that trade unions regard the European level as roughly equal to the national level (60%) in terms of importance, or possibly even more important. The EU has had a positive impact on the trade unions' work, and the importance of the EU dimension is expected to grow. The trade unions' operations at the European level very often (70%) affect their national activities. This may take the form of 'using Europe in argumentation', setting agendas or implementing European standards in the local environment (50% of the respondents said that they often use the 'Europe argument'; 40% use it only occasionally). The vice-chairman of ČMKOS described the situation this way:

> If we agreed on certain standards with employers at the EU level, and these standards are binding for us and them, we introduce them into collective bargaining, and obviously, without this channel it would have never been implemented and people would have never asked for it.[18]

This includes agreements with employers at the European level that are then implemented nationally.

A respondent gave an example of the positive impact Europe has had on the national representation of interests:

> Here we could look back in history, because we had become members of ETUC (EOK) before we joined the EU, and ETUC actually helped our trade unions with the integration and pre-accession process, expert- and money-wise. But we were part and parcel of the project and had an opportunity to take part in a number of things. So it has clearly been positive. And a current example would be that we jointly negotiate some European issues. And we have even expressed disagreement with some legislative drafts as for instance the Bolkestein Directive, which concerned services on the domestic market. So I would

---

17   Hix, S. / Goetz, K. H.: Europeanised Politics? European Integration and National Political Systems, in: Hix, S. / Goetz, K. H. (eds): Europeanised, London: Frank Cass, 2001, pp. 1–26.
18   Project interview, Summer 2007 (Cz-Gn07).

say that in some legislative proceedings concerning directives we have worked together and influenced some things just through the European level.[19]

At the national level, trade unions refer to the EU (50% very often, 50% sometimes) to gain support or justify their positions. Even more prevalent is the 'argument with Europe' used by employer associations. Trade unions mostly employ these arguments to very specific issues, such as the Social Dialogue, wages and salaries, pension reform, labour conditions, working hours, new forms of work (telework), equal opportunities, etc. Despite any misgivings they may have, some representatives of Czech trade unions hope that the European Social Dialogue will help to harmonize at least some social and labour conditions both in individual industries as well as more generally in individual member states.

The employers also believe that having European leverage helps the trade unionists to promote their interests at the national level as well. However, employers and experts are wary about the growing influence of the EU; they prefer the current balance between the national and European levels, which they believe should remain equal. They do not want to see either one become stronger.

9.4. Conclusion

The Social Dialogue as a method of promoting group interests is a traditionally legitimate part of the European social model. The European Social Dialogue can be defined as an exchange between social partners (employer organizations and trade unions) at the European level that addresses individual industries as well as more general issues. For their part, the trade unions received assistance from EU bodies in the pre-accession period; in their estimation, the transfer of know-how and networking proved to be the most important benefits. However, if the trade unions are to maximize their performance at the EU level, they will need to acquire more skills and re-examine their modus operandi.

The social partners in the Czech Republic interviewed in this study spoke positively about their integration within European structures, especially regarding the sharing of hard-to-access information and consulting. The trade unions in particular see great benefit in creating joint strategies for negotiating with employers, especially in industries dominated by supranational corporations (trading, heavy industry). They also appreciate the ability to comment on European legislation applicable to their individual industries. The European level of interest representation is as important for trade unions as the national level, and they expect the EU's significance to continue to grow.

---

19   Project interview, Summer 2007 (Cz-Gn08).

Monika Čambáliková

10. Slovak Trade Unions in EU Governance

10.1. Trade Unions in Slovakia

10.1.1. Development of Tripartite Negotiations

In Slovakia, the former socialist Confederation of Trade Unions (KOZ SR) remains dominant today, representing more than 90% of Slovak trade union members. The social partnership, in which the employees are represented solely by the KOZ, began to form at the beginning of the transformation period and was formally established in 1990, when Slovakia was still part of Czechoslovakia.

The main channel of political involvement became the tripartite Council of Economic and Social Agreement (RHSD). The social partnership in Slovakia was institutionalized in the specific context of 1990, when, paradoxically, some of the main actors, such as autonomous employer associations and standard trade unions, did not yet exist. Thus, the establishment of the tripartite body was inspired by the model from developed democratic societies *abroad* and initiated from *above* by the government rather than forged by the actors themselves.[1]

In this context, the following assumption is critical for understanding the dynamics in the tripartite:

> The fact that the state accepted the Confederation of Trade Unions as the exclusive representative of employees confirmed the exchange of the privileged standing of the trade unions for voluntary acceptance of certain restrictions on the trade union in the bargaining process.[2]

The KOZ preserves its privileged (monopoly) position in the tripartite due to the fact that no other trade union organization was able to meet the criteria of representativity established under the act on tripartite was created. As the government had an interest in tripartism and bargaining at the national level, it accepted the trade union representation that existed at that time.

According to the original charter of the RHSD, economic and social policies, wages and employment were the central issues of the tripartite bargaining, from which a General Agreement (GA) governing the conditions and relations in these spheres was

---

1   Čambáliková, M.: The Emergence of Tripartism in Slovakia, in: Ágh, A./ Illonszki, G. (eds): Parliaments and Organised Interests. The Second Steps, Budapest: Hungarian Centre for Democracy Studies, 1996, pp. 190–211.
2   Malová, D.: Reprezentácia záujmov na Slovensku. Smerom ku korporativizmu?, in: Sociológia, ročník, 1996 (Vol. 28), No. 5, pp. 403–415, here p. 409.

to be the outcome. As it turns out, the General Agreement is nothing more than a *gentleman's agreement*. Notwithstanding the collective agreement (concluded at the level of the enterprise or economic branch), the GA has never been legally enforced; it was and is 'only' politically binding and represents 'only' political and moral obligations.

The Tripartite Act, approved in 1999,[3] changed neither the principal content of the tripartite's activity nor the principal competencies of its actors in comparison with the original charter of the RHSD. In 2004 the act was revoked. Between 2004 and 2007 (and between 1991 and 1998), the tripartite body in Slovakia was regulated and guided by the statutes and rules adopted by the tripartite body itself. The new act governing the tripartite was approved by the parliament only in February 2007[4] and became effective as of 1 April 2007. Due to the fact that both acts on the tripartite respected the statutes and rules adopted by the tripartite body, the regulation of the tripartite body was not significantly changed in spite of the new laws.

Social partners were and are allowed to comment on drafts and bills of acts influencing economic and social development, employment and wage conditions. However, in compliance with the constitutional and legal system of the Slovak Republic, the tripartite partners, including the government, cannot guarantee that their comments will be incorporated in the final wording and provisions of law. The competence to adopt legislation is vested only in the Slovak national parliament. Members of the parliament are not bound by the comments and / or opinions of the RHSD, and drafts of acts submitted to the parliament by the MPs do not have to be submitted to the tripartite.

After the first years of the tripartite's activity, trade union representatives in Slovakia commenced (in addition to underlining the importance and advantages of this institution) to point out the problem of (non-)adherence to the agreements established by the social partners. The problem still exists. The report 'Standpoint of the Confederation of the Trade Unions of the SR to the activity of the RHSD' from January 1993 enumerates the positive aspects inherent in the tripartite itself and also lists the drawbacks based on its activities up to that point. The main drawback was deemed to be the 'conscious / deliberate and intentional omission of the tripartite (RHSD) from the decision-making process'. The trade union came to the conclusion that the

> RHSD from the formal point of view fulfils the criteria of the tripartite relations, but it has only limited relevance from the practical point of view and only partially fulfils its function from the point of view of the KOZ SR. Furthermore, the KOZ has – due to its participation in the RHSD – in the eyes of the public come to be viewed as the consenting partner of the government on issues (and in case of measures) with significant social impacts even in cases in which it disagrees with such measures.

Nevertheless, until 1997, the social partners in Slovakia drafted and signed a General Agreement every year. The respective GA defined relevant economic and social tasks

---

3   Act no. 106/1999 Coll. on Economic and Social Partnership.
4   Act no. 103/2007 Coll. on Tripartite Consultations at the National Level.

and specified the obligations of the individual social partners in this context. At the same time, the GA represented the framework and conceptual basis for collective bargaining at the branch and enterprise levels. The monitoring of the fulfilment of obligations agreed to under the respective GA was an important topic of the tripartite bargaining. Non-fulfilment, especially on the part of the government, was the subject of criticism.

In the middle of 1997, the KOZ withdrew from the tripartite bargaining. Contradictory interpretations of the reasons for the breakdown of the tripartite bargaining and mutual recriminations for the violation of rules and agreements deepened the conflict, especially between the KOZ and the government. As time went on, conflicts started to emerge within the KOZ: representatives of some of the trade unions associated in the KOZ deemed the decision of the KOZ's Board not to bargain in the tripartite as ill-advised. They feared that an entire year of tripartite inactivity could lead to the opinion that the tripartite was not necessary for the functioning of the state, which might set a dangerous precedent for the future. According to the aforementioned representatives, by refusing to participate, the KOZ had lost political influence at the national level, which weakened the stance of the trade union in bargaining with employers at the enterprise and branch levels.[5] Due to conflicting views towards the government and towards the management of various firms, the unity within some of the individual trade unions and their organizations in enterprises started to erode as well.

After the parliamentary elections in 1998, trade union representatives at the KOZ congress in November 1998 observed that the new government[6] had not yet fulfilled its pre-election promises to the trade unions. The first new round of negotiations with the tripartite took place on 22 December 1998, whereby the draft of a new act on the tripartite was approved.[7] I. Saktor, the chairman of the KOZ, remarked, 'The act does not enable the imposition of penalties in case of breach of agreements.'[8] The act became effective *de jure*, but *de facto* it did not change much. Vice-chairman of the KOZ E. Machyna commented: 'We are sorry that restrictive measures were approved without consultation within the tripartite.'[9]

After three years of abstaining from drafting a General Agreement, the parties signed the GA for 2000. However, in the years that followed, the social partners did not manage to conclude any GAs.

---

5   Interview with J. Blahák (Vice-president of the KOZ), Národná obroda, 24 March 1998.
6   The so-called first Dzurinda government (1998–2002).
7   The adoption of the new act on tripartite was often interpreted as a certain form of remuneration of the new government to the trade unions for their political support and activities during the time it was in the opposition.
8   Pravda, 28 December 1998, p. 1.
9   Pravda, 3 June 1999, p. 1.

After parliamentary elections in 2002, the situation for the trade unions became even worse. The right-wing government[10] continued to pursue the creation of a 'favourable environment for foreign investments' and liberalized the Labour Code with the aim of enhancing the flexibility of the labour market. The requests the trade unions made in the tripartite arena were denied. The government proposed to revoke the tripartite act altogether.

The representatives of the KOZ again started to join forces with the parliamentary opposition and organize a petition for a referendum for early elections. The vote for early elections (3 April 2004) was invalid[11], and only served to broaden the split among the electorate and trade union members. The organization of the petition and referendum on early elections as well as the declared political alliance with the opposition political party SMER again had a negative influence on tripartite bargaining and social partner relations.

However, the trade unions (KOZ) might see some positive changes under the government formed after the 2006 parliamentary elections; Robert Fico's new government has been cooperating with the KOZ. As a result, new amendments have been added to the Labour Code and the Act on Collective Bargaining (which now allows the extension of upper level collective agreements), and a new act on tripartite consultations has been passed.

10.1.2. The Influence of Trade Unions on National Politics

Formal institutional and legal preconditions for the activities of the social partnership and Social Dialogue were created relatively quickly after 1989. However, with regard to the social partnership (tripartite) and its actors (including the trade unions), the following points should be kept in mind: 1. this institution did not arise spontaneously from civil society, i.e. 'from below', but was created 'from above' by the government; 2. the trade unions (formerly the Revolutionary Trade Union Movement – Revoluční odborové hnutí – ROH) serving as an actor in this institution were not legitimized by civil society, but were vested with authority (again) by the government; and 3. it was neither civil society nor the trade union membership base but rather (again) the government (*de facto* and also *de jure*) that guaranteed the monopoly of employee interest representation to the trade unions. On the other hand, neither civil society in a broader (national) context nor employees in the narrower sense (at the enterprise or branch level) created any alternative institutions and / or actors in this sphere: the trade unions not associated with the KOZ have few members, are not representative *de jure* (they did not meet the criteria for representativeness defined in the act on the

---

10   The so-called second Dzurinda government (2002–2006).
11   Only 35.96% of the electorate took part in the referendum; the law requires more than 50% to take part.

tripartite and / or in the bylaws of the tripartite body) and are also *de facto* insufficiently endorsed by labourers as legitimate representatives in the system of the social partnership.

At first sight, it appears that the trade unions belonging to KOZ have managed to put themselves in a strong position: at the beginning of the post-socialist transformation, they represented a unified trade union base with developed organizational structures and a huge membership; the institutional as well as legislative framework enabled (and continues to enable) trade unions to participate in the decision-making processes at all levels; their property and monetary income allows them to be financially independent, autonomous and active. So why has their influence been relatively weak all along? It seems that their real weakness paradoxically originates from their (formal) strength. 'The weakness of the trade unions in Slovakia is caused mainly by its transformational path, in which preservation of the legal continuity, property and privileged stance towards the government was preferred.'[12] 'Gifts' that trade unions obtained from the government and heritage, which they got from the former ROH, turned out to be 'Greek gifts'.

To the public (including members of the trade unions), monopoly access to participation in the decision-making processes also meant monopoly responsibility – including for any negative impacts (especially in the first years of the transformation) of the inevitable economic reforms. Slovak trade unions probably gave too much attention to 'big policy': they joined with political parties, which was – on the non-crystallized political scene – not always effective for the protection of the employees' interests and not clearly transparent for the public. The Board of the KOZ fought for democracy or a 'democratic style of government' on the national level. However, in the opinion of its members, it often failed in negotiations for higher wages and neglected the enterprise level.

But employees, including members of the trade unions, gave priority to higher wages and the situation in the enterprise.[13] Even the KOZ's efforts to institutionalize or legally increase the influence of the trade unions have often been understood (and especially interpreted by the media) as something that is profitable for KOZ board members, but irrelevant for employees. The management of the trade unions has

---

12   Malová, D. / Rybář, M.: Organizované záujmy, in: Slovensko 2006. Súhrnná správa o stave spoločnosti, Bratislava: IVO, 2006, pp. 284–298, here p. 286.

13   E.g. Research ,The Quality of Working Life in the Electronic Industry' showed that the most important tasks for the trade union according to workers were: securing wage increases (in 2000 90.6% of trade union members considered this very important) and protecting job security (87% very important). Only 18% considered it very important to increase the influence of the trade unions (Čambáliková, M.: Dual Identity and / or 'Bread and Butter'. Electronics Industry Workers in Slovakia 1995–2000, in: Smith, Simon (ed.): Local Communities and Post-Communist Transformation Czechoslovakia, the Czech Republic and Slovakia, London, New York: RoutledgeCurzon, 2003, pp. 105–126, here p. 120).

not managed to mobilize its members; trade union membership has been eroding. At the beginning of the transformation process in 1990, the KOZ represented 2.4 million employees (almost 100% trade union density), at the end of 1993 1.5 million, in 1998 only 850,000, and today only slightly more than 500,000. In other words, trade union density has fallen to one-fourth of all employees.

Slovakia provides a formal legislative platform for participation of the social partners at all levels and in all spheres, which is compatible with the EU guidelines. However, it was confirmed that the formal preconditions (for institutions and actors) of the neocorporativist policy – especially at the beginning of the post-socialist transformation process – are often *de facto* 'empty structures'.[14] Formally, the tripartite's status as an advisory body with original actors and working pursuant to the original statute was preserved in Slovakia. However, working and wage conditions as well as employee-employer relations are increasingly governed by collective agreements (at the branch as well as enterprise level) and bargained for by the employees' negotiators, i.e. individual trade unions.

10.2. Representation of Slovak Trade Unions at the EU Level

10.2.1. Formal Institutions and Memberships

Despite the help that the EU provided to the Slovak trade unions prior to Slovakia's accession in 2004 (and which is by and large evaluated positively by them), the trade union representatives felt only partially prepared for the work at the EU level at the moment of accession. In spite of the fact that most of them feel that the situation has improved since then, it seems that the Slovak trade unions are still more passive observers and grateful recipients than active (co-) creators of European policy.

The representatives of the Slovak trade unions still do not exploit the existing range of possibilities for participation in the decision-making processes at the EU level. They are active in the European Economic and Social Committee (EESC) and participate in the EU-level Social Dialogue. They are able to exert influence – and obtain information – mainly via their membership in European umbrella institutions. However, up to now they have not taken (or, to be more precise, have mostly ignored) opportunities to exert influence, such as e.g. by participating in direct consultations with the European Commission, members of the European Parliament or national representatives in the Council of Ministers.

---

14   Čambáliková, M.: Tripartismus in der Slowakei – Leere Struktur oder außerparlamentarische Form der Interessenvertretung?, in: Zeitschrift für Gemeinwirtschaft, 2001 (Vol. 38), No. 6, pp. 27–46.

However, especially at the branch level, Slovak trade unions representatives use the different options available to them, including close cooperation with the respective branch-level trade unions from other EU member states. This cooperation varies significantly among particular branch-level trade unions, however: e.g. Slovak Metalworkers' Federation KOVO (OZ KOVO) engages in bilateral cooperation and is also active in the framework of the European Metalworkers' Federation. The Miners' Trade Union, on the other hand, does not go beyond the bilateral international cooperation, which limits them to cooperation with the Czech mining trade unions. The representatives of OZ KOVO also take advantage of other options and forums for acquiring influence (*de facto* all options and forums that are used by the KOZ), but the Miners' Trade Union itself is not directly active in any organizational structures or institutions at the EU level, and therefore enters into the decision-making processes at the EU level only via its membership in KOZ.

All interviewed representatives of the Slovak trade unions cited their membership in the EESC as the most important avenue for participation and representation of the trade unions' interests at the EU level. In this respect, the representatives of the OZ KOVO also consider their membership in the European Metalworkers' Federation as an important tool with respect to EU-level participation.

The Slovak trade union representatives characterized their cooperation with the European umbrella associations as positive. Only two exceptions were detected in this respect: Vice-chairman of the KOZ for economic policy and social partnership and member of the EESC expressed mixed feelings about such cooperation based on his personal experience[15] (he said that 'there is too much bureaucracy within such a big colossus'); a second respondent, vice-chairman of the Trade Union of Mines had had no personal experience[16] with the trade unions' interest representation at the EU level and therefore had no opinion.

The Slovak trade unions' participation in the decision-making processes at the EU level, has not changed over the years. Only the vice-chairman of the KOZ for economic policy and social partnership (and a member of the EESC) expressed the opinion that communication with the European institutions had 'improved' over the years, but immediately added that: 'We are not successful in communicating with Slovak members of the European Parliament'.[17] It is probably not a coincidence that the Slovak trade union representatives expressed the opinion that nothing had changed with regard to their participation in the decision-making processes or enhancing their influence at the EU level in recent years, but at the same time, all of them anticipate change for the better in the years to come.

---

15 Project interview, Summer 2007 (SK-Gn01).
16 Project interview, Summer 2007 (SK-Gn05).
17 Project interview, Summer 2007 (SK-Gn01).

10.2.2. Assessment of the Trade Unions' Influence and Participation at the EU Level

The influence of the trade unions at the EU level in comparison with other inter-est groups was assessed as average by most of the interviewees from Slovak trade unions. Only two respondents[18] assessed it as relatively high; however, both of them lacked direct personal experience with EU-level trade union participation. Both of these respondents assumed that the influence of the trade unions at the EU level had increased in recent years. But the majority of the Slovak trade union representatives (including those who are active at the EU level and in its structures) believe that the trade unions' influence at the EU level (in comparison with other interest groups) has decreased in recent times.

In comparing the influence and power of the trade unions at the national and EU levels, study participants pointed out that the standing and influence of the Slovak trade unions at the national level significantly depends on the national government or rather on its political orientation and composition. According to the trade union repre-sentatives as well as employer association representatives, the influence of the Slovak trade unions at the national level versus the EU level was significantly lower during Dzurinda's term; but since Fico took office, the trade unions' influence in Slovakia has increased. The Slovak social partners assessed the standing of the trade unions at the EU level as stable and their degree of influence as relatively high; they described it as unstable and varyingly effective at the national level, however. It is widely believed that despite possible (but uncertain) short-term advantages, the position of the Slovak trade unions is less advantageous than that of the trade unions at the EU level.

In our survey only one-third of the representatives active at the EU level expressed the opinion that the activity of the Slovak trade unions significantly contributes to the representation and furthering of the trade unions' interests at the EU level. The other two-thirds felt that the activities and influence of the Slovak trade unions is not signif-icant at the EU level. The respondents' reasoning was mainly predicated on the official size of their membership base. Those who think that the contribution of the Slovak trade unions is significant on the EU level base their assumption on the fact that: 'We are full members; we fulfil all of our obligations. We bring new thoughts, new culture and new knowledge.'[19]

The assessment of the importance of the trade unions' influence at the EU level is closely connected with the satisfaction of the Slovak trade union representatives with their role and performance at this level. The majority of the Slovak trade union rep-resentatives (almost all of whom are active at the EU level) are not satisfied with the

---

18   Member of the EESC and Expert (Legal Advisor) of KOZ (Project interview, Summer 2007, SK-Gn07) and vice-chairman of the Trade Union of Mines (Project interview, Summer 2007, SK-Gn05).
19   Project interview, Summer 2007 (SK-Gn04).

activities and performance of the Slovak trade unions at the EU level. In general, they assume that: 'It is possible to work better at the EU level'[20] and consider it difficult to 'increase their influence at this level'.[21]

The Slovak trade union representatives do not consider themselves significantly active in the representation of the trade unions' interests at the EU level; the Slovak employers' representatives do not perceive themselves as actively involved at this level either.

In contrast, most of the Slovak trade union representatives expressed satisfaction with their role and performance at the national level. However, in most cases, the satisfaction was not without reservations. While the representatives are pleased with their own activity[22] and legitimacy, they also cited numerous internal as well as external problems that remain to be solved and overcome.[23] The representative of the Miners' Trade Union expressed stronger dissatisfaction with the performance and role of his 'own' trade union at the national level; his opinion was probably shaped by the difficult and worsening position of this branch of industry in general and by the restrictions in the working and wage conditions of the workers who are represented by this particular trade union.

It seems that the representatives of the Slovak trade unions deem themselves as responsible for the advocacy and furthering of their interests primarily at the national level. Therefore, they are more sensitive with respect to the assessment of their performance at the national level; they defend their activities and legitimacy more rigorously there. They feel more needed, more competent and more powerful at the national level than at the EU level. They consider the EU (i.e. relevant European institutions) as their protector and patron – an entity that does not need their support and help, but is able to provide these things to them. They therefore see their principal challenge as fulfilling their role and tasks at the national level, which is where they feel irreplaceable and most needed, competent and prepared.

The Slovak employer representatives also confirm that the Slovak trade unions have a bigger influence at the national level than at the EU level. With respect to the representation of the trade unions' interests at the EU level, the Slovak trade

---

20   Vice-chairman of the KOZ for economic policy and social partnership and member of the EESC, (Project interview, Summer 2007, SK-Gn01).
21   Vice-chairman of OZ KOVO, (Project interview, Summer 2007, SK-Gn03).
22   'Partially I am satisfied, partially not… But I cannot say that I am not satisfied due to the fact that I am responsible and liable for the performance and I should change it if it is not good. It also depends on the communication with the members, expertise and other capacities' (vice-chairman of the KOZ for economic policy and social partnership and member of the EESC), (Project interview, Summer 2007, SK-Gn01).
23   'In the last eight years the pressure of the media has significantly harmed the trade unions: the assertion that everything left-wing and social is bad and should be denied and that the trade unions impede social and economic development has been harmful to the trade unions' (vice-chairman of OZ KOVO), (Project interview, Summer 2007, SK-Gn03).

unions are according to the Slovak employer representatives neither a hindrance nor a help regarding the performance of the European trade unions: 'They are absolutely unnoticeable.'[24]

The social partners in Slovakia do not question each other's legitimacy, which is an important precondition for an effective social partnership at all levels. However, this does not mean that the Social Dialogue is unproblematic in Slovakia. And, as the findings of the survey show, their interaction at the EU level also needs some ironing out. The representatives of the main Slovak employer associations assert that they in fact do not cooperate with the Slovak social partners at the EU level.

The Slovak employer association representatives often expressed critical attitudes towards the Slovak trade unions at the EU level. They described the trade unions as opponents that obstructed the measures they had approved. 'That might sound strong, but it's the truth. They are not merely one of the competitors: they are the main competitor. They are not constructive partners. For instance, they always vote with the EESC and always vote against all of the employers 'proposals.'[25]

10.3. Europeanization of Slovak Trade Unions

The pressure of the requirements and criteria of the EU have had a positive effect on the trade unions' standing as social partners. Slovakia, as an associated country and later member state of the EU, felt obligated to strengthen its democratic institutions, including those related to the social partnership. As a member state, Slovakia has also encouraged the seeking of consensus and agreement, which is enabled by the institutions of the social partnership. Simply said, the EU has not only fortified the legitimacy of the trade unions as an actor in the social partnership, but has also legitimized the trade union policy connected with the principle of the European social model. Therefore, it is not surprising that the Slovak trade union representatives unanimously agreed that the EU has had a positive effect on their performance and standing.

The values of the 'model Europe' and the policy based on this model led the Slovak trade union representatives to advocate an increase of the EU's influence on national policy. This type of policy is not merely close to their policy in principle, but has also facilitated the furthering and protection of the trade unions' interests. Understood in

---

24 Chairman of the Entrepreneurs Association of Slovakia (ZPS) and chairman of the committee for international and EU affairs of the National Union of Employers (RUZ) and member of the EESC, (Project interview, Summer 2007, SK-An01); Chairman of the committee for international and EU affairs of the National Union of Employers (RUZ) and member of the EESC and registered lobbyist in the European Parliament, (Project interview, Summer 2007, SK-An02).

25 Member of the committee for international and EU affairs of the National Union of Employers (RUZ), member of the EESC and registered lobbyist in the European Parliament, (Project interview, Summer 2007, SK-An02).

this way, EU policy can represent a legitimate social-democratic alternative to the policy of the current national government, be it strongly liberal, conservative or reformist. At the same time, principles and standards valid in the EU serve to protect employees. 'The Slovak employers would have crushed us were it not for the EU. The Slovak employers were inclined to embrace early capitalism. However, they respect the EU and the EU provides us with protection.'[26] When some of the Slovak trade union representatives stated that the influence of the EU on the national policy of the member states should be decreased, they were mainly referring to the 'excessive bureaucracy' and 'excessive administrative difficulty'.

In contrast to the Slovak trade union representatives, the representatives of the Slovak employer associations took a more critical stance on EU policy and its influence. 'At least in some spheres', they deemed EU influence as negative; however, they clarified that it is not negative for the 'work of our association, but for our members – individual firms / enterprises' and that

> the negative influence mostly has to do with the excessive regulation of the (otherwise) praiseworthy goals, such as the protection of health and safety at work, protective social laws as such, protection of the environment, protection of the consumer, etc. The enterprise is regulated from the moment it commences production, or rather even before that. Its production is regulated in order to protect the environment, the employees and their health; the products are regulated in order to protect the customer, etc. The aim is positive and we should applaud it. However, the reality is such that the regulation is much too detailed – so detailed that it has no meaning and is often counterproductive.[27]

The representatives of the Slovak employers and enterprises also rejected 'considerations about and proposals for the harmonization of the tax-system': 'For instance, the EU is active in harmonizing taxation issues, which is an example of the negative influence as we do not consider such harmonization as desirable; we wish to decide for ourselves in this sphere.'[28] Accordingly Slovak employer association representatives do not deem it desirable to further increase the influence of the EU on the national policy of the member states.

Slovak trade union and employer association representatives are both critical of the 'detailed' regulation and regulation of 'unimportant matters' from the EU level. However, with respect to regulation and harmonization in general (i.e. of 'frameworks and basic rules'), their opinions differ: the trade unions require it, but the employers are opposed to it.

26　Member of the EESC and Expert (Legal Advisor) of KOZ, (Project interview, Summer 2007, SK-Gn07).

27　Chairman of the Entrepreneurs Association of Slovakia (ZPS), chairman of the committee for international and EU affairs of the National Union of Employers (RUZ) and member of the EESC, (Project interview, Summer 2007, SK-An01).

28　Member of the committee for international and EU affairs of the National Union of Employers (RUZ), member of the EESC and registered lobbyist in the European Parliament, (Project interview, Summer 2007, SK-An02).

Trade union and employer representatives alike are fully aware of the importance of the representation of their interests on the national and EU levels: 'Regarding issues that fall within the competence of the national level, the representation at the national level is more important. But there is a tendency that more and more matters have to be solved at the EU level.'[29] Reflecting this situation, Slovak employers particularly defend their interests aggressively at both the national and EU levels. It seems that the representatives of the Slovak employers are more active at the EU level than the Slovak trade union representatives are. They use the many institutional forms available to increase their influence and to participate in the decision-making processes at the EU level, and it seems that they are also active informally and individually.

The representatives of the Slovak employers, for example, cooperate with the individual members of the European Parliament (at the EU level) much more often than Slovak trade union representatives do.

In comparison with the trade union representatives, the employer representatives evaluated the European Commission or rather consultations provided by the European Commission more positively.

> The EC really consults with the employers' as well as trade unions' representatives on all drafts and bills of new EU laws and reflects their opinions and standpoints. There is better access (almost free access for the employer associations as well as trade union representatives) to the people who prepare the laws at the EU level than at the national level.[30]

The Slovak trade union representative expressed a different opinion:

> With regard to the final decision of the European Commission or the European Parliament, we are not able to influence it (nor often evaluate it) as we lack the feedback from the EC as well as the EP. We are trying to obtain it, but we do not have it.[31]

On the other hand, it seems that the Slovak trade unions are more confident and satisfied with their cooperation with and activity in the EESC.

> Based on my own experience with consultations about social and employment issues in the EESC, I think that we as the trade union representatives are organized and disciplined and thus we are able to enforce our standpoint. The employers are very vehement, but sometimes lack consensus and are less organized. Thanks to that we are able to implement our standpoints in the EESC. However, only recommendations and standpoints for the EC and the EP are approved by the EESC.[32]

---

29   Chairman of the Entrepreneurs Association of Slovakia (ZPS) and chairman of the committee for international and EU affairs of the National Union of Employers (RUZ) and member of the EESC, (Project interview, Summer 2007, SK-An01)

30   Member of the committee for international and EU affairs of the National Union of Employers (RUZ), member of the EESC and registered lobbyist in the European Parliament, (Project interview, Summer 2007, SK-An02).

31   Vice-chairman of KOZ SR for economic policy and social partnership and member of the EESC, (Project interview, Summer 2007, SK-Gn01).

32   Vice-chairman of KOZ SR for economic policy and social partnership and member of the EESC, (Project interview, Summer 2007, SK-Gn01).

Slovak employer representatives were more critical of the EESC for the following reason:

> There are quantitatively represented three segments in the EESC – employees, employers and so-called organized civil society, which in practice usually means that the employers are outvoted 2:1 in all issues. This is due to the fact that 'organized civil society' contains representatives who are (in their opinions) very close to the trade unions.[33]

The employer representatives appear to have less informed as well as less positive attitudes towards the Social Dialogue at the EU level than the trade union representatives have. The employer representatives prefer the decentralization of the Social Dialogue:

> Leading the Social Dialogue at the EU level is meaningless. Leading it at the level of enterprise is more meaningful. Maybe the Social Dialogue at the national level might be of some importance, but I personally think that the Social Dialogue should occur at the workplace. I also have some doubts with respect to the branch-level Social Dialogue and national-level Social Dialogue; the latter is more about politics than solving real problems. The Social Dialogue at the EU level can only try to solve the issues. But the issues should be solved where they emerge - at the workplace.[34]

The Slovak employer representatives *sometimes* use the EU as an argument in support of their position and / or activities at the national level: 'Like everyone, we also use it when it is convenient for us.'[35] The survey confirmed what can be observed in Slovak society: Slovak trade unions *often* use the EU as an argument in support of their position and / or activities at the national level. Similarly, the effort of the trade unions to apply and implement (protective) laws and EU requirements to the maximum possible extent in Slovakia and to influence their standing and activities at the national level is obvious and transparent. 'As trade union representatives we very often refer to the EC and EU in general.'[36] Recently, Slovak trade union representatives have referred to the EU, especially with regard to the argumentation supporting the amendment of the Labour Code (which became effective on 1 September 2007).

---

33 Chairman of the Entrepreneurs Association of Slovakia (ZPS) and chairman of the committee for international and EU affairs of the National Union of Employers (RUZ) and member of the EESC, (Project interview, Summer 2007, SK-An01).
34 Chairman of the Entrepreneurs Association of Slovakia (ZPS) and chairman of the committee for international and EU affairs of the National Union of Employers (RUZ) and member of the EESC, (Project interview, Summer 2007, SK-An01).
35 Member of the committee for international and EU affairs of the National Union of Employers (RUZ) and member of the EESC and registered lobbyist in the European Parliament, (Project interview, Summer 2007, SK-An02).
36 Vice-chairman of the KOZ for economic policy and social partnership and member of the EESC, (Project interview, Summer 2007, SK-Gn01).

11. Conclusion

11.1. Introduction

The preceding country studies have presented the empirical evidence for the integration of trade unions from Poland, the Czech Republic and Slovakia into EU governance. The focus has been, first, on the actual (and not merely formal) inclusion of trade unions from the new member states in decision-making processes on the EU level and second, on the Europeanization of trade unions from the post-socialist member states. In this concluding chapter the country studies will be put in a broader comparative and analytical context. The interview results quoted here are documented in the appendix.

11.2. Engagement on the EU Level

11.2.1. Channels of Influence

In order to assess the trade unions' engagement at the EU level, it must first be determined in what form the trade unions from the new member states have been integrated into political decision-making processes at the EU level. Based on the structure of trade union organizations, modes of influence and relevant forums at the EU level, different categories of engagement can be delineated.

In this book we have summarized the channels for trade unions to exert influence on political decision-making processes at the EU level in the following way: (1) direct consultations with the European Commission, (2) consultations with national representatives in the Council of Ministers, (3) direct consultations with the EU Parliament, (4) participation in the Social Dialogue, (5) involvement in the European Economic and Social Committee (EESC), (6) engagement in transnational umbrella organizations and networks. An office in Brussels is also frequently cited as a way to obtain influence. However, an office in and of itself does not guarantee involvement in decision-making processes. It can just facilitate the pursuit of the avenues listed above.

With respect to the channels of influence, there are four relevant forums for political decision-making for trade unions: (1) the European Commission or the appropriate Directorate-General, (2) the Council of Ministers or the appropriate national representation at the Council of Ministers or the relevant working group, (3) the EU Parliament or the responsible parliamentary committee and (4) the Social Dialogue. The fifth and sixth channels of influence listed in the previous paragraph offer organizations (members of the EESC or European umbrella organizations) an alternative channel of access to the relevant forums of decision-making.

The thirteen trade unions from Poland, the Czech Republic and Slovakia surveyed in this study barely exert any influence on decision-making processes via direct consultations with EU organs. Direct consultations with the European Commission are a rare exception and were cited by only two of the thirteen trade unions. Consultations with the national representatives in the Council of Ministers were mentioned by three trade unions. Consultations with the European Parliament occur somewhat more frequently. Five of the trade unions polled have access to the Parliament, mostly because some trade union members are MEPs. In summary only the three largest national umbrella organizations from Poland and the Czech Republic have any meaningful access to direct consultations.[1]

One reason for the limited use of direct consultations could be that none of the trade unions from the post-socialist member states has an office in Brussels.[2] The responsible trade union members from the new member states tend to travel to Brussels only when they have a concrete appointment there.[3] Their interests are instead represented by a European umbrella organization (10 of the 13 trade unions), via the Social Dialogue (9) and by the Economic and Social Committee (8).[4] Accordingly, only 3% of the interviewees felt that their trade union was capable of representing their interests on the EU level adequately. The great majority depend on a European umbrella organization to further their interests, and roughly a third relies on cooperation with individual trade unions.[5]

Of the thirteen trade unions from Poland, the Czech Republic and Slovakia included in the study, eleven are members in a European umbrella organization, mostly in ETUC or in the relevant industry organization.[6] However, Józef Niemiec from Poland's Independent and Self-Governing Trade Union Solidarność (NSZZ Solidarność) is the only trade union representative from the three countries under review to hold a leadership position in one of the corresponding European umbrella organizations.[7]

The fixation on the European trade union federations is also underscored by the fact that nearly every trade union questioned named these as the best cooperation

---

1   Project Questionnaire, Summer 2007, Question Q16.
2   See the contribution by Brigitte Krech in this volume.
3   Nevertheless, two-thirds of the interviewed trade union representatives consider an office in Brussels important. Project Questionnaire, Summer 2007, Question Q21.
4   Project Questionnaire, Summer 2007, Question Q16.
5   Project Questionnaire, Summer 2007, Question Q18.
6   Two trade unions – the Confederation of Arts and Culture (KUK) from the Czech Republic and the Union of Workers in Mines, Geology and Oil Industry (OZ PBGN) from Slovakia – are not represented at the European level at all. Project Questionnaire, Summer 2007, Question Q17 (open responses).
7   See the contribution by Brigitte Krech in this volume.

partners on the EU level. Three trade unions cited the European Economic and Social Committee as a valuable partner, and the All-Poland Alliance of Trade Unions (OPZZ) and its industry federations specified Polish members of the European Parliament.[8] The participation of the Polish, Czech and Slovak trade unions in the decision-making processes at the EU level thus takes place almost exclusively via EU-wide umbrella organizations or through membership in EU committees (the Social Dialogue, the European Economic and Social Committee).

As explained in the introduction, the most influential trade unions from the new member states were consciously chosen for this investigation. Based on these findings, it can be assumed that trade unions from the post-socialist member states by and large have no other channels of influence at the EU level. The fact that the Social Dialogue has not led to a single relevant political decision since the eastern expansion[9] means that not even a handful of the trade unions from the new member states are represented in the relevant forums of political decision-making at the EU level. The trade unions from the new member states primarily rely (if they are active at the EU level at all) on collective interest representation through the European trade union movement.

In contrast, large German trade unions for example additionally exert influence via direct consultations with the European Commission, national representatives in the Council of Ministers and the European Parliament.[10] Of the six major employers' federations from the countries under study, which were included in the project, two have a permanent representative in Brussels.[11]

11.2.2. Satisfaction

The trade union representatives from the new member states are not dissatisfied with this situation, however. The interviewed representatives perceive cooperation with the European umbrella organizations as overwhelmingly positive. Only 4% reported having had primarily negative experiences.[12]

The influence of the European trade union representation at the EU level is perceived as comparatively great. The trade unions and employer associations are seen

8   Project Questionnaire, Summer 2007, Question Q22 (open responses).
9   At the same time, the trade unions from the new member states agree with nearly all European trade unions that the social partners should not play a larger role on the EU level in the future. (Questionnaire from a project conducted by the Friedrich-Ebert-Stiftung from spring 2005 to early 2006 with respect to the positions of representatives of national trade unions, employer federations and parties vis-à-vis European economic and social policy, here: Question 37, unpublished).
10   Project Questionnaire, Summer 2007, Question Q16. Responses of the German trade union representatives, not included in the appendix.
11   See European Public Affairs Directory 2007.
12   Project Questionnaire, Summer 2007, Question Q19.

as equally strong in this arena; the majority of employer representatives and experts agreed with this assessment.[13] However, the groups were far from unanimous in their assessment of the trends in recent years. In equal measure, respondents described the trade unions' influence as having grown, remained the same or declined.[14]

At the same time, the trade unions from the new member states appear to over-estimate their own impact. 70% of the interviewed trade union representatives vs. only 30% of the employer representatives were of the opinion that trade unions from the countries under review significantly advance the trade unions' interests at the EU level.[15] The trade unions from the new member states also evaluate their individual role at the EU level critically. Only a slim majority was satisfied with their role at the EU level; satisfaction with their performance at the national level is greater.[16]

11.3. Europeanization

11.3.1. Perception of the EU

According to Radelli's[17] definition, Europeanization as the transfer of rules, values or behaviours from the EU level to the national level is only possible when the levels are interlinked. With respect to the trade unions, the first requirement for Europeanization is incorporation into the EU level for trade union related work and the recognition of the EU as an important decision-making level.

As described in the previous section, the large trade unions from the countries under review are at least linked to the EU level by means of EU umbrella organizations and committees. The trade union representatives from Poland, the Czech Republic and Slovakia participating in this project attribute great importance to the EU. More than half of them consider the EU and national levels to be of equal importance, while one-third thinks that the EU is even more important than national politics.[18] This assessment also holds true with respect to the importance of interest representation for one's own trade union. Only about one tenth of the respondents consider the EU level to be less important than the national level.[19]

---

13 Project Questionnaire, Summer 2007, Question Q26, 26a.
14 Project Questionnaire, Summer 2007, Question Q27, 27a.
15 Project Questionnaire, Summer 2007, Questions 30, 30a.
16 Project Questionnaire, Summer 2007, Questions 31, 32.
17 'Europeanisation consists of processes of a) construction, b) diffusion and c) institutionalisa-tion of formal and informal rules, procedures, policy paradigms, styles, "ways of doing things", and shared beliefs and norms which are first defined and consolidated in the EU policy proc-ess and then incorporated in the logic of domestic (national and subnational) discourse, polit-ical structures and public policies.' Radaelli, Claudio M.: Europeanisation. Solution or Problem?, in: European Integration Online Papers, 2004 (Vol. 8), No. 16, pp. 3–4.
18 Project Questionnaire, Summer 2007, Question Q1.
19 Project Questionnaire, Summer 2007, Question Q3.

At the same time, the role of the EU is viewed very positively. Nearly 90% report that the EU has a positive effect on their own trade union work.[20] Accordingly, two-thirds of the interviewed trade union representatives hope that the influence of the EU on national politics will grow in the future.[21] The trade union representatives are not exceptional in their positive assessment of EU membership: the polled employer representatives share a similar view[22] and the populations of the countries under review are also for the most part favourably disposed to the EU.[23]

As described in the introduction, trade union representatives directly responsible for EU relations were interviewed. It can thus be assumed that due to their direct responsibility, they systematically rate the role of the EU more highly in comparison to other trade union representatives. This is also apparent insofar as the experts interviewed in the project rate the importance of the EU for trade union work more reservedly than the trade union representatives themselves. This explains why one-third of the experts but only one-tenth of the trade union representatives rank the EU level as less important than the national level for the trade unions from the countries under examination.[24]

At the same time, the groups polled, i.e. the trade union representatives from the three countries under study and the experts contend that for the trade unions from Poland, the Czech Republic and Slovakia, the EU is of great significance and plays a positive role in trade union work.[25] It is also worth noting that the surveyed trade union representatives are the representatives of their trade unions at the EU level and therefore potentially the main agents of Europeanization. For the Europeanization of trade unions their conduct is therefore of greater importance than that of the other trade union members.

11.3.2. Europeanization Tendencies

Based on the positive evaluation of the EU, the question now is whether the trade union representatives in fact attempt to transfer ideas, concepts or values from the EU level to the national (and subnational) levels, and if they succeed in doing so, whether a meaningful exchange and a behavioural or normative harmonization is actually taking place between Brussels and the new member states with respect to the trade unions. This issue is not only important for an understanding of national trade union

---

20   Project Questionnaire, Summer 2007, Question Q4.
21   Project Questionnaire, Summer 2007, Question Q2.
22   Project Questionnaire, Summer 2007, Questions Q2, Q4.
23   78% of the Polish population, 61% of the Czech population and 58% of the Slovak population believe that their countries have benefited from EU membership (Standard Eurobarometer No. 67, June 2007, http://ec.europa.eu/public_opinion/archives/eb/eb67/eb67_en.htm).
24   Project Questionnaire, Summer 2007, Questions Q3, Q3e.
25   Project Questionnaire, Summer 2007, Questions Q3, Q3e, Q4.

activity, but it is also relevant for the long-term capacity of trade unions to effectively integrate themselves into decision-making processes on the EU level.

All of the interviewed trade union representatives agree that the activities on the EU level influence the work of their trade unions on the national level. Roughly half believe this is often true and half perceive it as sometimes true.[26] A similar view is expressed with respect to the importance of the EU's standards.[27] In summary, the trade union representatives as well as the employer representatives believe that the EU influences their activity at the national level. In fact, the EU is actively used by both groups as an argumentation aid at the national level. More than half of the interviewed trade union representatives and employer representatives claim to frequently use the EU to justify arguments at the national level or to support their position or activities.[28] External experts also found this to be true.[29]

From the trade unions' perspective, Europeanization most importantly means that the EU supports their interest representation at the national level insofar as its guidelines and standards bolster the trade unions' position in negotiations with the government or employers. Furthermore, the trade unions do not have to grapple with implementing worker-friendly regulations on their own; they receive backing from European law and EU standards.

The representative of a national Polish trade union explained:

> It is certainly true that membership in the EU can hinder the government from acting without consulting the social partners. EU membership also offers an additional arena for the protection of Polish workers' rights, for example through the Fundamental Rights Charter. [...] When the Polish government wanted to change the European directive on weekly working hours without consulting us, we found out about it – among other things – thanks to our participation in the European Trade Union Confederation and we had a chance to present our own opinion. The result was that the government's action without consulting the public could be hindered. Membership in the European Federation of Trade Unions thus represents an additional information source. It enables one to learn not only about European opportunities, but also about national ones.[30]

Representatives of the Slovak trade unions mentioned the revision of the labour code as a current national debate, in which the harmonization of EU regulations was a central issue. On the other hand, representatives of the Czech trade unions mentioned a broad spectrum of topics from wage issues to job security and from telework to pension reform; in each case, they explicitly used the relationship to the EU to fuel their argumentation in the national debate.[31]

---

26   Project Questionnaire, Summer 2007, Question Q33.
27   Project Questionnaire, Summer 2007, Question Q34.
28   Project Questionnaire, Summer 2007, Question Q35.
29   Project Questionnaire, Summer 2007, Question Q35e.
30   Project interview, Summer 2007 (PL-Gn04).
31   The appendix on the guided interviews provides an overview.

The Polish trade union representatives in particular pointed out the importance of their own engagement at the EU level. The coordinator of the Department for Foreign Relations in NSZZ Solidarność elaborated:

> Through our cooperation in the European Trade Union Confederation, we have a deci-sive influence on the formation of certain directives. [...] The interesting thing is that just now at the ETUC Congress in Seville [2007], Józef Niemiec, a Solidarność representative, was elected for his second term of office. The former chairman of Solidarność was also in charge of the preparation of ETUC's representation for the so-called Bolkestein Directive over services in the European internal market. This also enables members of the EU to have their 'own people' in important committees.[32]

However, only one interviewee, the chairman of the Polish Federation of Metalworkers' Trade Unions 'Metalowcy', spoke of a 'genuine' Europeanization with respect to the internalisation of European ideas:

> I might not even notice that I use the European Union or European directives [as argu-ments] in a discussion because to me some points are self-evident and I already act and talk this way. However, I prefer not to use the phrase 'Because the EU wants it that way' at meetings.[33]

His deputy, however, emphasized the aspect of a European trade union solidarity that also leads to internal conflicts of interest, and is as such a conscious decision:

> Signing the declaration of accession to the Metalworkers' Federation, we have pledged to support the activities of the Federation for the benefit of other trade unions in other countries. In some ways, these actions are part of our statutory obligation. Hence, when there are protest actions somewhere we back them. Of course, sometimes it is inconven-ient for us, because when manufacturing is going to be shifted from France to Poland, we should be glad and not block it. Sometimes philosophy and diplomacy are necessary to reconcile these interests.[34]

In summary, in their own estimation, the large trade unions from Poland, the Czech Republic and Slovakia exhibit significant Europeanization tendencies; this has also been observed externally. Some of the key tendencies include citing EU regulations in national reform debates as well as exploiting membership in European umbrella organ-izations to obtain information. In addition, the large Polish trade union federations per-ceive themselves as a shaping force in the European trade union movement.

11.4. Causal Relationships

Various forms of Europeanization and the associated different causal relationships can be identified for the large trade unions under review from the three new member states Poland, the Czech Republic and Slovakia. The trade unions' attempts to transfer con-crete regulations and standards from the labour market and social policy arenas from

---

32 Project interview, Summer 2007 (PL-Gn01).
33 Project interview, Summer 2007 (PL-Gn08).
34 Project interview, Summer 2007 (PL-Gn07).

the EU level to the national level are very important. However, this does not necessarily mean total acceptance of decisions made at the EU level, but rather instrumentalisation of EU standards to improve one's own negotiating position on the national level. The director of the NSZZ Solidarność's Department for International Affairs explains: 'When we feel it's the right thing to do, we invoke the European Union.'[35] The trade union representatives are aware that support for the EU in their countries is limited. A Polish trade union representative explained:

> This is not an argument: 'The EU wants it this way.' We speak out whenever regulations implemented in Poland go in the wrong direction or stray from the European standards. But we don't do it the way it was done during the accession negotiations, when it was said: 'Now we have to conduct very hard reforms because the EU demands it.' At that moment, support for the EU dropped among some groups. 'We have to do it because the EU wants it' is not an argument. We have to do it so that there won't be legal inconsistencies later on.[36]

This form of Europeanization is thus predicated on opportunism rather than on conviction. Accordingly, EU guidelines considered undesirable are not accepted. Europeanization in this sense serves to compensate for organizational and programmatical weaknesses in national policy as well as for comparatively weak national labour market and social standards.

This suggests that as the harmonization of national regulations and EU standards increases, this form of Europeanization will lose most of its relevance. When the employees' situation ceases to benefit from the adoption of EU standards and when the trade unions can no longer bolster its positions with EU guidelines, then EU regulations and standards will no longer be cited by the trade unions in their arguments.

Another form of Europeanization of the trade unions from the post-socialist member states occurs via membership in an umbrella organization, which is viewed very favourably.[37] Access to important information relevant to the individual trade union is especially valued.[38] The large Polish trade unions also mention their opportunities to shape policy as an important benefit of membership in these organizations. The deputy chairman of the Polish metalworkers' union 'Metalowcy', which belongs to the OPZZ, put it this way:

> EU membership offers two major benefits: contacts and greater room for manoeuvre for trade unions. The contact with the deputy chairman of the European Parliament enabled discussions to take place about the Commission's green book and the curtailing of employees' rights contained therein. Thanks to membership, the negotiation framework for trade unions has also been broadened; the protection of Polish employees' rights can now be represented on the European level: 'there is still someplace to air one's grievances.' The EU also provides support in resolving conflicts on the national level. Aside from these

---

35   Project interview, Summer 2007 (PL-Gn05).
36   Project interview, Summer 2007 (PL-Gn03).
37   Project Questionnaire, Summer 2007, Question Q19.
38   See also the appendix with the guided interviews.

things, membership in the European Metalworkers' Federation [EMF] also furnishes support for national protest actions. [39]

Accordingly, membership in European umbrella organizations is linked to two forms
of Europeanization. On the one hand, information transfer from the European level to
the national level is involved. This form of passive profiting from membership is predominant. However, it will likely cease to be important in the long term once the trade
unions' EU competence grows and interest in adopting EU regulations, as described
above, wanes.

On the other hand, membership in European umbrella organizations also means
active engagement at the EU level, especially for the large Polish trade unions. In this
case, an internalised Europeanization via networking and collaboration is more likely
to occur. The key factor is the development of European solidarity in the trade union
movement.

In this respect the debate on the EU Service Directive (Bolkestein Directive) was
a crystallisation point for the post-socialist member states. The planned liberalization benefited service providers from countries with low standards, such as the post-
socialist member states. The public debate was focussed on the symbolic figure of the
'Polish plumber', who would benefit from the liberalization at the expense of work-
men from the old member states. The great majority of the political elites in the post-
socialist EU member states thus supported the original version of the directive. The
trade unions meanwhile feared social dumping and wanted to codify the national
standards for all service providers. In the conflict between the national public opinion
and the European trade union position, the large trade unions from the post-socialist
member states decided overwhelmingly in favour of European trade union solidarity. The Polish trade unions for example found themselves in opposition to all of the
political parties represented in parliament.[40]

NSZZ Solidarność's coordinator for the Department for Foreign Relations
explained:

> Through our contribution to the policy of the European Trade Union Confederation [ETUC]
> we exert significant influence on the shape of some directives. For example, concerning
> the Directive on Services in the Internal Market, Solidarność was one of the organizations
> that gave its opinion on the Directive as it was being prepared. When it was necessary,
> we also demonstrated with 60,000 other trade union representatives.[41]

The Chairman of the National Committee for the Trade Union of Miners in Poland
spoke in similar terms:

> EU membership provides contacts to other national trade union organizations, for exam-
> ple in Germany and Sweden. It is therefore a source of new knowledge and is useful in

---

39   Project interview, Summer 2007 (PL-Gn07).
40   See the contribution by Katarzyna Gajewska in this volume.
41   Project interview, Summer 2007 (PL-Gn01).

the mutual exchange of experience. An example is the activities on the European level, such as the participation in protests in Strasbourg and Brussels against the Bolkestein Directive.[42]

A colleague in the Department for European and International Relations of the Czech trade union federation ČMKOS confirmed this perspective:

> Together we take part in negotiations on the European level, for example in actions meant to demonstrate our opposition to particular legislative proposals. The so-called Bolkestein Directive about service provision in the European market also fell into this category. I can tell you that we have attempted to exert influence on the European level in several of these legislative processes.[43]

However, the development of European trade union solidarity in the post-socialist member states should not be overestimated for a number of reasons. First of all, it requires an EU-wide, unified trade union position, which is rarely given.[44] Second, active European solidarity in the post-socialist EU member states is limited – including in the case of the Service Directive – to the few large trade unions that have the capacity for engagement at the EU level. Whether they possess the potential to act as a Europeanizing force on the national level is questionable. Third, it must be kept in mind that European solidarity was made easier for the trade unions in that the Service Directive primarily pertained to companies, and the members of the trade unions from post-socialist member states showing their solidarity were for the most part not directly affected. A true test case for trade union solidarity not only against the national public, but also against the interests of its own members, is yet to come.

---

42   Project interview, Summer 2007 (PL-Gn06).
43   Project interview, Summer 2007 (CZ-Gn08).
44   The following offers a recent assessment: Busemeyer, Marius R. / Kellermann, Christian / Petring, Alexander / Stuchlík, Andrej: Overstretching Solidarity? Trade Unions' National Perspectives on the European Economic and Social Model, Friedrich Ebert Stiftung, Berlin, 2007. For a more direct focus on the countries under review, see the contribution by Andrej Stuchlík, Christian Kellermann, Alexander Petring and Marius R. Busemeyer in this volume.

Appendices

Analysis of the Questionnaires

Within the context of the project more than 40 trade union representatives, more than 10 representatives of employers' unions and more than 20 experts from politics and consultancy were interviewed. From each of the trade unions and employers' unions executive members were selected who were responsible for the relations of their organization to the EU (heads of department and members of the board, respectively). In order to obtain reliable information concerning the position of the organizations, for each organization at least two representatives were interviewed, thus ensuring that details on the position of the interviewee's organization were not distorted by personal preferences of an outsider.

The questionnaire was designed by Heiko Pleines and then critically examined by the project partners, the members of the project advisory board and other experts. The final German version of the questionnaire was translated into the four other interview languages (English, Polish, Slovak and Czech); the translations were then reviewed and corrected by native speakers using back-translation.

The interviews were conducted as face-to-face interviews by the partner institution responsible for the country in question in the form of personal conversations. The completed questionnaires and the recorded guided interviews are being centrally archived at the Research Centre for East European Studies.

The questionnaire with a total of 43 questions is divided into 7 parts:
1. importance of the EU in the interviewee's personal estimation
2. introduction of the country to the EU (before the accession of the country to the EU)
3. requirements of the EU Commission on lobbyists (accountability)
4. ways of exerting influence at the EU level
5. potential of exerting influence and contentment
6. connections between EU and national level
7. information on the interviewee.

In the following pages, the questionnaires with the answers of the trade union and employers' representatives from Poland, the Czech Republic and Slovakia as well as those of the experts are reproduced. Open answers are not reproduced here. Selected answers from the guided interviews are given in the following part of the appendix. For the list of respondents see p. 193.

If the questions differ in the way they are formulated, this is indicated by slashes (your trade union / your organization / the trade unions from our country). If the questions are directed at employers' representatives or experts and relate to the trade unions, the answers are cited separately.

Importance of the EU

Q1. What is your personal assessment of the importance of the EU in comparison to national politics?

	Trade unions	Employers' associations	Experts
significantly more important	11%	22%	25%
slightly more important	21%	56%	6%
equally important	54%	11%	44%
slightly less important	14%	11%	25%
significantly less important	0%	0%	0%

Q2. What general role of the EU do you think is desirable? The impact of the EU on national policy

	Trade unions	Employers' associations	Experts
should grow	61%	44%	38%
should stay the same	19%	44%	56%
should decrease	13%	11%	6%
no answer	6%	0%	0%

Q3. How important is interest representation at the EU level for your union / for your association in comparison to the national level?

	Trade unions	Employers' associations
significantly more important	7%	11%
slightly more important	18%	0%
equally important	57%	89%
slightly less important	7%	0%
significantly less important	4%	0%
no answer	7%	0%

Q3e. How important is interest representation at the EU level for trade unions from our country in comparison to the national level?

	Experts
significantly more important	0%
slightly more important	13%
equally important	56%
slightly less important	31%
significantly less important	0%
no answer	0%

Q4. How does the EU impact the work of your union / of your association / of trade unions? The EU ...

	Trade unions	Employers' associations	Experts
... has a positive effect	89%	70%	75%
... has no effect	7%	0%	19%
... has a negative effect	4%	20%	0%
don't know	0%	10%	6%

Q5+. Does your union take part in EU projects?

	Trade unions*
as submitter of the project	32%
as project partner	58%
no	6%
no answer	3%

multiple answers for Poland, Czech Republic

Preparations for EU Membership

Q6. Did the EU help your union / trade unions from our country prior to accession in 2004 to prepare for participation at the EU level?

	Trade unions	Experts
yes	86%	100%
no*	14%	0%

if no, continue with question Q9

Q7. How? (multiple answers possible)

	Trade unions	Experts
financial support	15%	16%
training or seminars for union employees	25%	27%
organization of international contacts and networks	24%	16%
supply of information	25%	27%
other	7%	11%
no answer	4%	4%

Q8.   Was this EU support for your union / the unions generally

	Trade unions	Experts
very helpful	25%	25%
sufficiently helpful	57%	38%
not very helpful	4%	13%
not helpful at all	0%	25%
no answer	14%	0%

Q9.   Did you in 2004 have the impression that your union was / trade unions from our
        country were well prepared for its work at the EU level?

	Trade unions	Experts
yes	50%	19%
somewhat	46%	38%
no	4%	31%
don't know	0%	13%

Q10.   Has anything changed since then?

	Trade unions	Experts
yes, for the better	75%	56%
yes, for the worse	21%	0%
no, not at all	4%	31%
don't know	0%	13%

Accountability

Q11.   The European Commission compiled a list of requirements for social partners active
        at the EU level. The main requirements are representativeness, accountability and
        transparency. Are you familiar with these requirements?

	Trade unions	Employers' associations	Experts
very familiar	64%	78%	38%
somewhat familiar	21%	22%	31%
I have heard about them before	4%	0%	13%
This is the first time I have heard about them	11%	0%	19%

Q12. Do you think your union / your association fulfils the requirements for representativeness, accountability and transparency?

	Trade unions	Employers' associations
yes, completely	89%	100%
somewhat	11%	0%
no	0%	0%
don't know	0%	0%
no answer	0%	0%

Q12a. Do you think that trade unions from our country fulfil the requirements for representativeness, accountability and transparency?

	Employers' associations	Experts
yes, completely	66%	41%
somewhat	22%	35%
no	11%	0%
don't know	0%	12%
no answer	0%	12%

Q13. Do you consider it fair that the European Commission imposes requirements on organizations that advise it?

	Trade unions	Employers' associations
yes, in any case	68%	89%
yes, under certain circum-stances	29%	11%
no, under no circumstances	0%	0%
no answer	4%	0%

Q14. In your opinion, how should these requirements be interpreted?

	Trade unions	Employers' associations	Experts
strictly	64%	67%	56%
less strictly	21%	33%	25%
only very loosely	4%	0%	0%
no answer	11%	0%	13%
don't know	0%	0%	6%

Q15. Do you think it is necessary to specify and expand these requirements, or is it
     sufficient to allow them to serve as a rough guideline?

	Trade unions	Employers' associations	Experts
specify and expand	43%	67%	50%
rough guideline	50%	33%	31%
no answer	7%	0%	13%
don't know	0%	0%	3%

Channels of Influence

Q16. In which ways does your union / your association try to exert influence at the EU
     level? (multiple answers possible)

	Trade unions	Employers' associations
direct consultations with the European Commission	6%	12%
direct consultations with the European Parliament	10%	12%
consultations with national representatives in the Council of Ministers	13%	4%
via the EU Social Dialogue	20%	23%
via the European Economic and Social Committee	20%	23%
via membership in an European umbrella organization	24%	15%
others	5%	12%
don't know	0%	0%

Q16a. According to your experience, in which ways do trade unions from our country try
      to exert influence at the EU level? (multiple answers possible)

	Employers' associations	Experts
direct consultations with the European Commission	7%	4%
direct consultations with the European Parliament	10%	9%
consultations with national representatives in the Council of Ministers	7%	7%
via the EU Social Dialogue	20%	22%
via the European Economic and Social Committee	23%	28%

	Employers' associations	Experts
via membership in an European umbrella organization	23%	26%
other	10%	0%
don't know	0%	4%

Q18. Does your union / your association represent interests at the EU level mostly alone or in cooperation with other unions / other associations? (multiple answers possible)

	Trade unions	Employers' associations
mostly alone	3%	21%
in cooperation with other unions	30%	43%
via an umbrella organization like the ETUC	67%	36%

Q18e. Do trade unions from our country represent their interests at the EU level mostly alone or in cooperation with other unions?

	Experts*
mostly alone	5%
in cooperation with other unions	36%
via an umbrella organization like the ETUC	45%
don't know	14%

* multiple answers for Czech Republic and Slovakia

Q19. What the general assessment of your union / your association regarding collaboration with European umbrella organizations?

	Trade unions	Employers' associations
positive	79%	67%
mixed	14%	22%
negative	4%	0%
don't know	4%	11%

Q20. Does your union / your association cooperate with social partners from our country at the EU level?

	Trade unions	Employers' associations
on a regular basis	50%	44%
occasionally	29%	22%
barely ever	21%	22%
no answer	0%	11%

Q20e. Do trade unions from our country cooperate at the EU level with social partners from our country?

	Experts
on a regular basis	31%
occasionally	38%
barely ever	19%
no answer	13%

Q21. Do you think direct representation via an office in Brussels is

	Trade unions	Employers' associations
important	68%	78%
helpful under certain circumstances	29%	22%
unnecessary	4%	0%
don't know	0%	0%

Q21e. Do you think in the case of trade unions from our country direct representation via an office in Brussels is

	Experts
important	44%
helpful under certain circumstances	38%
unnecessary	13%
don't know	6%

Q25. Besides traditional forms of direct consultation, the European Commission has developed new modes of governance including – for instance – internet based consultations, the open method of coordination, voluntarily agreements, voluntarily self-commitment and codes of best practices. What is your organization's position towards these new forms of collaboration?

	Trade unions	Employers' associations
we know about and use them	57%	67%
we know about them but do not use them	36%	22%
we do not know about them	4%	11%
don't know	4%	0%

Q25e. Besides traditional forms of direct consultation, the European Commission has developed new modes of governance including – for instance – internet based consultations, the open method of coordination, voluntarily agreements, voluntarily self-commitment and codes of best practices. In your opinion what is the position of trade unions from our country towards these new forms of collaboration?

	Experts
we know about and use them	19%
we know about them but do not use them	50%
we do not know about them	13%
don't know	19%

Influence Potential and Satisfaction

Q26. How do you assess the overall influence of trade unions at the EU level compared to other interest groups?

	Trade unions	Experts
relatively great	50%	56%
average	46%	38%
relatively small	4%	6%

Q27. Has that changed in the last few years?

	Trade unions	Experts
yes, the unions' influence has increased	25%	19%
yes, the unions' influence has decreased	32%	44%
no, the unions' influence has stayed the same	36%	31%
don't know	4%	6%
no answer	4%	0%

Q26a. How do you assess the overall influence of employers' associations at the EU level compared to trade unions?

	Employers' associations
greater	30%
equal	50%
smaller	10%
don't know	10%

Q27a. Has that changed in the last few years?

	Employers' associations
yes, the employers' influence has increased	33%
yes, the employers' influence has decreased	22%
no, the employers' influence has stayed the same	33%
no answer	11%

Q28. How do you assess the role of employers' associations / trade unions at the EU level? The employers' associations / trade unions are

	Trade unions*	Employers' associations**
constructive partners	36%	36%
an opponent that blocks actions	33%	50%
one competitor among many	15%	7%
don't know	12%	0%
no answer	3%	7%

* multiple answers for Poland
** multiple answers for Poland, Slovakia

Q28e. How do you assess the relationship between trade unions and employers' associations at the EU level? For the trade unions the employers' associations are

	Experts*
constructive partners	41%
an opponent that blocks actions	29%
one competitor among many	29%

* multiple answers for Poland, Slovakia

Q29. How do you assess the influence of your union / trade unions from our country at the EU level in comparison to the national level?

	Trade unions	Employers' associations	Experts
greater	29%	11%	13%
the same	25%	67%	13%
smaller	39%	0%	75%
don't know	7%	22%	0%

Q30. Do you think that your union / trade unions from our country provide an important contribution to the unions' interest representation at the EU level?

	Trade unions	Experts
yes	71%	63%
no	29%	25%
don't know	0%	13%

Q30a. How do you evaluate the role of trade unions from our country at the EU level?

	Employers' associations
They strengthen the influence of trade unions at the EU level.	33%
They make no difference.	56%
They make it more difficult for trade unions to present a common position.	11%

Q31. Are you satisfied with the role your union plays at the EU level?

	Trade unions
yes	61%
no	39%

Q32. Are you satisfied with the role your union plays at the national level?

	Trade unions
yes	75%
no	25%

Connections between the EU and the National Level

Q33. Do the activities of your union / your association / trade unions from our country at the EU level influence its / their work at the national level?

	Trade unions	Employers' associations	Experts
often	54%	56%	19%
occasionally	46%	44%	75%
never	0%	0%	6%

Q34. Do the EU requirements influence the work of your union/ your association / of trade unions from our country at the national level?

	Trade unions	Employers' associations	Experts
often	46%	78%	56%
occasionally	50%	22%	38%
never	4%	0%	6%

Q35. Does your union / your association use the EU as an argument to justify or support its position or activities?

	Trade unions	Employers' associations
often	61%	56%
occasionally	39%	44%
never	0%	0%

Q35e. Do trade unions from our country use the EU as an argument to justify or support their position or activities?

	Experts
often	63%
occasionally	31%
never	6%

Personal Information

Q38. How do you assess your personal influence within your union / your association / your organization?

	Trade unions	Employers' associations	Experts
I am one of the central decision makers	64%	67%	38%
I can create constructive majorities	29%	22%	31%
I am often isolated	0%	0%	0%
Central decisions are made without me	0%	0%	0%
I am a consultant	7%	11%	6%
don't know	0%	0%	6%
no answer	0%	0%	6%

Q39. Do you belong to a political party?

	Trade unions	Employers' associations	Experts
yes	32%	0%	19%
no	68%	100%	81%

Q40. How would you describe your political orientation?

	Trade unions	Employers' associations	Experts
communist/socialist	7%	0%	0%
social democrat	86%	11%	38%
conservative/Christian democrat	0%	11%	13%
nationalist	0%	0%	0%
liberal	4%	33%	19%
green/ecological	0%	0%	13%
other	4%	44%	13%
no answer	0%	0%	6%

Q42. What is your educational level?

	Trade unions	Employers' associations	Experts
college/univer-sity degree (BA, MA, Diploma)	75%	100%	94%
apprenticeship (after secondary school degree)	21%	0%	6%
secondary school degree	4%	0%	0%
Primary school degree	0%	0%	0%

Q43. What foreign languages do you speak fluently? (multiple answers possible)

	Trade unions	Employers' associations	Experts
German	10%	14%	3%
English	22%	29%	44%
French	6%	14%	9%
Greek	0%	4%	0%
Italian	0%	0%	3%
Norwegian	2%	0%	0%
Russian	29%	21%	19%
Swedish	10%	0%	0%
Spanish	0%	4%	0%
Czech	14%	11%	16%
Hungarian	2%	4%	6%
no language	6%	0%	0%

Excerpts from the Guided Interviews

Within the context of the project more than forty trade union representatives, more than ten representatives of employers' unions and more than twenty experts from politics and consultancy were interviewed. From each of the trade unions and employers' unions executive members were selected who were responsible for the relations of their organization to the EU (heads of department and members of the board, respectively). In order to obtain reliable information concerning the position of the organizations, for each organization at least two representatives were interviewed, thus ensuring that details on the position of the interviewee's organization were not distorted by personal preferences of an outsider. The list of respondents is given at the end of this paper.

The interviews were conducted by the partner institution responsible for the country in question in the form of personal conversations. The completed questionnaires and the recorded guided interviews are being centrally archived at the Research Centre for East European Studies.

In what follows, the answers to some of the key questions from the guided interviews are reproduced in excerpts. As many respondents insisted on anonymity, the interviewees are designated by abbreviations that identify country (CZ: Czech Republic, PL: Poland, SK: Slovakia) and group (Gn: trade unionists of the new member states, An: employers of the new member states, Ex: experts). Only responses of trade union representatives from Poland, the Czech Republic and Slovakia are presented in the following pages. Within the main questions the answers are arranged to the greatest possible extent according to topic.

How do you Assess the Role of the EU for the Work of your Trade Union? Please Give Examples.

[Summary: the role of the EU for trade union work is on the whole assessed positively. This often applies to the implementation of directives and standards relating to labour law. Besides this, networking at the European level plays an important role for the trade unions. Moreover, via the integration in European trade union associations' influence on both EU policies politics and national politics can be increased.]

PL-Gn01:

I have to define the concept 'European Union'. For me as a trade union official, this concept refers to our presence in our umbrella organization, which represents us vis-à-vis various European institutions. Among these are the European Commission, the Parliament and the Council.

Through our cooperation in the European Trade Union Confederation [ETUC], we exert a decisive influence on the drafting of many directives, for example, on the drafting of the directive on services in the European Single Market. Solidarność was one of the organizations that submitted a statement on the directive that was being drafted. When it became necessary, we also demonstrated together with 60,000 other trade unionists.

It is interesting that with Józef Niemiec a representative of Solidarność has been elected for a second term at the ETUC congress in Seville [in 2007]. The former chairman of Solidarność was also responsible for the drafting of the statement of the ETUC on the so-called Bolkestein directive on services in the European Single Market.

Additionally, membership in the EU makes it possible to have 'one's own people' in important committees and institutions.

Moreover, accession to the EU also meant the implementation of certain directives and standards in Poland. This in turn had a positive influence on the trade union and labour world in the broadest sense. One example: Directive No. 14 of 2002 on the rights of employees to information and consultation[1], on the basis of which employees' councils were appointed in firms in which trade unions are not represented.

PL-Gn07:

Membership in the EU offers above all two different advantages: contacts and an enlarged scope of action for the trade unions. For example, talks on the Green Paper of the Commission and the restrictions of employee rights contained in this Paper were made possible via contacts to the Deputy Chairman of the European Parliament.

Membership in the EU has also enlarged the scope of action for trade unions, the rights of Polish employees can now also be protected at the European level: 'there is somebody else to whom one can tell one's troubles'. Moreover, the EU offers support for the resolving of conflicts at the national level.

Apart from these issues, membership in the European Metalworkers' Federation (EMF) also means support for national protests.

[Summary: the EU plays a significant role for the work of trade unions by supporting trade union positions in negotiations with the state or with employers via EU directives and standards. Therefore, the implementation of regulations which are beneficial to employees does not have to be pushed through solely by the trade unions; they are supported by European law and by standards laid down at the European level.]

---

1   Framework Directive for informing and consulting employees (Directive 2002/14/EC).

PL-Gn04:

It is a positive factor that membership in the EU prevents the state from acting without consulting both sides of industry. Moreover, membership in the EU offers an additional arena for the protection of Polish employee rights, e.g., via the Charter of Fundamental Rights. I would like to mention two examples of this:

When the Polish government wanted to change the European Working Time Directive without consulting us, we found out about this project amongst others through our membership in ETUC. This enabled us to comment on this. Ultimately, this prevented the government acting without consulting society.

A further example was the declaration of the prime minister concerning provisos and restrictions in the application of the Charter of Fundamental Rights.

We act both at the national and at the European level, as we are of the opinion that the Poles expressed their support of an EU based on the Charter of Fundamental Rights in the referendum. In the same moment that Poland became a member of the EU, the Charter was recognised as the basis for the future organization of Europe.

Thus, membership in ETUC is an additional source for information. We can inform ourselves not only on European, but also on national matters.

PL-Gn02:

A positive, but so far still too small, influence of the EU can be felt due to the fact that some regulations relating to labour law were included in the Charter of Fundamental Rights. The implementation of directives and standards relating to labour law in Poland also put an end to the discussions on certain topics at the national level. By their implementation, [these directives and standards] have become law and thus binding. However, many areas are still regulated at the national level; e.g., working time is still a bone of contention between trade unions and employers. Working time should be included in the catalogue of fundamental rights.

Increasing standardisation of law is a positive influence of the EU.

PL-Gn05:

The EU helps with the implementation of regulations and standards relating to labour law in Poland. Moreover, membership in the EU has a positive effect on the drafting and introduction of a social model and a culture of negotiation in Poland.

[Summary: the increased networking of the trade unions throughout Europe does not only lead to an exchange of information; rather, trade unions can represent and assert their positions on a major scale at the European level.]

PL-Gn06:

EU membership promotes contacts to other national trade union organizations, e.g. in Germany and Sweden. Because of this, EU membership is also a source of new knowledge and an aid for the mutual exchange of information. Examples of this are activities at the European level such as the participation in protests in Strasbourg and Brussels against the Bolkestein directive.

CZ-Gn08:

A current example is the following: together, we participate in negotiations at the European level; e.g., during activities that are supposed to demonstrate our resistance to certain legislative proposals, such as the Bolkestein directive on services in the European single market. Therefore I can say: in some of these legislative processes we attempted to exert influence via the European level.

PL-Gn08:

In the course of EU membership there will also be an integration of the trade unions at the European level. The exchange of experiences and opinions are being intensified, new contacts are being intensified and new views of some social problems, because a comparison to other countries is made easier. There are good personal contacts to colleagues from Germany, Italy, Spain and France. These contacts have a positive effect on the development of the trade union federation.

The introduction of European Works Councils [EWC] and the creation of works councils in companies in which no trade union is represented are positive effects.

PL-Gn10:

The cooperation with CESI (Confédération Européenne des Syndicats Indépendants) and with DBB (Deutscher Beamtenbund) can be assessed as very positive. One of the deputy chairpersons of CESI is from Forum (Forum Związków Zawodowych, FZZ); thus, membership in the EU permits the placing of one's own representatives in committees and institutions at the EU level. Cooperation at the European level leads to the acquisition of new knowledge and experience.

CZ-Gn08:

We have to go back in history. We became members of ETUC even before accession to the EU. The EU already helped us before membership during the accession process. Above all, this concerns information, but also the integration into various projects.

Thus, we had the occasion to participate in various activities even then. This was definitely positive.

[Summary: apart from these topics, which were mentioned most of all, the EU also plays a role for trade union work in other areas; for example, the EU played a positive role for the creation of the employees' social charter, for the development of the Social Dialogue and of collective negotiations, for pensions and for miners' working conditions (CZ-Gn01). The EU moreover exerts influence via the Directives on Working Time[2] and Services[3] (CZ-Gn03, CZ-Gn05), as well as in the area of industrial policy (CZ-Gn05). Trade unions aim at creating the same conditions for everybody as far as working time and the Directive on Services are concerned (CZ-Gn03); on the other hand, they do not aim for, and take a negative view of, the transition to more flexible employment relationships as supported by EU Commissar Vladimír Špidla from the Czech Republic (CZ-Gn01).

The EU plays a role for trade union work in the area of energy policy (CZ-Gn02). Trade unions view improving the quality of trade union work and of trade union officials as well as the development of European Works Councils from a pan-European point of view (CZ-Gn06). They also single out improved exchange of information for praise (CZ-Gn10).]

CZ-Gn07:

The Social Dialogue and the values contained in the so-called European Social Model, which are valid throughout Europe, can be viewed positively. The Social Dialogue is part of the Social Model, which, while differing form country to country, does have common characteristics. The Social Dialogue is codified in EU documents, its committees meet regularly, and the agreements of the two sides of industry are respected. Thus, by structuring civil society, the Social Dialogue and the European Social Model also lead to a strengthening of democracy.

[Summary: during the interviews, the Slovak trade union representatives often underlined the positive influence of the European level, such as the directives of the EU Commission or the 'Green Paper on Labour Law', on trade union work at the national level.]

SK-Gn01:

When the labour law was amended, we as trade unions often quoted the regulations of the European Commission during the negotiations. Moreover, EU regulations now are observed to a greater extent.

---

2   Council Directive 93/104/EC of 23 November 1993, amended by Directive 2000/34/EC of the European Parliament and of the Council of 22 June 2000.
3   Directive on services in the internal market, Directive 2006/123/EC, commonly referred to as the Bolkestein directive.

[Summary: the Green Paper 'Modernising labour law to meet the challenges of the 21st century' of the EU Commission also played an important role for other respondents (SK-Gn03, SK-Gn05, SK-Gn07) when the labour law was amended.

In addition, SK-Gn02 underscores the adoption of European norms at the national level, which SK-Gn06 specifies and applies in particular to social matters; e.g., certain standards for social protection, to which Slovakia would not conform without accession to the EU, are associated with the EU.

SK-Gn04 sees effects of the EU on trade union work for the following issues: the problem of multinational corporations, questions of national legislation, the question of workers of temporary employment agencies (in this case e.g. the Austrian model for the protection of agency employees) and the cooperation and help of trade unions in the metal-processing sector; e.g., trade union members who are not working in their home country are entitled to free legal assistance rendered by the 'cooperating trade union' in the host country. SK-Gn04 singled this out for especial praise.]

Does your Trade Union Use the EU as an Argument for the Justification or Support of its Positions or Activities at the National Level?

[Summary: at the national level, the EU is used less to justify and more to support trade union positions. Trade unions in particular refer to standards of the EU in labour law conflicts with employers or the state.]

PL-Gn03:

The directive relating to working time. In this area, there are problems relating to the Polish health system, in which standby duty is not counted as working hours. However, by its verdicts the European Court has established standards according to which standby duty should be counted as working hours. We are trying to solve this problem.

PL-Gn02:

If we discuss the labour market, working time or qualifications, we often refer to the standards of the EU.

CZ-Gn04:

We used the EU and European standards as argument and support in the area of labour law relations.

[Summary: the EU seems to play an especially important role as support for trade unions' arguments for disputes on negotiated wages and salaries and for questions of payment.]

PL-Gn05:

When we consider it appropriate, we refer to the European Union, for example, when we discuss fixed-term employment contracts. In this case, we used the directive in order to convince the government to limit the number of fixed-term contracts. This was during the term of office of the last government. And yes, indeed, the law that was passed in Poland limited this number [i.e., of fixed-term employment contracts]. Thus, according to the law, since 1 May 2004 no more than a certain number of fixed-term contracts can be carried out.

However, whether we referred to this directive or not: European legislation is binding. It could well be that some else would have referred to [this directive]. In spite of this: yes, we used this argument in our favour.

PL-Gn04:

Recently, we sent a letter to the president concerning the ratification of the article on just pay for work. Generally, we also refer to the Charter of Fundamental Rights and to many directives which above all deal with social standards and remuneration [for work].

We also refer to European average values and to European standards concerning minimum wages for various areas of life, e.g. in the health system. It was said earlier that the minimum wage should be 60% of the average income. We are now campaigning for increased wages and in particular as far as the minimum wage is concerned we refer to the principles of the EU.

PL-Gn06:

Yes, for example in respect to the level of remunerations for work in the European Union and in Poland and also in respect to the pensions system. [...] I also know other examples when 'provisional pensions' or other solutions were accepted both by governments and also by trade unions and became certain standards. Why then don't we use European models as examples?

[Summary: a significant number of Slovak trade union representatives (SK-Gn01, SK-Gn04, SK-Gn05, SK-Gn06, SK-Gn07, SK-Gn08) cited the amendment of the labour law as a concrete example. In this case, the EU seems to have been an important support for the trade unionists' arguments.]

SK-Gn02:

The amendment of the labour law. Quoting European regulations directives was a strong argument.

[Summary: in Poland, trade unions referred to the liquidation of, and the subsidies meted out to, the German mining industry in order to assert their claims to a restructuring of the Polish mining industry that was more socially acceptable.]

PL-Gn09:

Sometimes we refer to statements of the EU or use them as references. For example, in respect to restructuring programmes and subsidies in the German mining industry. Several times we raised the issue how the German government deals with this problem, albeit without success. All successive prime ministers declared that we are not the Federal Republic and cannot afford such things. Supposedly, we are also a significantly smaller net payer in the EU and also receive significantly less. And that was it.

PL-Gn10:

Yes, we use the EU. However, at the national level there is more or less no one left who needs convincing; at any rate, not the partners with whom we are dealing, that is, the representatives of the employers' and employees' organizations (OPZZ, Solidarność). Within these organizations, no one has to be convinced that such argumentations are right.

In respect to employees' affairs in which we tried to act it was always the best realisation that the given situation has already occurred in the European Union. For example, during the restructuring of the mining industry. In this case, we received a helpful consultation how the mining industry could be saved. Our reformers wanted to liquidate the mining industry very quickly, whereas the European Coal and Steel Community told us: stay calm and don't permit this to come about. We have liquidated mining for decades; do not permit this to happen in your country within the space of four or five years. This is not possible.

[Summary: besides regulations pertaining to labour law, conflicts pertaining to negotiated rates, the amendment of the Slovak labour law and the restructuring in the Polish mining industry, various special cases were quoted, in which the trade union used the EU to supports its arguments.]

CZ-Gn01:

We used the EU as support for our arguments for the Social Dialogue, and when discussing pensions, wages and work conditions.

CZ-Gn02:

In respect to the pension reform, we referred to a difference between Germany and the Czech Republic: in Germany, miners work 25% less shifts during their working life than miners in the Czech Republic.

CZ-Gn04:

In respect to overtime in transportation, in cinemas, theatres, etc.

CZ-Gn05:

Comparisons were made at the European level in the areas of working time, restructuring of the steel industry and taxation of firms.

CZ-Gn07:

In our case, the problem was telecommuting, which is only just beginning in the Czech Republic; we know, however, that e.g. in the Netherlands 25% of employees work according to this model. Therefore, we are trying to gain experience over there; amongst other things, in order to see what it does to society.

CZ-Gn08:

We refer to the EU in all questions pertaining to the social acquis, for example, also in the case of the reform of the Lisbon strategy, of the employment strategy or of social integration – and of course, there is the question of equal opportunities for men and women, which is very important for me, since I spend a lot of time on this issue.

CZ-Gn09:

Interoperability of employees in railway traffic.

CZ-Gn10:

Questions of wages, collective negotiations and occupational safety.

SK-Gn03:

Recently, we again used the European example in the question of collective bargaining above the company level, when we ascertained in the course of a survey that in the majority of EU countries this is in force.

PL-Gn01:

We used arguments of ECTU in order to underline the importance of finding a solution for the implementation of the directive on information and consultation rights. In the end, it became a law on European Works' Councils. In this case it was important that trade unions had the last word in the formulation of the law. I mean the Directive No. 14 of the year 2002.

[Summary: apart from the support of trade union positions at the national level by using European standards during conflicts with governments or employees, the shunting off of responsibility to Brussels is also viewed critically.]

PL-Gn03:

'The EU wants it thus!' is no argument. If certain regulations which are implemented in Poland go in the wrong direction and deviate from European standards, we point this out. But then we don't do it the way it was done during the negotiations: we now must carry out harsh reforms because the EU demands it. In this moment, approval of the EU went down among certain groups in society. We have to do it this way, so that there are no legal contradictions later on.

PL-Gn07:

Yes, since by signing the declaration to accede to the European Metalworkers Federation (EMF) we have so to speak committed ourselves to supporting the activities of the federation to support other trade unions, in other countries as well. This is a part of the duties established in the statutes. Therefore we send support whenever there is a strike anywhere. Of course, this doesn't always suit our purposes, as when production is transferred from France to Poland we should really be glad and not block such transfers. Sometimes you need philosophy and diplomacy in order to integrate your interests.

PL-Gn08:

In my opinion, it can be good if I cite the European Union or EU directives in discussions as arguments without noticing it. This is also because of the fact that there is a lot that is a matter of course for me. Therefore, I also act accordingly. I don't even notice it, I just do or say it. However, if during meetings there is the possibility of using the phrase 'Because the EU wants it thus!' – no, on the whole I don't use it.

[Summary: the trade union representatives seem to use the EU to support their arguments especially in order to assert trade union positions in conflicts with governments or employers. For the most part, the issue is the implementation of European standards which are supposed to improve the condition of the employees. At least according to the respondents, effects that are negative for the trade unions are not simply foisted off on Brussels without further reflection.]

Translation from German: Matthias Neumann

List of Respondents (Abbreviation of Organization and Number of Interviewees)

	Poland	Slovakia	Czech Republic	Brussels	Germany
National trade unions	2 Solidarność 2 OPZZ 2 FZZ 2 FZZ Metalowcy 2 ZZG	5 KOZ SR 2 OZ KOVO 2 OZ PBGN	4 ČMKOS 2 ASO 1 KUK 1 KOVO 2 OS PHGN	1 DGB 1 UPA 1 UGT 1 GMB	2 DGB 2 IG Metall 2 IG BCE
European umbrella associations of trade unions	-	-	-	1 ETUC 1 EMF (Metall) 1 EFFAT	-
National employers' associations	1 KPP 1 PKPP Lewiatan 1 BCC	2 RUZ 1 AZZZ	1 SP CR 1 Economic Chamber 1 SCMVD		-
European umbrella associations of employers	-	-	-	2 CEEP	-
Political administrations	2 Ministry of Labour	1 Ministry of Labour 1 MEP	1 MEP	2 EU Commission (DG Employment)	-
Experts	2 academics 1 NGO	2 academics	2 academics 2 NGO	1 NGO 2 analyst	-

About the Authors

Dr. **Marius R. Busemeyer** is a research associate at the Max Planck Institute for the Study of Societies in Cologne. His research interests are comparative political economy, processes of institutional change in education and training systems as well as the politics of European integration. He has published in the Journal of European Public Policy, West European Politics, German Policy Studies and Politische Vierteljahresschrift.

Dr. **Monika Čambáliková** is a senior research fellow at the Institute of Sociology, Slovak Academy of Sciences. In addition, she is a member of the Scientific Board of the Institute of Sociology and editor-in-chief of the Slovak sociological journal Sociologia. Her fields of work include the labour market, social policy, industrial relations, the social dialogue, social partnership and regional development.

Joanna Einbock (MA) studied English linguistics, social psychology and European studies at Leibniz University of Hanover. Currently she works as a research assistant on EU-funded projects at uni transfer, the University's research and technology contact office. She is also a research associate at the Koszalin Institute of Comparative European Studies (KICES). Her research interests focus on the activities of Polish trade unions at the EU level.

Dr. **Katarzyna Gajewska** finished her Ph.D. at the Graduate School of Social Sciences of the University of Bremen in the summer of 2008. Her dissertation investigates the trade union response to the recent developments in the European integration in the field of transnational cooperation and mobilization with emphasis on case studies involving British, German, Latvian, Polish and Swedish trade unions.

Dr. **Christian Kellermann** is a research fellow in the International Policy Analysis Unit at the Friedrich Ebert Foundation in Berlin, where he focuses on European economic and social policies as well as on global financial markets and governance issues.

Dipl-Geo. **Brigitte Krech** is a freelance researcher in Brussels. She has had several years of working experience in EU institutions (research division/European Parliament; DG RELEX/European Commission) as well as NGOs (WWF EPO, Eurogroup for Animals). She regularly takes part in OSCE missions to the Western Balkans and Caucasus. Her main research interest is the representation of civil society at the EU level. During her studies at the School of Slavonic and East European Studies (University of London) and at Corvinus University of Budapest, she focused on Central and Eastern Europe.

Aleksandra Lis is a Ph.D. candidate in sociology and social anthropology at the Central European University in Budapest. One of her core research areas is organizational change in the post-socialist EU member states.

Dr. **Zdenka Mansfeldová** is a senior researcher and head of the Department of the Sociology of Politics at the Institute of Sociology, Academy of Sciences of the Czech Republic. Her research focuses on political institutionalization and representation of interests in both political terms (parties and parliament) and the non-political meso-structures of social interests.

Alexander Petring (MA) is a research fellow at the Social Science Research Center Berlin (WZB). His research interests are comparative political economy, democratic theory and European integration.

Dr. **Heiko Pleines** is Head of the Department of Politics and Economics at the Research Centre for East European Studies and Lecturer in Comparative Politics and European Studies at the University of Bremen. One of his major research interests is the representation of interest groups from the post-socialist member states in EU governance.

Andrej Stuchlík is a political scientist and is currently completing his Ph.D. at the Free University Berlin while working for the EU Policy Department of the Friedrich Ebert Foundation. Previously, he was a lecturer at the postgraduate Andrássy University Budapest. His research includes European social policy and social policy transformation in the Visegrád countries.

Dr. **Janna Wolff** is a research fellow and lecturer at the Jean Monnet Centre for European Studies at the University of Bremen. Her main areas of teaching and research are the European Union's institutional integration and its Neighbourhood Policy, with particular reference to democracy promotion.

Series Subscription

Please enter my subscription to the series *Changing Europe*, ISSN 1863-8716, as follows:

starting with
☐ volume # 1
☐ volume # ___
    ☐ please also include the following volumes: #___, ___, ___, ___, ___, ___,

☐ the next volume being published
    ☐ please also include the following volumes: #___, ___, ___, ___, ___, ___,

☐ 1 copy per volume   OR   ☐ ___ copies per volume

Subscription within Germany:

You will receive every volume at 1st publication at the regular bookseller's price – incl. s & h and VAT.

Payment:

☐ Please bill me for every volume.

☐ Lastschriftverfahren: Ich/wir ermächtige(n) Sie hiermit widerruflich, den Rechnungsbetrag je Band von meinem/unserem folgendem Konto einzuziehen.

Kontoinhaber: _____Kreditinstitut: _____

Kontonummer: _____Bankleitzahl:_____

International Subscription:

Payment (incl. s & h and VAT) in advance for

☐ 10 volumes/copies (€ 319.80)   ☐ 20 volumes/copies (€ 599.80)
☐ 40 volumes/copies (€ 1,099.80)

Please send my books to:

NAME_____DEPARTMENT_____

ADDRESS _____

POST/ZIP CODE_____COUNTRY _____

TELEPHONE _____EMAIL_____

date/signature_____

A hint for librarians in the former Soviet Union: Your academic library might be eligible to receive free-of-cost scholarly literature from Germany via the German Research Foundation. For Russian-language information on this program, see
    http://www.dfg.de/forschungsfoerderung/formulare/download/12_54.pdf.

Please fax to: **0511 / 262 2201 (+49 511 262 2201)**
or mail to: *ibidem*-Verlag, Julius-Leber-Weg 11, D-30457 Hannover,Germany
or send an e-mail: ibidem@ibidem-verlag.de

ibidem-Verlag

Melchiorstr. 15

D-70439 Stuttgart

info@ibidem-verlag.de

www.ibidem-verlag.de
www.edition-noema.de
www.autorenbetreuung.de

www.ingramcontent.com/pod-product-compliance
Lightning Source LLC
Chambersburg PA
CBHW050711280326
41926CB00088B/2934